I0050011

INTERNATIONAL DEVELOPMENT IN FOCUS

Port Development and Competition in East and Southern Africa

Prospects and Challenges

Martin Humphreys, Aiga Stokenberga, Matias Herrera Dappe, Atsushi Iimi, and Olivier Hartmann

WORLD BANK GROUP

© 2019 International Bank for Reconstruction and Development / The World Bank
1818 H Street NW, Washington, DC 20433
Telephone: 202-473-1000; Internet: www.worldbank.org

Some rights reserved

1 2 3 4 22 21 20 19

Books in this series are published to communicate the results of Bank research, analysis, and operational experience with the least possible delay. The extent of language editing varies from book to book.

This work is a product of the staff of The World Bank with external contributions. The findings, interpretations, and conclusions expressed in this work do not necessarily reflect the views of The World Bank, its Board of Executive Directors, or the governments they represent. The World Bank does not guarantee the accuracy of the data included in this work. The boundaries, colors, denominations, and other information shown on any map in this work do not imply any judgment on the part of The World Bank concerning the legal status of any territory or the endorsement or acceptance of such boundaries.

Nothing herein shall constitute or be considered to be a limitation upon or waiver of the privileges and immunities of The World Bank, all of which are specifically reserved.

Rights and Permissions

This work is available under the Creative Commons Attribution 3.0 IGO license (CC BY 3.0 IGO) http://creativecommons.org/licenses/by/3.0/igo. Under the Creative Commons Attribution license, you are free to copy, distribute, transmit, and adapt this work, including for commercial purposes, under the following conditions:

Attribution—Please cite the work as follows: Humphreys, Martin, Aiga Stokenberga, Matias Herrera Dappe, Atsushi Iimi, and Olivier Hartmann. 2019. *Port Development and Competition in East and Southern Africa: Prospects and Challenges.* International Development in Focus. Washington, DC: World Bank. doi:10.1596/978-1-4648-1410-5 License: Creative Commons Attribution CC BY 3.0 IGO

Translations—If you create a translation of this work, please add the following disclaimer along with the attribution: *This translation was not created by The World Bank and should not be considered an official World Bank translation. The World Bank shall not be liable for any content or error in this translation.*

Adaptations—If you create an adaptation of this work, please add the following disclaimer along with the attribution: *This is an adaptation of an original work by The World Bank. Views and opinions expressed in the adaptation are the sole responsibility of the author or authors of the adaptation and are not endorsed by The World Bank.*

Third-party content—The World Bank does not necessarily own each component of the content contained within the work. The World Bank therefore does not warrant that the use of any third-party-owned individual component or part contained in the work will not infringe on the rights of those third parties. The risk of claims resulting from such infringement rests solely with you. If you wish to re-use a component of the work, it is your responsibility to determine whether permission is needed for that re-use and to obtain permission from the copyright owner. Examples of components can include, but are not limited to, tables, figures, or images.

All queries on rights and licenses should be addressed to World Bank Publications, The World Bank Group, 1818 H Street NW, Washington, DC 20433, USA; e-mail: pubrights@worldbank.org.

ISBN: 978-1-4648-1410-5
DOI: 10.1596/978-1-4648-1410-5

Cover photo: © mtcurado/istockphoto.com. Used with permission; further permission required for reuse.
Cover design: Debra Naylor/Naylor Design Inc.

Contents

Boxes

Figures

Maps

Photo

Tables

Foreword

International trade patterns have changed markedly in recent years, in terms of both trade partners and volumes. Over the past decade, Africa's trade has slowly trended away from developed countries and toward emerging economies. Whereas Western European countries accounted for the bulk of Africa's trade in the late 20th century, countries like China, India, Indonesia, Russia, and Turkey have since grown in importance as export destinations for the resource-rich economies. Emerging economies have also become origins of a significant share of imports for nearly all African countries, the total trade of the latter with China increasing twenty-fold in the last two decades. The changing trade relationships and needs require that Africa's external transport connections evolve as well.

The changing structure and intensity of international trade is increasing the region's infrastructure needs and demand for more specialized transport and logistics services at the maritime gateways and on the key trading corridors: Africa has 16 landlocked developing countries, which represent 30 percent of the region's population, and which are entirely dependent on the key trading corridors through neighbors for access to the sea. Trade costs for these countries tend to exceed the global average 3 to 4 times. In some of these countries, transport costs represent upwards of a quarter of the final price of goods, including crucial production inputs such as fertilizer and fuel. Connections to gateway ports are key to allow these countries to engage in global trade and value chains. In other words, East and Southern Africa's ports are the nodes of entry not only to their coastal host countries but also the landlocked hinterland. Investments in ports will have implications far beyond the port gates. Against this backdrop, the existing port facilities and current operational practices in the East and Southern Africa region are inadequate, with insufficient capacity to serve not only their coastal countries, but also the hinterland of landlocked nations. The visible result has been high ship waiting times, high berth occupancies, congestion on both the land and maritime side, and increased costs.

East and Southern Africa now stand at a pivotal moment. The accelerating growth of its consumer class is rapidly increasing the demand for imported goods and, hence, the need for improvements in containerized cargo transport services that would allow delivering the goods efficiently and at minimum cost. New discoveries of oil and gas resources have the potential to transform regional markets, provide significant revenues for government, and improve living standards. They will also require further investment in infrastructure capacity to support exploitation, some of which might be quite urgent. However, this growth and prosperity will require not only new infrastructure on both the maritime and landside, but also policy reforms, the greater use of specialized private operators, and the leveraging of private investment, both to deliver transport infrastructure and to ensure its efficient use.

This book assesses the capacity expansion needs, the operating efficiency, and the landside access gaps of the fifteen main ports in East and Southern Africa within the context of these broader global and regional trends. In doing so, it provides detailed policy recommendations for each of the ports regarding the needed port and access infrastructure, the port sector regulations, and the institutional and management approaches to port operation and development.

The World Bank looks forward to working closely with member countries, other development partners, and the private sector to deliver solutions and results that will help bring the region's development vision to life.

Guangzhe Chen
Senior Director, Transport
The World Bank

Foreword

Over the last two decades, the countries of East and Southern Africa (ESA) have taken concrete steps to improve the efficiency of their transport networks and to reduce the costs of trade. These actions have included significant physical investment in the main regional corridors, increased attention to intermodal connectivity, and implementation of trade facilitation measures to enable cross-border trade and to smooth the intraregional movement of labor. These efforts have also led to improvements in the region's performance as evaluated by the international Logistics Performance Index, with most ESA countries climbing in the ranking relative to their global peers. Today, the region is better connected and more resilient to economic shocks than it was at the turn of the century. Improved connectivity and reduced trade costs have contributed to a rapid rise in the consumer class, reaching 8–10 million in Ethiopia, Kenya, and Tanzania, and surpassing 35 million in South Africa.

The positive developments notwithstanding, the region's growth and progress in poverty reduction going forward will require not only significant investment in infrastructure, including in roads, rail, sea ports, and logistics platforms. It will also necessitate bold policy reforms that promote the efficiency of transport service provision, improve transport safety, and ensure that improved connectivity helps boost firm productivity, country competitiveness, and human capital, while helping reduce existing spatial economic imbalances. Countries would have to continue making progress toward economic integration and allowing people to get the full benefits of economic integration. Infrastructure connectivity is critical, but by no means sufficient, as it needs to be accompanied by "soft" policy and regulatory reforms, creation of value chains, and trade facilitation measures.

Despite impressive reductions in the average poverty rates, Sub-Saharan Africa (SSA) remains home to more than half of the world's poor, exceeding 410 million, and in individual countries the inequality between the bottom 40 percent and the rest has grown in recent years. Just five ESA countries alone — Ethiopia, Kenya, Madagascar, Mozambique, and Tanzania — jointly represent about a quarter of SSA's poor population. Employment in low-productivity, informal agricultural activities remains dominant in much of the region, the overall share of agricultural employment remaining at about 30 percent.

Progress in poverty reduction in ESA is threatened by several factors, some internal and some external to the region. Investment remains low and the investment climate is still weak. Recent global trends, such as the projected softening in the global economic growth, are raising vulnerabilities; commodity prices remain volatile; and global financial conditions are tightening, especially in emerging markets and low-income countries.

A critical area for the future growth of the region — and one where transformation from the *status quo* will be required — concerns the availability of infrastructure financing. One solution to addressing the region's growing infrastructure needs, at least in part, lies in bringing in private capital. To accelerate this much needed transition, the World Bank Group (WBG) has embraced Maximizing Finance for Development (MFD) as its approach to helping countries systematically leverage all sources of finance, expertise, and solutions to support sustainable growth. Of course, such an approach requires careful attention to country macroeconomic stability and debt levels, and to the overall investment climate needed to encourage private investment.

Consistent with the MFD approach, the new Africa Strategy, endorsed by the World Bank Board in 2019, aims to accelerate poverty reduction and increase shared prosperity in SSA through three main avenues. First, it aims to create sustainable and inclusive growth, including through digital transformation and maximizing private finance. Second, the Strategy intends to strengthen the region's human capital. And finally, it aspires to build resilience to fragility and climate change. With these objectives in mind, the WBG is providing assistance to the region's governments in implementing important structural reforms, including in trade policy and regulation, competition policy, and investment policy. Regional integration remains a key priority for the WBG and is an important way to increase trade, diversify economies, and address diseconomies of scale emerging from small domestic markets. All of these are necessary for creating the jobs that will be needed to fuel growth over the coming years and decades.

This timely study outlines recommendations for the fifteen main ports on the ESA coastline to guide decision making and policy in port capacity expansion, hinterland connectivity, and leveraging of private investment and digital technologies to enhance operational efficiency and maximize the impact of ports on boosting economic growth and reducing vulnerabilities. Thus, the objectives of this analytical work are directly aligned with the pillars of the Africa Strategy and the increasing centrality of MFD in the World Bank Group's country and sector strategies.

Deborah L. Wetzel
Director of Regional Integration
Africa and Middle East and North Africa
The World Bank

Acknowledgments

This report was prepared by a team led by Martin Humphreys (Lead Transport Economist, Transport Global Practice, South Asia Unit) under the overall direction of Aurelio Menendez (Practice Manager, Transport Global Practice, West Africa Unit), Ben Eijbergen (Practice Manager, Transport Global Practice, East Africa Unit), and Maria Marcela Silva (Practice Manager, Transport Global Practice, Southern Africa Unit), with contributions from the following members of the Transport and Trade and Regional Integration Global Practices: Aiga Stokenberga (Transport Economist, Transport Global Practice, West Africa Unit), Matias Herrera Dappe (Senior Economist, Transport Global Practice, South Asia Unit), Atsushi Iimi (Senior Economist, Transport Global Practice, Southern Africa Unit), and Olivier Hartmann (Senior Private Sector Specialist, Global Trade and Regional Integration Unit). Tim Bushell (Infrastructure Advisor, U.K. Department for International Development, Dar es Salaam), was an external member of the team.

Assistance with transport and trade data identification and assembly was provided by Keith Garrett (Senior Geographer, Development Economics and Chief Economist). Spatial analysis and mapping support was provided by Charles Fox (Analyst, Sustainable Development Chief Economist). Tatiana Daza (Senior Program Assistant, Transport Global Practice, East Africa Unit) and Lisa Warouw (Program Assistant, Transport Global Practice, West Africa Unit) provided coordination and logistical support.

External inputs and comments were provided by Professor Jean-Claude Thill, Behnam Nikparvar, Faizeh Hatami, Adrienne Hua, and Paul H. Jung at University of North Carolina at Charlotte, Professor Lourdes Trujillo and her team at the University of Las Palmas, Gran Canaria, Professor Hercules Haralambides at Erasmus University Rotterdam, and Maritime Transport Business Solutions (MTBS).

The team would also like to express their gratitude to Biju Ninan Oommen (Senior Port and Maritime Transport Specialist, Transport Global Practice, Southeast Asia and Pacific Unit), Gylfi Palsson (Lead Transport Specialist,

Transport Global Practice, East Africa Unit), and Gael Raballand (Lead Public Sector Specialist, Governance Global Practice, Anglophone Africa Unit) for their comments on the draft report.

This work would not have been possible without financial support from the Tanzania Corridors for Growth Multi-Donor Trust Fund (TCFG), administered by the World Bank, with a financial contribution from UK aid.

About the Authors

Olivier Hartmann joined the World Bank in 2010 and is currently in the Trade and Regional Integration unit, working primarily on improving transport and logistics along the African corridors. He is also contributing to the Regional Integration pillar of the Africa Transport Policy Program (SSATP). Prior to that, he worked for the Port Reunion Authority (Reunion Island) and as Secretary General of PMAESA (the port industry association for East and Southern Africa), where he was involved in trade facilitation and multimodal transport in Sub-Saharan Africa. After PMAESA, he worked for the Northern Corridor, which is serving the landlocked countries of East Africa from the port of Mombasa, where he designed the model Transport Observatory for the corridor.

Matias Herrera Dappe is a Senior Economist in the Transport Global Practice of the World Bank. He has worked in the field of infrastructure and economic policy for more than 15 years, focusing on the economics of infrastructure investment, particularly transport, performance benchmarking, competition, and auctions. Before joining the World Bank, he worked in consulting and think tanks advising governments and companies in Latin America, North America, and Europe. He has written extensively on the topics mentioned. He holds a doctorate in economics from the University of Maryland, College Park.

Martin Humphreys is a Lead Transport Economist in the South Asia Unit of the Transport Global Practice of the World Bank. He has been working in the transport sector for nearly 30 years in a number of countries/regions, including, inter alia, United Kingdom, Denmark, Eastern Europe, the Russian Federation, South Asia, Central Asia, the South Caucasus, the Baltic States, the Western Balkan countries, and East and Southern Africa. His experience covers roads, railways, inland waterways and maritime ports, public-private partnerships, and trade and transport facilitation in post-conflict, fragile, and low- and middle-income countries. Humphreys has a first degree in economics and a master's degree and doctorate in transport economics.

Atsushi Iimi is a Senior Economist in the Transport Global Practice of the World Bank, where he specializes in development economics related to the Bank's transport operations in Africa. He joined the World Bank in 2006 after earning a doctorate in economics from Brown University. Before joining the Bank, he also worked at the International Monetary Fund (IMF) and Japan International Co-operation Agency/Overseas Economic Cooperation Fund, Japan. His research interests include spatial analysis, rural accessibility, evaluation of transport and energy projects, growth, and public expenditure. His research on these topics has been published in scholarly journals such as the *Review of Industrial Economics*, *Journal of Urban Economics*, *Journal of Applied Economics*, *Development Economies*, and *IMF Staff Papers*.

Aiga Stokenberga is an Economist in the Transport Global Practice of the World Bank, where she works on economic and spatial analyses that inform urban transport and regional corridor planning strategies in Sub-Saharan Africa. She has previously worked in the fields of sustainable energy, logistics, and trade integration, while at the World Resources Institute and as part of the Latin America and the Caribbean Unit of the World Bank. Her published research spans the fields of urban economics and transport planning. Stokenberga holds a master's degree in international energy policy from Johns Hopkins University School of Advanced International Studies (SAIS) and a doctorate in environment and resources, with a focus on urban land use, from Stanford University.

Abbreviations

2PL	second-party logistics
3PL	third-party logistics
4PL	fourth-party logistics
APMF	Agence Portuaire Maritime et Fluviale (Maritime and River Port Authority of Madagascar)
BCP	border crossing point
BPA	Berbera Port Authority
CAGR	compound annual growth rate
CCECC	China Civil Engineering Construction Corporation
CD	chart datum
CdM	Cornelder de Moçambique
CDN	Corredor de Desenvolvimento do Norte (Northern Corridor Development Authority)
CFM	Portos e Caminhos de Ferro de Moçambique (Mozambican Ports and Railways Authority)
CHEC	China Harbour Engineering Company
CMPH	China Merchants Port Holdings
DPFZA	Djibouti Ports & Free Zones Authority
DWT	deadweight tonnage
ESA	East and Southern Africa
eTKM	eTheKwini Municipality (Durban)
GDP	gross domestic product
GRT	gross registered tonnage
GT	gross tonnage
ICD	inland container depot
IMF	International Monetary Fund
ISO	International Organization for Standardization
IT	information technology
KPA	Kenya Ports Authority
LAPSSET	Lamu Port–South Sudan–Ethiopia Transport
LCDA	LAPSSET Corridor Development Authority
LOA	length overall

LSBCI	Liner Shipping Bilateral Connectivity Index
MPA	Mauritius Ports Authority
MPDC	Maputo Port Development Company
P/TOS	port/terminal operating system
PA	port authority
PCS	port community system
PdN	Portos do Norte (Ports of the North, Nacala)
PDSA	Port de Djibouti S.A.
PMAESA	Port Management Association of Eastern and Southern Africa
PPP	public-private partnership
R&D	research and development
RTG	rubber-tired gantry crane
SCA2D	Stratégie de Croissance Accélérée de Développement Durable (Accelerated Sustainable Development Growth Strategy)
SCP	Société Comorienne des Ports (Comoros Port Authority)
SGR	standard gauge railway
SPAT	Société du Port à Gestion Autonome de Toamasina (Autonomous Port Authority of Toamasina)
SSA	Sub-Saharan Africa
STS	ship-to-shore
TEMPI	Transnet eTheKwini Municipality Planning Initiative
TEU	twenty-foot equivalent unit
TICTS	Tanzania International Container Terminal Services
TNPA	Transnet National Ports Authority
TO	terminal operator
TPA	Tanzania Ports Authority
TPT	Transnet Port Terminals
ULCC	ultra-large container carrier
ULCS	ultra-large container ship
UNCTAD	United Nations Conference on Trade and Development
ZMA	Zanzibar Maritime Authority
ZPC	Zanzibar Ports Corporation

Overview

Between 2005 and 2015, the countries of Sub-Saharan Africa displayed strong and consistent economic performance, averaging gross domestic product (GDP) growth of 5 percent per year, despite the global financial crisis in 2009. Growth slowed notably in 2015–16, averaging about 1.2 percent, and recovery continued to be modest in 2017, with overall regional growth at 2.5 percent and varying performance across the region's countries. Robust growth was observed in non-resource-intensive countries such as Ethiopia, Kenya, Rwanda, and Tanzania in contrast to Angola, Nigeria, and South Africa (World Bank 2017).

In East and Southern Africa (ESA), freight volumes have been growing at 9 percent per year through some of the key ports, with transit consignments to land-locked countries growing at 16.5 percent per year until relatively recently. These growth trends are expected to continue in the medium term.

Against this backdrop, many of the main ports have struggled to meet the challenge of current growth, let alone that projected over the medium to long term. The result in many cases has been high ship waiting times, high berth occupancies, and congestion on both the land and maritime side, among other things; all contributing to increased transport costs.

The response has seen all the ESA ports either implementing or planning significant capacity enhancements, primarily relying on public investment. In addition to the proposals to develop existing ports, there are also plans—at various stages of preparation and implementation—to develop new greenfield ports at Lamu in Kenya, now under construction, and Bagamoyo in Tanzania, now in the planning stage.

This report presents the findings from a number of separate strands of work, which collectively seek to answer the following questions: (1) Are the proposed capacity enhancements justified by current and projected demand?; (2) What is the current performance of the ports, relative to regional and global peers, in terms of spatial and operating efficiency?; (3) Which ports are likely to become regional hubs, and which are more likely to become subregional or feeder ports?; (4) Is the current approach to increasing capacity—a balance between maritime capacity enhancement and rectifying other impediments to port efficiency—appropriate in the ESA subregion?; and (5) What are the other necessary actions for the main ports[1] from an institutional, policy, and operational perspective to ensure the ports deliver what is needed to enable local and regional economic development and trade?

THE MAIN FINDINGS

The study confirms the need to increase maritime capacity in the ports of ESA, but with certain caveats: Overall container demand in the fifteen ESA ports is predicted to begin exceeding total current capacity by between 2025 and 2030; capacity gaps are already visible in some ports in terms of dry bulk handling; and demand for liquid bulk handling is expected to exceed capacity in a number of ports by 2020–25.

However, the development plans and subsequent expansion of the individual ports, and the actual and proposed development of greenfield ports, need to reflect the trends in the shipping industry, the potential role of the port relative to both existing and new competing ports, the spatial and operating efficiency of the port, and landside access issues.

Not every port will have the opportunity to develop as a regional hub, with geographical location and proximity to main shipping routes, available draft, and appropriate infrastructure being crucial considerations. Based on the analysis undertaken in this study, and the ongoing port and hinterland development, a more likely scenario for ESA is for Durban and Djibouti to emerge as the regional hubs.

The development of any port as a regional hub port in ESA faces several challenges: First, many of the ports serve only one transport corridor, so diversion from other corridors is difficult; second, the movement toward a hub-and-spoke system is slightly slower in ESA than in West Africa; third, many ports simply lack the necessary attributes to develop into a hub; and finally, some investment appears to be diverted to less-viable port facilities.

There is a need to improve the operating efficiency in all the ports. The analysis shows that the average technical efficiency of container terminal operations in the 10 ports (Beira, Dar es Salaam, Durban, East London, Maputo, Mombasa, Nacala, Port Louis, Djibouti, Toamasina) falls in a range of 44–53 percent for the 2000–10 data set in the defined sample of matching ports.[2] In other words, the ports in ESA are less than half as productive as the most efficient ports in the matched data set of similar ports across the world, in terms of efficiency of container-handling operations.

The ranking is constant, more or less, across the different models: Durban, Mombasa, Dar es Salaam, and Port Sudan are the most efficient ports in terms of container handling; Beira, East London, and Nacala are the least efficient. Globally, the port of Mombasa, based on this data set, is the most technically efficient port, and ranks as the 43rd most efficient container port in the defined sample of matched ports. Dar es Salaam and Durban follow at 64th and 70th positions, respectively, for container operations. These are the rankings in the sample of 110 matched ports of similar size and scope, not the ranking globally among all ports. All the ESA ports would rank well below the most efficient ports in the world.

The analysis also reveals that the main factors that contribute to driving higher efficiency in container handling in these ports are (1) the presence of specialist international terminal operator(s); (2) the existence of an effective rail connection to the port; (3) the existence of transshipment traffic; (4) a higher score on the Connectivity Index; and (5) reduced vessel time at berth. Not all ports meet the five criteria (Mombasa and Durban, for instance, are publicly operated); if the aspiration is to make them globally competitive, it will require movement on all five factors.

There is a need for greater integration in the supply chain. The global port industry has for some time been impacted by vertical and horizontal integration among producers (port operators and port authorities), terminal operators, shipping lines, and land transport.

Within the maritime industry, a key example of horizontal integration is in container shipping alliances, where shipping lines pool their respective fleets and move containers on one another's behalf, to extend their service offerings and geographic coverage in a manner analogous to code-sharing by the airlines. In the port subsector, the most important trend is the development of global specialist terminal operators that operate container terminals internationally, with enhanced cooperation between the respective ports. In some contexts, this can give rise to concerns over anticompetitive practices (World Bank 2015).

An example of vertical integration by public-sector entities in the port sector concerns the role of the port authority (PA) or terminal operator (TO) as cluster manager. In this role, PAs or TOs are involved in the development or operation of rail and road hinterland links via logistics platforms, to offer efficient and reliable transport services to shippers and ensure sufficient flows of goods through the port (Baccelli, Percoco, and Tedeschi 2008).

In the ESA port sector, vertical integration is visible, but to a lesser extent than it is in the more economically developed countries. Also, vertical integration in some countries in the project region is driven by the public sector authorities themselves, while in developed countries these trends are usually driven by the private sector. The degree of vertical integration is strongest in the ports of Djibouti, Mombasa, Toamasina, Port Louis, Durban, and the three Mozambican ports.

Improving landside access is crucial: One challenge faced by all the ESA ports, almost without exception, is the need to improve landside access. In the case of many, the issue of landside access is more important than improving maritime access and capacity. There are three main constraints: (1) limited or no intermodality; (2) limitation in the quality of the road infrastructure, and delays at the border-crossing points; and (3) congestion at the port-city interface.

Limited or no intermodality: Current connectivity from ESA's ports to hinterland destinations still depends primarily on a road network of variable quality and coverage. Despite this, road transport moves a majority of cargo to and from the region's ports: More than 70 percent of all cargo to or from the ports is carried by road transport. If one excludes South Africa, the figure increases to 90 percent. A significant part of the ESA railway network is in a poor state, and most lines are single-track and not electrified— the exception being South Africa.

Roads and borders: While the core regional road network on the main trading corridors is in good to fair condition, there are still some sections in poor condition, and some with missing links. But a major issue across the region, with the exception of South Africa, is the efficacy and the efficiency of road maintenance. Despite substantial investments in road infrastructure in recent years, limitations in management, poor enforcement of axle-load restrictions, inadequate maintenance practices, and insufficient resources continue to lead to premature deterioration of the roads and increased transport costs.

Also, the border crossing points, despite improvements in many locations, remain significant points of delays and additional costs: An analysis of the road corridor on the Southern North-South Corridor revealed—for the movement of a consignment between Durban and Lusaka—border posts were responsible for 15 percent of total monetary costs (comprising 1 percent, 1 percent, and 13 percent) and 37 percent of total travel time (comprising 13 percent, 11 percent, and 13 percent) through Beitbridge, Chirundu, and Kasumbalesa, respectively.

The port-city interface: The final major challenge for many of the ESA ports in terms of land access is what is known as the port-city interface. The evolution and development of ports create a number of benefits for their host cities and countries. Ports and their related services and industries create substantial employment for local workers. As port traffic has grown, port-related labor demand has increased, usually unskilled and from the immediate vicinity of the port. While increased containerization and mechanization in a port has diminished the number of unskilled cargo handlers, generally ports remain significant local employers at the heart of an economic cluster.

Despite the benefits, the negative impacts of ports on cities—both direct and indirect—are substantial. These externalities range from environmental issues (such as air emissions, water pollution, or soil pollution) to congestion issues and safety risks. Port-induced city congestion is the most notable negative externality in and around the ESA ports. Many cities grew around the existing port, with roads running through the city centers and suburbs, and few have successfully addressed these concerns in a substantive manner.

There is a need to improve stakeholder engagement in many ports. The relationship between the port and its stakeholders—including, but not only, the users of the port—is an essential component of good management and operation. This group includes the users of the port, the other public agencies involved in the port, and the authorities responsible for the land areas outside the port. For example, if there is no collaborative dialogue with the revenue authority, spatial and operating efficiency could be impeded. Currently, the dialogue is not equally strong and formalized across the ESA ports; and in some it is ad hoc and informal.

There is a need to introduce modern management systems. Despite the importance of comprehensive information management systems, in a number of the ports the current modus operandi in the terminals is characterized by operational and administrative procedures for which approval and information exchange is carried out on paper, in offices at multiple locations inside the port operations area. Also, imported cargo in cars and trucks is subject to customs inspection inside the operational area of the port. Agents, customs officers, and truck drivers walk between offices inside the operations area, adding to safety and security risks. All of this obstructs efficient cargo and equipment flow, and results in operational delays.

Although many ports in the ESA region provide services that could be part of a port community system (PCS), such as single-window, tracking-tracing, automatic data interchanges, or truck appointment systems, there are only three that operate a full PCS: Port Louis, Durban, and East London. In some cases, specialist terminal operators have invested in terminal operating systems and gate management systems. In other ports, there is little movement toward a substantive PCS, with some terminals operated by the port authority still running inefficient, paper-based PA/TO systems, such as at the publicly operated berths in Dar es Salaam port.

There is also an overreliance on public investment in port development and expansion. Ports require considerable infrastructure in order to fulfill their function and compete successfully. The necessary infrastructure is large, lumpy in an economic sense, and expensive. Traditionally, the development of ports has relied on public investment, which remains the predominant approach in the ESA countries. However, elsewhere in the world, this reliance on the public purse changed in the 1980s, with private investment being used for equipment and the initial superstructure, and more recently for financing the construction of entire terminals, including quay walls, land reclamation, and dredging, along with the superstructure.

There is another advantage to utilizing the experience of specialist terminal operators. Ports and terminals benefit from the participation of private terminal operators, not only in terms of leveraging private capital and reducing the level of necessary public investment, but also in the transfer of expertise, managerial incentives, and technologies. A transaction can be designed to protect the strategic interests of a country, but a specialist operator can also provide a port with a competitive edge relative to regional peers. Many ports in West Africa show the efficiency improvements of moving to a landlord model and bringing in a specialist terminal operator.

Finally, the institutional framework for all the ports needs strengthening to ensure the most efficient use of the infrastructure. The primary weakness in all the ESA countries, with the singular exception of South Africa, is the lack of an independent regulator with sufficient resources and capacity to ensure effective auditing, monitoring, and tariff regulation in the port sector. For example, in seven of the countries, the PAs regulate themselves in terms of the scale and structure of tariffs (Djibouti, Kenya, Zanzibar in Tanzania, the Comoros, Madagascar, Mauritius, Mozambique).

Also, despite the explicit objective of a number of governments to move toward the landlord port management model, in many countries in the region, port operations are still carried out in whole or in part by the PAs themselves, using their own employees (Kenya, Tanzania in part, Zanzibar), or by publicly owned companies working as operators (Mauritius, South Africa). While neither model is ideal, the latter, at least, offers the advantage of transparency with respect to the profit and costs of port operations, and the avoidance of implicit cross-subsidization.

Increasing maritime capacity without adequately considering these latter issues will inhibit the realization of the full benefit from any maritime capacity enhancement and also constrain the efficiency of a port.

NOTES

1. The report covers the main ports in ESA: Djibouti, Berbera, Lamu, Mombasa, Dar es Salaam, Zanzibar, Nacala, Maputo, Beira, Durban, Port Louis, East London, Toamasina, Mahajanga, and Moroni.

2. For each port in the study, the analysis identified 11 matching ports of similar size and scope: 5 in Africa, 2 in Latin America, and 4 in Asia. The aggregate list of 110 ports represents the matched sample.

REFERENCES

Baccelli, O., M. Percoco, and A. Tedeschi. 2008. "Port Authorities as Cluster Managers." *European Transport* 39: 44–58. https://www.openstarts.units.it/bitstream/10077/5984/1/Baccelli _Percoco_Tedeschi_ET39.pdf.

World Bank. 2015. *PPP Knowledge Lab Comoros*. https://pppknowledgelab.org/countries /comoros.

——. 2017. *World Development Indicators*. https://databank.worldbank.org/data/source/world -development-indicators.

1 Introduction

WHY WAS THIS STUDY UNDERTAKEN?

Between 2005 and 2015, the countries of Sub-Saharan Africa displayed strong and consistent economic performance, averaging gross domestic product (GDP) growth of 5 percent per year, despite the global financial crisis in 2009. Growth slowed notably in 2015–16, averaging about 1.2 percent, and recovery continued to be modest in 2017, with overall regional growth at 2.5 percent and varying performance across the region's countries. Robust growth was observed in non-resource-intensive countries such as Ethiopia, Kenya, Rwanda, and Tanzania, in contrast to Angola, Nigeria, and South Africa (World Bank 2017).

In East and Southern Africa (ESA) specifically, freight volumes have been growing at 9 percent per year through some of the key gateway ports, with transit consignments to landlocked countries growing at 16.5 percent, albeit with some recent flattening of that growth.

In the medium term, the global demand for Africa's natural resources, which account for 70 percent of the region's exports—much of which will pass through its maritime ports—is likely to remain strong. As the individual economies continue to grow, the demand for consumer goods, vehicles, construction materials, and agricultural inputs will increase, further raising volumes moving through the region's maritime ports.

Against this backdrop, many of the existing ports have struggled to meet the challenge of current growth, let alone the growth projected over the next 20–30 years. Many are spatially and operationally inefficient, lack specialist terminal operators and modern technology, display limited functional integration, and suffer restrictions on maritime and landside access.

The result in many cases has been, among other things, high ship waiting times, high berth occupancies, and congestion on both the land and maritime sides, all contributing to increased costs. There is also the related tension between the port and the host city, reflecting the asymmetry in the distribution of benefits and costs for gateway ports—known as the problem of the port-city interface.

The response to these pressures has seen all major ports either implementing or planning significant capacity enhancements, primarily relying on public investment. Along with proposals for the existing ports, there are also plans—at various stages of preparation and implementation—to develop new "greenfield" ports at Lamu in Kenya and Bagamoyo in Tanzania.

While projected demand growth appears to support the proposed enhancements in maritime capacity, there is concern that there is insufficient focus on other key challenges facing the port sector: The need to improve spatial and operational efficiency, introduce modern information technology systems, attract and retain specialist terminal operators, reduce the burden on the public purse through partnerships with the private sector, improve functional integration in the logistics chain, and improve landside access and the port-city interface. Addressing these issues in the right manner could deliver both increased efficiency and capacity at lower cost, thereby obviating the immediate need for significant capital investment, and potentially reducing the scale of the required public investment. More importantly, greater efficiency raises the attractiveness of a port relative to its competitors.

There is a related concern about some of the investment plans, in the sense that the justification for some is an aspiration to develop as major regional hubs serving the subregional network of feeder ports with an expanded hinterland and attracting more transshipment consignments. However, not every port will be able to develop into such a role, and some are likely to be deceived in their ambitions. Elements such as geographical location, proximity to the main shipping lanes, available water depths, and the preferences of the shipping lines will force some ports to focus on subregional markets or specific commodity groups, irrespective of investments made or planned. In certain cases, additional investments could be required.

This report presents the findings of a number of separate strands of work, which collectively seek to answer the following questions: (1) Are the proposed capacity enhancements justified by current and projected demand?; (2) What is the current performance of the ports, in spatial and operating efficiency, relative to regional and matched peers globally?; (3) Which ports are likely to become regional hubs, and which are destined to become subregional or feeder ports?; (4) Is the current balance between maritime capacity enhancement and the other impediments to port efficiency appropriate in the ESA subregion?; and (5) What are the other necessary actions for the main ports[1] from an institutional, policy, and operational perspective, to ensure that the ports deliver what is needed to enable local and regional economic development and trade?

The report covers the 15 main ports on the ESA coast: Beira, Berbera, Dar es Salaam, Djibouti, Durban, East London, Lamu, Mahajanga, Maputo, Mombasa, Moroni, Nacala, Port Louis, Toamasina, and Zanzibar (map 1.1).

AN OUTLINE OF THE REPORT

Chapter 2 provides an overview of the evolution of economic growth and trade in countries in the hinterlands of the ports of interest, and a summary of the overall and transport-specific costs of trade in the ESA region. The chapter then outlines the role of maritime ports in driving growth and trade.

Chapter 3 provides an overview of the 15 ports, summarizing their current operational status, trends, capacity, and recently implemented and ongoing or

MAP 1.1

Ports included in the study

Source: World Bank.

planned capacity expansion projects. It also provides an overview of the recent growth in volumes handled by the ports, together with regional trends.

Chapter 4 evaluates the recent performance and status of the ESA ports from several perspectives, benchmarking ports against one another and against matched global comparators to the extent possible. The report uses three broad sets of indicators to provide an indication of the relative performance of ESA ports: spatial and operating efficiency; maritime access and connectivity; and technical efficiency.

Chapter 5 reviews the various challenges facing the port sector in ESA in more detail. Among these are the changes taking place in global shipping markets, such as the cascading effect; consolidation among shipping lines; gaps in the policy, legal, and institutional frameworks relative to best-practice benchmarks; and poor access and limited intermodality.

Chapter 6 discusses the prospects of the ESA port sector going forward. This includes an analysis of the competitive landscape of the ports, and the drivers of port choice from the shippers' point of view; an aggregate and disaggregate estimate of the increase in volume and hinterland shares for the different ports; and the implications of these trends for investment needs.

Finally, chapter 7 provides the key conclusions, followed by more specific recommendations for each of the 15 ports.

NOTE

1. The report covers the 15 main ports in ESA: Djibouti, Berbera, Lamu, Mombasa, Dar es Salaam, Zanzibar, Nacala, Maputo, Beira, Durban, Port Louis, East London, Toamasina, Mahajanga, and Moroni.

REFERENCE

World Bank. 2017. *World Development Indicators.* https://databank.worldbank.org/data/source/world-development-indicators.

2 The Role of the Port in International Trade

AFRICAN ECONOMIC GROWTH

Africa has demonstrated strong economic growth over the past 10 years, resulting in a compound annual growth rate (CAGR) of 3.7 percent. Total gross domestic product (GDP) in the countries served by the ports in this study grew to an aggregate US$762.7 billion in 2016, measured in constant 2010 US$. The largest share is accounted for by South Africa, with a total GDP of US$421.3 billion, followed by Kenya with a GDP of US$55.4 billion, and Ethiopia with a GDP of US$52.3 billion. At the other end of the scale, the GDPs of the Comoros and Djibouti amounted to US$1.1 billion and US$1.6 billion respectively.

There has also been significant population growth in the subregion, with East and Southern Africa (ESA)'s population growing at a CAGR of 2.8 percent over the period 2006–16. The total population grew from just over 400 million inhabitants in 2006 to approximately 530 million inhabitants in 2016. This growth is expected to continue, with the entire continent expected to surpass 2 billion inhabitants before 2040. In absolute terms, Ethiopia is the most populous country in ESA, with just over 100 million inhabitants in 2016. In relative terms, population growth was the largest in Swaziland, at a CAGR of 4.2 percent in 2006–16, followed by Burundi (3.5 percent) and Uganda (3.4 percent).

GDP per capita in 2016 ranged between US$198 in Burundi and US$9,700 in Mauritius. There is a large difference in GDP per capita between the top four countries—Mauritius, South Africa, Botswana, and Swaziland—and the remaining ESA countries. Over 2006–16, Ethiopia demonstrated the highest growth in GDP per capita, at 7.4 percent per year, followed by Rwanda with 4.7 percent (World Bank 2017).

With the growth trends of GDP and population expected to continue, a key aspect for many African countries is to limit the volatility of economic growth through diversification. At present, most ESA countries remain characterized by low economic diversification, overdependence on the agricultural sector and on imports of finished goods, and an overreliance on commodity exports as the main drivers of economic growth. Both Mauritius and South Africa have diversified their economies, with sectors other than mining or tourism contributing significantly to GDP, whereas at the other extreme Botswana and Swaziland have a more limited export base focused on diamonds and sugar cane.

THE GROWTH AND GEOGRAPHY OF AFRICAN TRADE

Over the last 15 years, Africa's total trade has increased at about 12 percent annually. In 2016, Sub-Saharan Africa (SSA) exported a total of US$332 billion worth of goods and services and imported goods and services worth US$396 billion (World Development Indicators). Much of this was shipped through the main ports of the region. While the value of SSA exports of bulk commodities has declined since the end of the global resources boom in 2010, imports have continued to grow, overtaking exports in value terms (PwC 2018). SSA imports are dominated by containerized cargo, while exports are mainly raw materials and agricultural products, which are mostly handled as bulk freight. Most ESA countries have an abundance of natural resources, including large deposits of coal, iron ore, and precious metals. These commodities are mined and exported either to neighboring countries or globally, and frequently represent the largest drivers of economic growth in these countries.

For ESA, exports of precious metals and minerals represent a significant share in value terms. Copper and copper products in 2016 represented nearly 80 percent of Zambia's exports; and nickel and other minerals exports consti-tuted about 20 percent of Zimbabwe's exports. Aluminum and alloys repre-sented close to a quarter of Mozambique's; another 12 percent of Mozambique's exports, worth nearly US$0.5 billion, were represented by coal and coke. Gold represented over 18 percent of South Africa's exports in 2016, worth US$17.5 billion (Center for International Development 2018). Nevertheless, South Africa's economy is among the most diversified in SSA, with commodi-ties accounting for approximately 13 percent of GDP and 60 percent of mer-chandise exports by value (PwC 2018).

A second major group of key products exported by the region's countries are agricultural cash crops such as tobacco, tea, cocoa, and coffee, which in 2016 represented about 70 percent of Malawi's exports, 48 percent of Zimbabwe's, and about 25–28 percent of Uganda's and Kenya's.

In terms of trade partners, the share of intraregional trade in Africa remains limited. As a share of total exports in value terms, other African countries in 2016 represented less than 5 percent in Djibouti, South Sudan, and Somalia; and it was in the 20–30 percent range in most other countries in the region. An exception is Uganda, where exports to the rest of Africa reached 53 percent as a share of its total exports in value terms (Center for International Development 2018). Imports from the rest of Africa were considerably higher than exports in the landlocked countries of Malawi, Zambia, and Zimbabwe, reaching 37 percent, 64 percent, and 55 percent, respectively, in value terms in 2016. In contrast, imports from African partners were significantly lower than exports in the case of Kenya, South Africa, Tanzania, and Uganda.

European countries continue to represent a significant share of the region's trade, typically in the range of 20–40 percent in value terms. There is also an increase in the trade volumes between African countries and China: In 2000,

China-Africa trade amounted to US$10 billion. Since then, this figure has risen more than twentyfold, peaking at over US$220 billion in 2014 (*Financial Times* 2017). In 2016, China accounted for more than 40 percent of Zambia's exports in value terms, 37 percent of Zimbabwe's, and 19 percent of South Africa's. The ESA countries heavily reliant on China for imports include Djibouti (54 percent of all its imports in value terms in 2016), Kenya (36 percent), and Tanzania (34 percent).

India is also becoming an increasingly important trade partner for individual countries in the ESA region, with nearly a third of Somalia's imports in value terms coming from India in 2016. In most other countries in ESA, India's imports represent between 5 and 10 percent of total goods and services (Center for International Development 2018).

THE COST OF TRADE

The state of Africa's primary road network has improved considerably in the last three decades, with the share of roads in good condition increasing from 20 percent to about 50 percent. Despite these improvements, transport and trade costs and prices have not decreased proportionally, as the benefits from the improvements in physical infrastructure are partly diminished by the time lost at the national borders (Fitzmaurice and Hartmann 2013),[1] at the maritime gateways, and in overcoming the soft barriers.

Moreover, international trade costs for the region are further increased by the relatively small shipment sizes and asymmetric flows, leading to high costs per unit of shipment. Unit costs are also elevated by the imbalance between the types of cargo imported and exported (containerized versus mostly bulk). Moving a unit (such as container) of cargo is 1.5–3.5 times more expensive in Africa than in comparable high-volume trade routes over a similar distance (PwC 2018).

The World Development Indicators (World Bank 2017) show that in 2014, it cost, on average, US$2,201 to export a container from Sub-Saharan Africa and US$2,931 to import one. These averages, however, mask significant disparities across countries. In ESA's landlocked countries, the costs of trade tend to be significantly higher than in the coastal countries and the island economies. For example, in 2014 it cost US$4,290 to import a container into the Democratic Republic of Congo and US$4,990 to import into Rwanda, compared with just US$910 and US$710 per container, respectively, into Djibouti and Mauritius.

The cost of imports and exports to or from a given country often varies quite significantly depending on the corridor used. For example, the cost of import by road into Malawi ranges from US$70 per ton on the Nacala corridor to US$178 per ton when using the Durban corridor. Still, despite the high costs and long lead times, significant cargo volumes are moved via Durban because of the route's high reliability in lead time and better port performance compared with the Beira and Nacala corridors (Ksoll and Kunaka 2016).

As a result, transport costs represent a sizable share of key imported production inputs in the region's landlocked countries. In Malawi, transport prices account for nearly a third of the delivered price of fertilizer (Ksoll and Kunaka 2016). The overall trade costs are directly influenced by cargo type and by the mode of transport, where a choice is available. As one example, the cost of moving one container carrying tobacco from Malawi to Beira is reported to be

US$3,800, whereas by rail to Nacala, if the service were reliable, the cost would be US$2,000 per container, for subsequent transshipment in Durban in both cases (Ksoll and Kunaka 2016).

The costs of trade can be expected to decline as trade volumes increase, because of the economies of scale characteristic of port and shipping operations—if other impediments are also addressed. In SSA overall, a 10 percent efficiency gain from economies of scale from higher throughput—if the average throughput at the major SSA ports is doubled (PwC 2018)—has been estimated to result in a savings of US$2.2 billion per year in logistics costs.

THE ROLE OF THE MARITIME PORT

Seaborne trade accounted for 80 percent of the total volume and 70 percent of the value of global trade in 2016. In absolute terms, total volume carried reached 10.3 billion tons. Seaborne trade by developing countries represented 59 percent and 64 percent of loaded and unloaded world tonnage, respectively. However, African countries accounted for just 7 percent and 5 percent of both magnitudes (UNCTAD 2017), with the former falling slightly from 2015, reflecting the impact of lower commodity prices.

Seaports along the ESA coast have evolved along with the hinterlands they serve and have played an important role in their economic performance (Suárez Bosa 2014). Ports and maritime trade stimulated the emergence of the money economy, the expansion of urban populations, and the growth of local markets for goods and services. Both local and global patterns played a role in the long-term evolution of the regional port system (Wang and Ducruet 2013). For instance, the length of the coastline of the larger countries in ESA and their relative population dispersions were key factors stimulating port concentration processes in a few major ports.

The transport revolution in the region was initially tied to colonial settlement and the exploration and exploitation of regional economic resources. Subsequently, rapid and sustained pre–World War I economic growth in ESA pushed forward the first large-scale reforms at major seaports: Mombasa (1896), Beira (1897), Dar es Salaam (1900), Maputo (1903), and Durban (1904). Most of these ports were connected with rail lines during this time to support the expansion of cash crop farming and mining production. However, there were some differences across the main ports in terms of the source of demand for their services. For example, while Durban and Maputo's growth was based on expansion of mining exports such as copper and chrome, Mombasa's sustained growth was dominated by general cargo shipping and bulk trade in grains and cash crops.

During the interwar period, structural changes in the shipping industry required further port reforms, and demanded considerable investment by colonial governments, such as in commodity export terminals. During this period, the concentration of port activity was intentionally increased, and the smaller local ports were definitively displaced by ocean-going trade networks.

The post–World War II economic boom, driven by external demand for raw materials and commodities, further promoted infrastructure investment and port development in ESA. However, the port-creation process during this time was less intense in Eastern Africa compared with the continent's Atlantic coast, where port throughputs multiplied as a result of recent oil discovery. In the next several decades, the ESA ports mostly played the role of external trade growth poles, while regional integration and trade within ESA slowed down.

While the containerization trend in global maritime shipping first emerged in the early 1970s, it was only in the late 1990s that the trend reached the entire East African coast. The expansion of containerization further reinforced the port hierarchies and concentration patterns already established. Containerization developed rapidly in South Africa already during the 1980s, allowing Durban to consolidate its position as the main regional port and encouraging the development of hub-and-spoke transport networks with Durban playing a central role (Fraser, Notteboom, and Ducruet 2014).

Moving forward, port competitiveness and positioning in global supply chains will further define Africa's ability to export and import (PwC 2018).

NOTE

1. In a study on total logistics costs on the Northern Corridor, estimates of the monetary costs of the delays were at US$247 per 24 hours for a truck, and US$137 for the goods: a total of US$384 for a loaded truck.

REFERENCES

Center for International Development. 2018. *Atlas of Economic Complexity*. http://atlas.cid .harvard.edu/explore/?country=71&partner=undefined&product=undefined&product Class=HS&startYear=undefined&target=Product&year=2016.

Financial Times. 2017. "Chinese Investment in Africa: Beijing's Testing Ground." https://www .ft.com/content/0f534aa4-4549-11e7-8519-9f94ee97d996.

Fitzmaurice, M., and O. Hartmann. 2013. "Border Crossing Monitoring along the Northern Corridor." Sub-Saharan Africa Transport Policy Program (SSATP) Working Paper No. 96, World Bank, Washington, DC.

Fraser, D. R., T. Notteboom, and C. Ducruet. 2014. "Peripherality in the Global Container Shipping Network: The Case of the Southern African Container Port System." *Geojournal* 81 (1): 1–13.

Ksoll, C. and C. Kunaka. 2016. "Trade and Logistics Background Paper for Malawi Country Economic Memorandum."

PwC. 2018. *Strengthening Africa's Gateway to Trade*. PwC.

Suárez Bosa, M., ed. 2014. *Atlantic Ports and the First Globalisation, c.1850–1930*. Palgrave Macmillan.

UNCTAD (United Nations Conference on Trade and Development). 2017. *Review of Maritime Transport*. UNCTAD.

Wang, C., and C. Ducruet. 2013. "Regional Resilience and Spatial Cycles: Long-Term Evolution of the Chinese Port System (221BC–2010AD)." *Tidjschrift voor Economische en Sociale Geografie* 104 (5): 521–38.

World Bank. 2017. *World Development Indicators*. https://databank.worldbank.org/data/source /world-development-indicators.

3 The Port Sector in East and Southern Africa

This chapter provides an overview of the 15 ports in the study, their operational status, current capacity, and ongoing or planned expansion projects for each. It also provides an overview of the recent growth in volume handled by the ports, some comment on general trends in volumes, and aggregate predictions of future growth.[1]

A REGIONAL PERSPECTIVE

The 15 East and Southern Africa (ESA) ports in the study vary markedly in the core characteristics of total capacity, port area, available equipment, and connectivity. For example, in 2017 the length of berth available for container vessels ranged from 308 meters in Maputo to 2,576 meters at Durban. Durban also has the largest amount of space allocated to container facilities, at more than one million square meters.

By contrast, the comparable areas in the ports of Djibouti, Dar es Salaam, Beira, and Mombasa fall between 200,000 and 250,000 square meters, and Maputo has a modest 150,000 square meters allocated.

This variation reflects, to a certain extent, the current role or function of each port, and its connectivity. In terms of the former, the report differentiates among global hubs, regional hubs, feeder ports, and regional ports. A port is referred to as a global hub when it is connected to the main global trade routes and is called on by mega ships of up to 20,000 twenty-foot equivalent units[2] (TEU) to transship cargo to both regional and global markets (for example, Rotterdam). There are no global hubs in the ESA region. A regional hub is smaller in scale and acts primarily as a transshipment hub to other ports in the region. Feeder ports are the ports that are not connected to the main trade routes and are primarily "feedered," or served, by the main shipping lines, via the regional hub ports. Regional ports, small or large, are those that have a specific focus on the port's direct hinterland, which determines the size of the port. The following section summarizes the salient points of the individual ports, and their current role in this typology of ports.

OVERVIEW OF THE MAIN PORTS

Djibouti

The port of Djibouti is located at the southern entrance to the Red Sea (map 3.1). Since 1998, the port has handled most of landlocked Ethiopia's maritime traffic, which moves to and from Addis Ababa by truck. Serving Ethiopia gives the port of Djibouti a vast hinterland. The port focuses on the transit traffic for Ethiopia and provides transshipment activities for containers destined for other ESA ports, as such acting as a regional hub at the northern end of the continent. The port has three main parts: the old port located in the city and the Doraleh Container Terminal opened in 2008 and the first phase of the Doraleh Multipurpose Port opened in 2013, which are both located to the west of the city.

Djibouti also acts as a key gateway port, and it is estimated that approximately 85 percent of the total throughput in the port of Djibouti comprises cargo destined for or coming from Ethiopia. The composition and volume of traffic handled at the port is shown in table 3.1. The port is connected to Ethiopia by road and rail. However, the condition of the road network has deteriorated in recent years. At the end of 2017, a new 756 km electrified railway became operational, linking the port of Djibouti to Ethiopia's capital, Addis Ababa. In the future, the new railway is not only expected to connect to Addis Ababa, but also to other landlocked east African countries such as Uganda and South Sudan (DPFZA 2017).

The Djibouti Ports & Free Zones Authority (DPFZA) is the governing authority that sets the rules, directives, and overarching principles for the smooth and efficient running of the port and free zones in Djibouti. Port Autonome International de Djibouti (PAID) was originally established as a

MAP 3.1
Location of Djibouti port

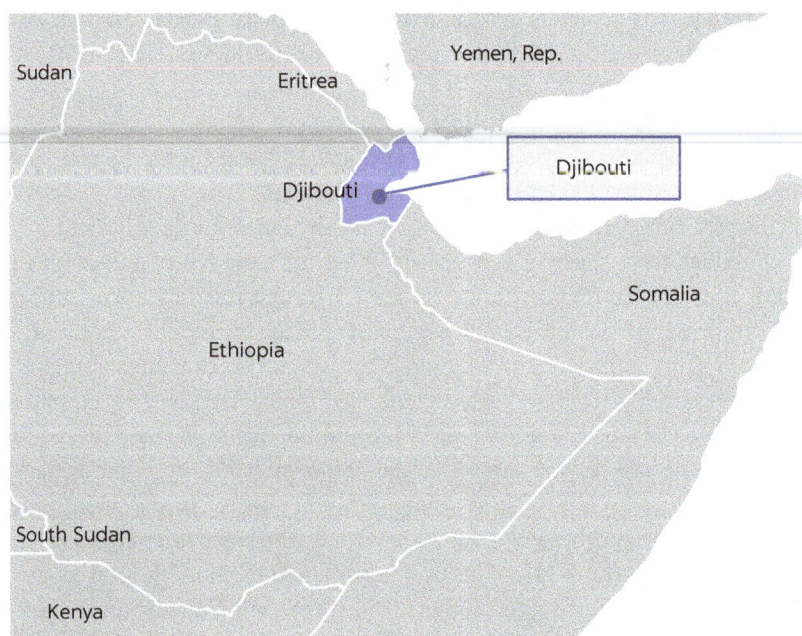

Source: World Bank.

TABLE 3.1 **Traffic composition and volume, Djibouti, 2012–16**

UNIT (thousands)	2012	2013	2014	2015	2016
Containers (TEU)	791	795	856	909	987
Containers (tons)[a]	7,915	7,947	8,561	9,094	9,872
General cargo (tons)	1,633	1,512	1,584	2,057	2,022
Dry bulk (tons)	2,378	2,422	2,527	2,904	4,295
Liquid bulk (tons)	2,749	2,970	3,892	3,818	3,767
Vehicles (tons)	194	199	165	216	208
Total (tons)	**14,869**	**15,050**	**16,729**	**18,089**	**20,164**

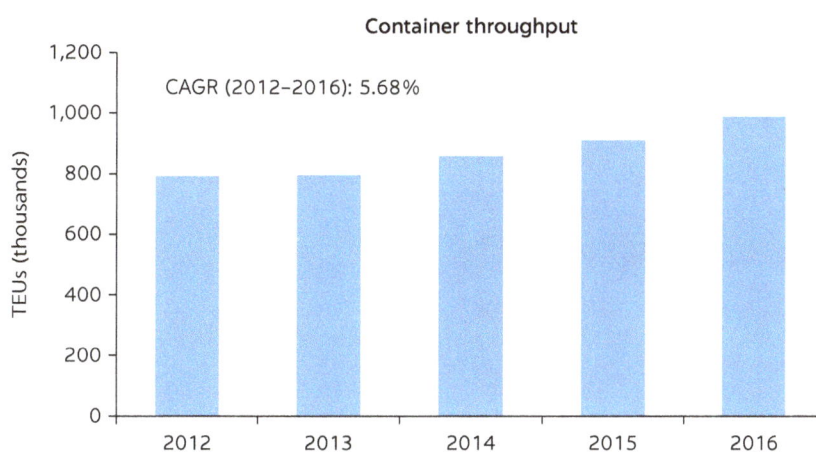

Container throughput

CAGR (2012–2016): 5.68%

Source: DPFZA.
Note: CAGR = compound annual growth rate; TEU = twenty-foot equivalent unit.
a. Estimated.

public company, managing and regulating the port of Djibouti. In 2012, PAID was transformed into a private company with shares, called Port de Djibouti S.A. (PDSA). China Merchants Holdings International (CMHI) then acquired 23.5 percent of the shares in PDSA. The remaining shares are owned by the DPFZA. The Doraleh Multipurpose Port is operated by a 100 percent subsidiary of PDSA, called DMPSA. The Doraleh Container Terminal was developed by DP World under a concession agreement in which they had a 33 percent share, but it was recently nationalized by the government after a dispute.

Berbera

The port of Berbera is strategically located in the northwestern region of Somalia, on the Gulf of Aden (map 3.2). The steep growth in the traffic handled by the port is shown in table 3.2. The Berbera Port Authority (BPA) and the Somaliland government have been in discussions with private partners regarding a large-scale infrastructure development project expanding the port of Berbera and constructing roads ("The Berbera Corridor") that would connect the port with Ethiopia. This project is a high priority for Berbera, which would derive substantial revenue, as well as for Ethiopia, which seeks improved access to the port to meet its domestic requirements. It is early in the development of the port, but the port is primarily a regional port.

MAP 3.2
Location of Berbera port

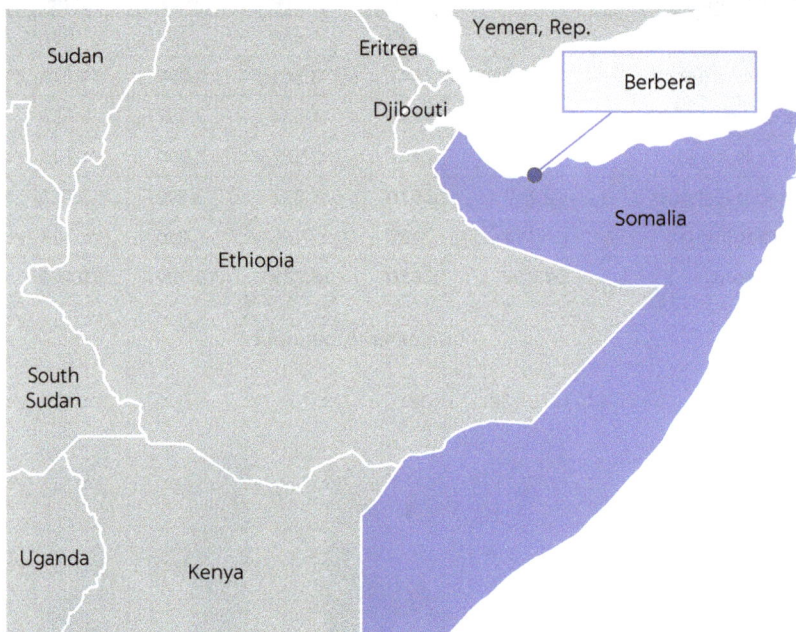

Source: World Bank.

TABLE 3.2 **Traffic composition and volume, Berbera, 2012–16**

UNIT (thousands)	2012	2013	2014	2015	2016
Containers (TEU)	36	38	53	73	92
Containers (tons)[a]	359	377	525	730	916
General cargo (tons)	443	394	450	394	404
Dry bulk (tons)	702	679	700	1,020	1,436
Liquid bulk (tons)	93	102	152	233	218
Vehicles (tons)	11	15	18	24	19
Total (tons)	**1,609**	**1,567**	**1,846**	**2,402**	**2,993**

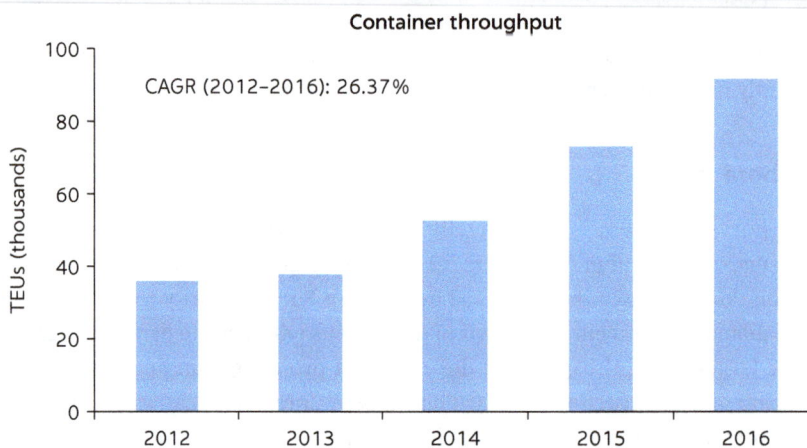

Container throughput

CAGR (2012–2016): 26.37%

Source: Berbera Port Authority.
Note: CAGR = compound annual growth rate; TEU = twenty-foot equivalent unit.
a. Estimated.

The port of Berbera is owned and operated by the Somaliland Administration through an autonomous (parastatal) body: the Berbera Port Authority. This parastatal organization has autonomous status for the management and operation of the port. Consequently, the BPA is free to order or execute works for the port infrastructure, to procure services for its own needs, and to hire and fire its own employees.

In late 2016, United Arab Emirates–based port operator Dubai Ports World announced it would set up a joint venture with 65 percent control, together with the government of Somaliland, to manage and invest in the port of Berbera. The investment of up to US$442 million will include a first phase of operational improvements and acquisition of terminal equipment, and a second phase with a 400-meter quay and 250,000 m² yard extension.

Mombasa

The port of Mombasa is Kenya's primary port, and the main gateway and exit port for cargo belonging to a large hinterland including the landlocked countries of Uganda, northern Tanzania, Burundi, Rwanda, South Sudan, and the eastern regions of the Democratic Republic of Congo (map 3.3). Using a regular feeder system, the port is connected to Mogadishu, Dar es Salaam, and transshipment hubs such as Djibouti, Durban, and Salalah. Mombasa is both a feeder port and an important regional port.

The port is home to two container terminals: The Mombasa Container Terminal and the newly constructed Kipevu Container Terminal, which was commissioned in April 2016 and has an annual capacity of 550,000 TEU in Phase I. The composition and volume of cargo handled at the port is shown in table 3.3. The port of Mombasa is connected via "The Northern Corridor" road

MAP 3.3
Location of Mombasa port

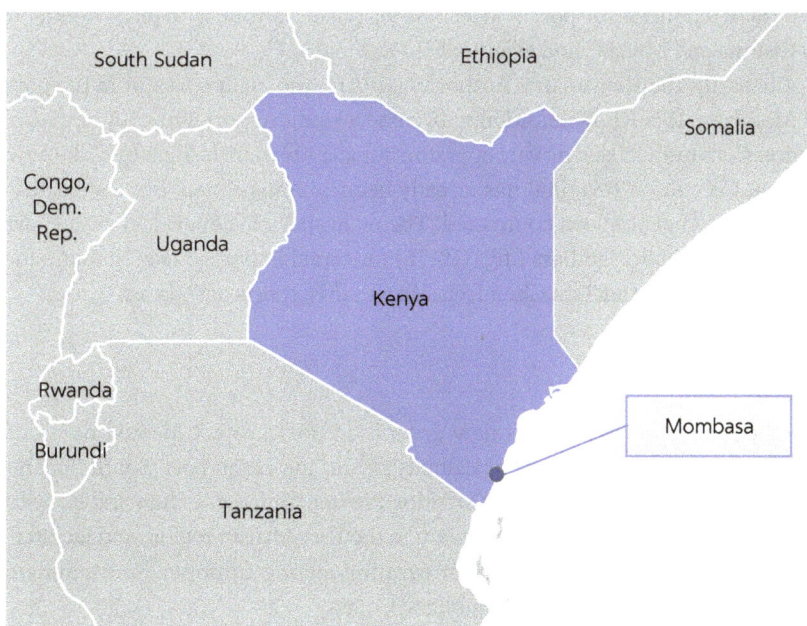

Source: World Bank.

TABLE 3.3 Traffic composition and volume, Mombasa, 2012–16

UNIT (thousands)	2012	2013	2014	2015	2016
Containers (TEU)	903	894	1,012	1,076	1,091
Containers (tons)[a]	8,723	8,838	10,047	10,276	10,615
General cargo (tons)	1,275	1,649	1,701	2,040	1,821
Dry bulk (tons)	4,917	4,978	5,653	6,928	7,053
Liquid bulk (tons)	6,825	6,637	7,237	7,272	7,728
Vehicles (tons)	180	205	237	216	147
Total (tons)	**21,920**	**22,307**	**24,875**	**26,732**	**27,364**

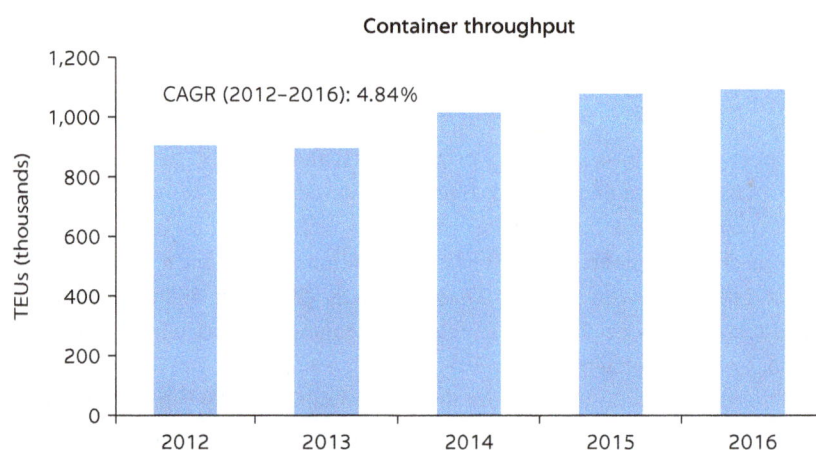

Container throughput

CAGR (2012–2016): 4.84%

TEUs (thousands)

2012 | 2013 | 2014 | 2015 | 2016

Source: Kenya Port Authority.
Note: CAGR = compound annual growth rate; TEU = twenty-foot equivalent unit.
a. Estimated.

network to its hinterland markets, though current road conditions highlight the need for quality improvements. The recently inaugurated standard gauge railway (SGR) connects the port of Mombasa via rail to Nairobi, with plans to extend to Kisumu and Malaba, and eventually to Kampala.

Currently, the Kenya Ports Authority (KPA) is the main operator in the port of Mombasa. It is KPA's ambition to become a landlord port authority, granting concessions to specialist private operators for all its terminals. Phase I of the new Kipevu Container Terminal has already been commissioned, but a specialist operator has not yet been contracted. The main specialist operators in the port are the Grain Bulk Handlers Ltd. (GBHL) for cereal imports, Base Titanium for titanium exports, and Tata Chemicals Magadi for exports of soda ash.

Lamu

The port of Lamu is Kenya's new greenfield port project located north of Mombasa (map 3.4). The port of Lamu is part of the Lamu Port–South Sudan–Ethiopia Transport (LAPSSET) Corridor Project, aimed at enhancing Kenya's position as a gateway and transport hub to the East African region, and facilitating trade and regional economic integration among Ethiopia, South Sudan, Rwanda, and the Democratic Republic of Congo.

The LAPSSET Corridor initiative envisages the development of 32 deep-sea berths. Three berths are currently under construction. Construction of the first

MAP 3.4
Location of Lamu port

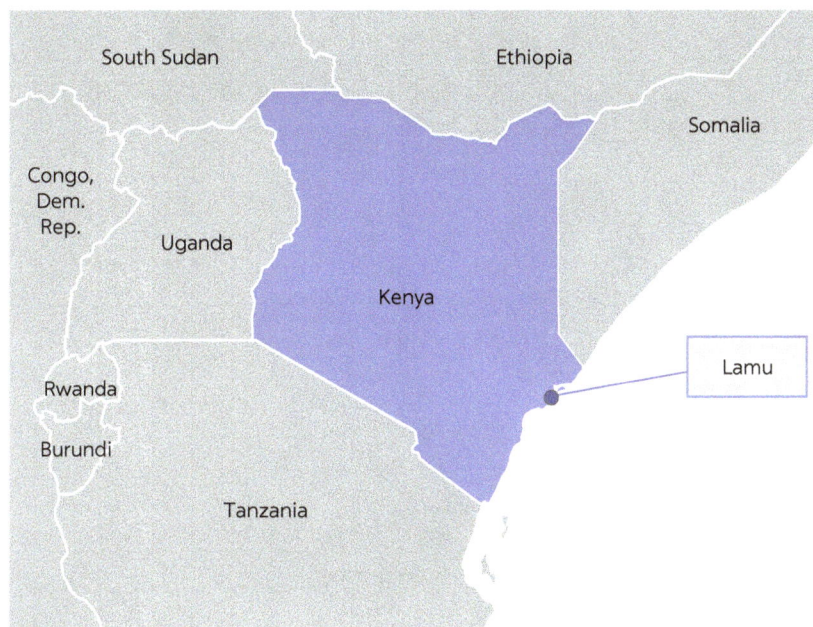

Source: World Bank.

berth was expected to be completed in 2018, while the other two berths are to be completed by December 2020. The three berths will consist of one container berth, one bulk berth, and one general cargo berth. Total investments for the first three berths have been reported to amount to US$480 million.

The KPA is responsible for management and operations in the port of Lamu. The role of The LAPSSET Corridor Development Authority (LCDA) is to take the development initiative, plan, coordinate, and ensure that all relevant government entities are joining forces and contributing to the realization of LAPSSET. With the first three berths being fully financed by public investment, the remaining 29 berths are proposed to be financed by the private sector. The government of Kenya plans to concession the operation of the first three berths to private sector operators and include the construction and operation of berths 4–6.

Dar es Salaam

The port of Dar es Salaam is located in the center of Tanzania on the coast of the Indian Ocean (map 3.5), and is the most important port of Tanzania, handling about 95 percent of Tanzania's international trade. The port has a large hinterland which includes the landlocked countries of Burundi, Rwanda, Malawi, Zambia, and the Democratic Republic of Congo. As a result, transit volumes represent approximately 35 percent of the total cargo throughput in the port of Dar es Salaam. The evolution of cargo volumes handled at the port of Dar es Salaam is shown in table 3.4. In terms of the typology, Dar es Salaam is considered an important regional port.

The port authority of the port of Dar es Salaam is the Tanzania Ports Authority (TPA). The container terminal in the port is operated by the Tanzania International Container Terminal Services (TICTS). TICTS is 70 percent owned

MAP 3.5
Location of Dar es Salaam port

Source: World Bank.

TABLE 3.4 **Traffic composition and volume, Dar es Salaam, 2012–16**

UNIT (thousands)	2012	2013	2014	2015	2016
Containers (TEU)	562	601	665	659	622
Containers (tons)	5,594	5,995	6,715	6,333	6,019
General cargo (tons)	291	492	425	377	328
Dry bulk (tons)	2,024	2,460	2,425	2,153	1,875
Liquid bulk (tons)	3,984	4,789	4,730	5,322	5,289
Vehicles (tons)	172	217	248	241	146
Total (tons)	**12,065**	**13,954**	**14,542**	**14,426**	**13,658**

Container throughput

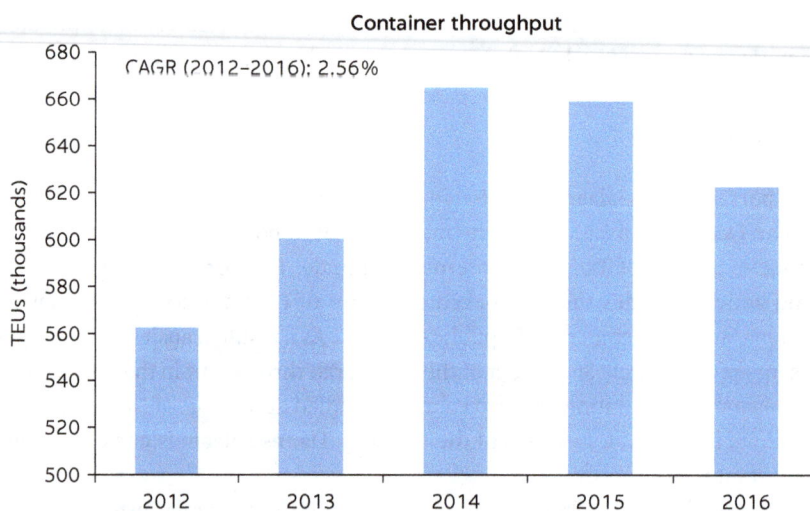

CAGR (2012–2016): 2.56%

Source: Tanzania Port Authority.
Note: CAGR = compound annual growth rate; TEU = twenty-foot equivalent unit.
a. Estimated.

by Hutchison Port Holdings, with Harbors Investment Ltd. of Tanzania holding 30 percent. TICTS was awarded a 10-year concession in 2000 to operate the Dar es Salaam container terminal, which was subsequently extended to 25 years in 2005. In 2017, the contract was renegotiated to increase and index the annual lease fee in 2018. The Ubungo inland container depot also reverted to TPA as part of the renegotiations.

Zanzibar

The port of Zanzibar, also referred to as the port of Malindi, is located on the western part of Zanzibar (map 3.6) and acts as the island's main port. With approximately 1.5 million passengers per year, Malindi has one of the busiest passenger terminals in the East African region. The port has one large berth of 240 meters, which is capable of handling 20,000 deadweight tons (DWT) vessels with a maximum draft of –10.0 m below chart datum (CD).[3] With just one mobile harbor crane (MHC), most ships are geared (have their own cranes) to handle cargo in the port of Zanzibar. Container and cargo volumes are relatively small (see table 3.5), as the port acts primarily as gateway to the island of Zanzibar.

Despite these volumes, the port of Zanzibar is severely congested, partly due to the limited expansion possibilities. Part of the 2007 Zanzibar Transport Master Plan is the construction of the new US$230 million greenfield Maruhubi Port, located 3 kilometers north of Malindi Port. Construction is ongoing, with financing from China's Exim Bank.

The port of Zanzibar is managed, operated and developed by the Zanzibar Ports Corporation (ZPC), a parastatal organization established under the ZPC Act No.1 of 1997. The ZPC is regulated by the Zanzibar Maritime Authority (ZMA),

MAP 3.6
Location of Zanzibar port

Source: World Bank.

TABLE 3.5 Traffic composition and volume, Zanzibar, 2012–16

UNIT (thousands)	2012	2013	2014	2015	2016
Containers (TEU)	65	71	79	75	77
Containers (tons)[a]	651	706	793	752	768
General cargo (tons)	139	141	158	265	288
Dry bulk (tons)	35	35	40	66	72
Liquid bulk (tons)	20	21	23	39	42
Total (tons)	845	903	1,014	1,122	1,170

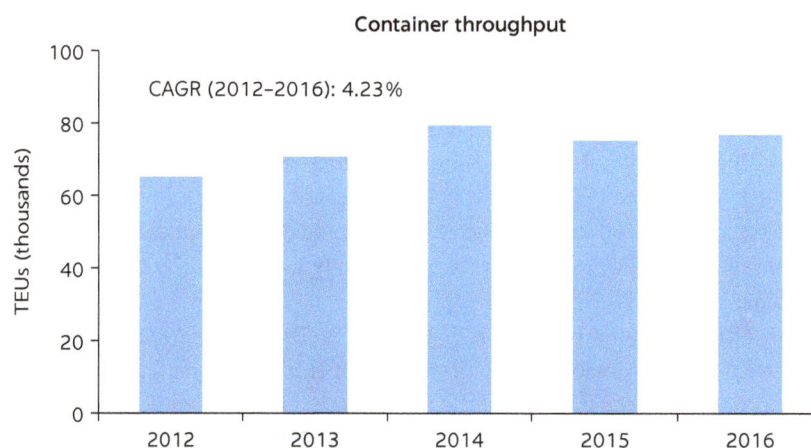

Container throughput

CAGR (2012–2016): 4.23%

Source: Zanzibar Port Authority.
Note: CAGR = compound annual growth rate; TEU = twenty-foot equivalent unit.
a. Estimated.

which focuses on safety, security, and tariff setting in the port of Malindi. The ZMA is a fully autonomous institution acting under the direct authority of the Zanzibar Ministry of Construction, Infrastructure, Communication, and Transportation.

Moroni

The port of Moroni is located on the west side of the largest island of the Union of the Comoros, Grand Comoros, approximately 300 kilometers from the African mainland (map 3.7). It is a small regional port, as illustrated by the small overall volumes handled (table 3.6).

The port handles imports of food and petroleum products, and exports comprising vanilla, spices, and flowers. Because of its low draft at quay (approximately 4.5 meters), large vessels are unable to berth inside the port. Consequently, larger vessels anchor outside the port and cargo is unloaded onto barges. The port faces several days of downtime each year during the cyclone season, which hampers berthing procedures between November and April. The port has two berths: one dedicated to containers and one handling general cargo and dry bulks.

The port of Moroni's formal regulatory body in the port authority of the Comoros is the Société Comorienne des Ports (SCP), which was created in 2013. As the establishment of SCP has not yet been implemented, the former Autorité

MAP 3.7
Location of Moroni port

Tanzania

Zambia

Malawi

Mozambique

Zimbabwe

Comoros

Mayotte

Moroni

Madagascar

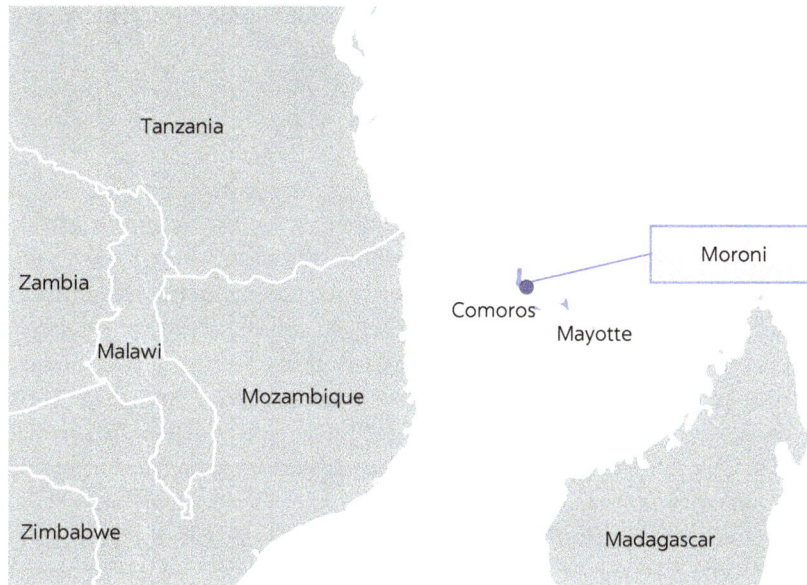

Source: World Bank.

TABLE 3.6 **Traffic composition and volume, Moroni, 2012–16**

UNIT (thousands)	2012	2013	2014	2015	2016
Containers (TEU)	17	17[a]	18	16	18
Containers (tons)[a]	167	173	179	163	183
General cargo (tons)	47	93	73	114	85
Dry bulk (tons)	5	9	7	11	8
Liquid bulk (tons)	50	53	56	35	14
Vehicles (tons)	0.6	0.5	0.3	0.1	0.2
Total (tons)	**269**	**328**	**316**	**324**	**291**

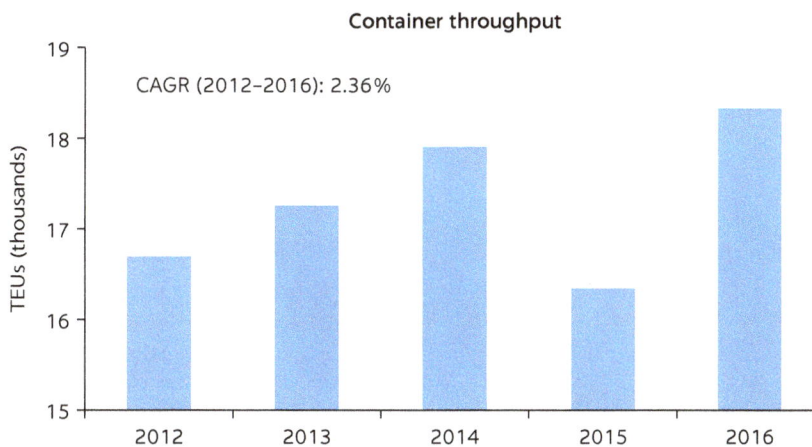

Container throughput

CAGR (2012–2016): 2.36%

Source: SCP.
Note: CAGR = compound annual growth rate; TEU = twenty-foot equivalent unit.
a. Estimated.

Portuaire des Comores is still responsible for executing policies on the island of Grand Comoreos. Bolloré Africa Logistics is in charge of the Moroni Terminal, which handles container and general cargo operations inside the port of Moroni. Their concession was granted in 2011 for 10 years.

Toamasina

The port of Toamasina is the main port of Madagascar, located on the east side of the country (map 3.8). Employment at the port represents approximately 35 percent of total employment in Toamasina—the second largest city in the country—underlining its importance for both the city and the country of Madagascar. The port handles approximately 90 percent of the container volumes of the country, via the concessioned Madagascar International Container Terminal, and some 90 percent of total trade volumes passing through the ports of Madagascar (recent trends in total cargo throughput at the port are summarized in table 3.7). The port is equipped to handle various cargo types, including bulk grain, roll on–roll off (Ro-Ro) and ship traffic. The sharp increase in the port's volumes are primarily from the increase of nickel and cobalt exports, originating from mines in Moramanga, located 80 kilometers east of the capital Antananarivo.

The port of Toamasina is managed and operated by the Société du Port à Gestion Autonome de Toamasina (SPAT). In June 2005, container operations were concessioned to International Container Terminal Services Inc. (ICTSI) for a period of 20 years. ICTSI is consequently in charge of operating, managing, financing, and developing the container terminal in the port of Toamasina. The port is a medium-sized regional port.

Mahajanga

The port of Mahajanga is a small regional port located on the west side of the island of Madagascar with direct access to the Mozambique Channel (map 3.9). The port of Mahajanga is the second port in the country and focuses on local

MAP 3.8

Location of Toamasina port

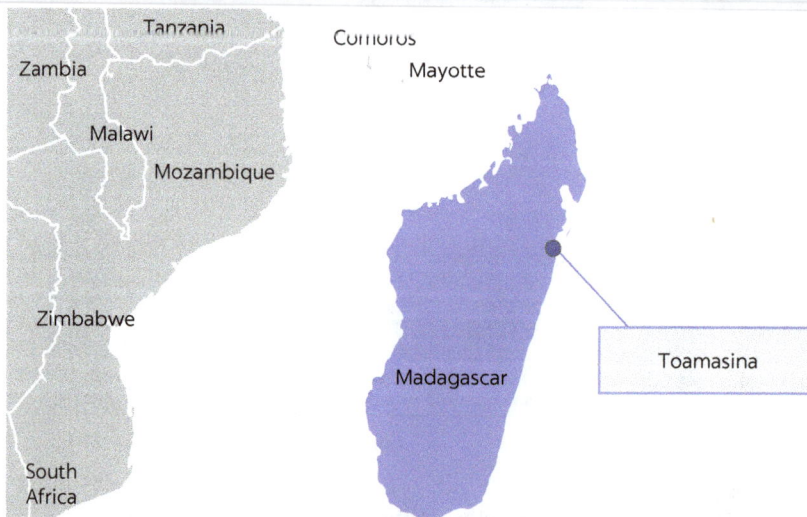

Source: World Bank.

TABLE 3.7 **Traffic composition and volume, Toamasina, 2012–16**

UNIT (thousands)	2012	2013	2014	2015	2016
Containers (TEU)	182	196	207	191	209
Containers (tons)[a]	1,824	1,963	2,070	1,913	2,091
General cargo (tons)	190	168	258	400	373
Dry bulk (tons)	1,248	1,579	2,448	2,749	2,439
Liquid bulk (tons)	806	786	776	937	992
Vehicles (tons)	21	22	19	20	26
Total (tons)	**4,089**	**4,518**	**5,571**	**6,019**	**5,921**

Container throughput

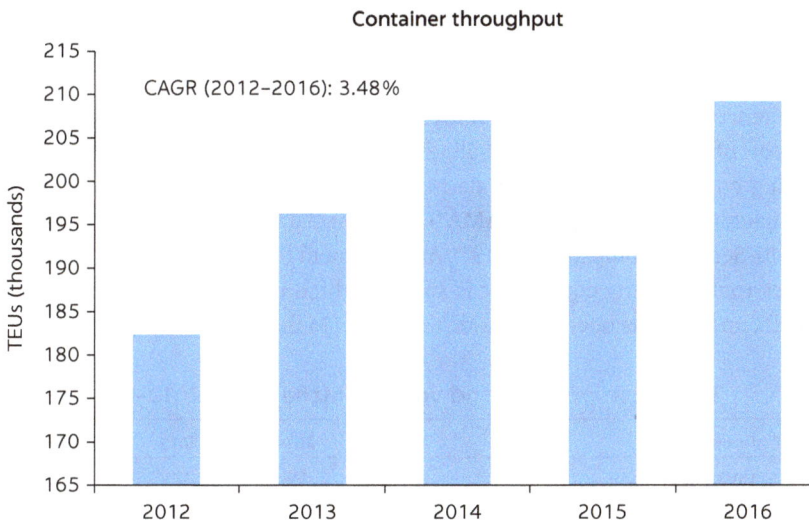

CAGR (2012–2016): 3.48%

Source: SPAT.
Note: CAGR = compound annual growth rate; TEU = twenty-foot equivalent unit.
a. Estimated.

MAP 3.9
Location of Mahajanga port

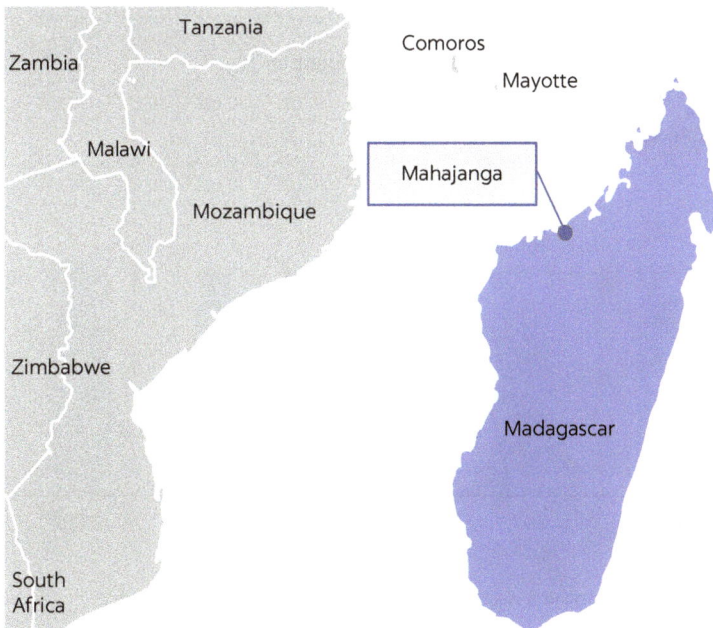

Source: World Bank.

traffic on the west coast of Madagascar, as illustrated by the comparatively small volumes handled (table 3.8). Large prawn farms in the vicinity of Mahajanga use the port to export their products. Because of its low water depth at berth, of only 4.5 meters below CD, the port of Mahajanga is capable of handling small to medium-sized vessels only, with an average vessel size of 800 twenty-foot equivalent units (TEU). The stated water depth is measured during high tide, and with a tidal range of roughly four meters, there is scarcely any water depth during low tide. This severely limits the operations and cargo handling activities in the port of Mahajanga.

The Economic Development Board of Madagascar (EDBM) has presented rehabilitation projects including the construction of new docks and dredging plans worth approximately US$12 million. The project aims to increase capacity and improve port efficiency. Studies toward this end have been conducted but need to be updated.

Agence Portuaire Maritime et Fluviale (APMF) is the representative body of the port of Mahajanga. Cargo handling operations are shared between the stevedoring companies Compagnie de Manutention de Mahjanga (Stevedoring Company of Mahajanga, "COMAMA") and Société d'Entreprises Multi-Services (Multi-Services Company, "SEMS"). An agreement between the two companies states that handling equipment is shared, which counts for reach stackers, trucks, and forklifts operating inside the port of Mahajanga.

TABLE 3.8 Traffic composition and volume, Mahajanga, 2012–16

UNIT (thousands)	2012	2013	2014	2015	2016[a]
Containers (TEU)	13	15	15	12	13
Containers (tons)[a]	125	151	151	121	130
General cargo (tons)	128	134	170	196	198
Dry bulk (tons)	14	15	19	22	22
Liquid bulk (tons)	n.a.	n.a.	n.a.	n.a.	n.a.
Vehicles (tons)	n.a.	n.a.	n.a.	n.a.	n.a.
Total (tons)	268	300	339	339	350

Container throughput

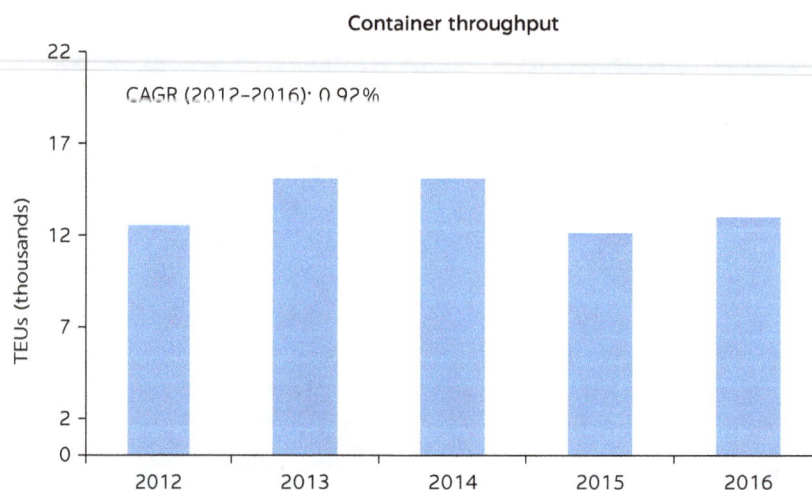

CAGR (2012–2016): 0.92%

Source: APMF.
Note: CAGR = compound annual growth rate; TEU = twenty-foot equivalent unit; n.a. = not applicable.
a. Estimated figures.

Port Louis

The port of Port Louis is largest port of Mauritius (map 3.10), handling approximately 99 percent of the total trade volume of the island. The port serves as both a gateway to the island of Mauritius, and as a transshipment hub for the East African region. In 2016, the port handled approximately 511,000 TEUs, with almost 50 percent of the volume being transshipment (see table 3.9). The port's major import products include food, petroleum products, and raw materials for the textile industry; export products include primarily sugar and textiles.

The port of Port Louis has several terminals, including the Mauritius Container Terminal (MCT), the Multipurpose Terminal (MPT), and the Cruise Terminal. Several development plans have been proposed by the Mauritius Ports Authority (MPA), including the increase of container handling capacity to 1 million TEU by 2025, of which 750,000 TEU would be transshipments. The project envisions four phases, to ensure that the port of Port Louis remains operational while the upgrading and expansion work is ongoing.

The MPA, set up under the Ports Act of 1998, is the governing authority in the port of Port Louis. Acting as a landlord port authority, it provides the main port infrastructure and superstructure, together with related facilities, marine services, and navigation aids. Container, general cargo, and bulk operations (excluding products through pipelines) are handled by the publicly owned company Cargo Handling Corporation Limited (CHCL), which has a 30-year concession agreement with the MPA.

MAP 3.10
Location of Port Louis port

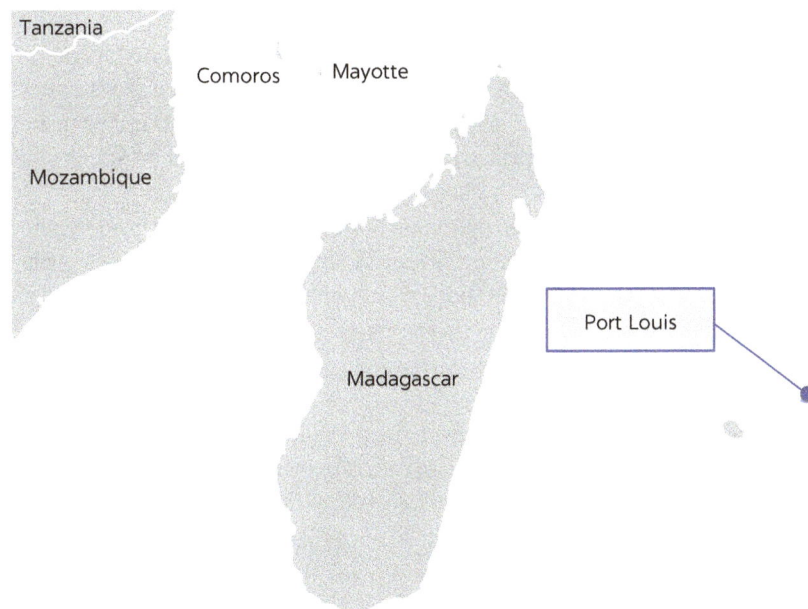

Source: World Bank.

TABLE 3.9 **Traffic composition and volume, Port Louis, 2012–16**

UNIT (thousands)	2012	2013	2014	2015	2016
Containers (TEU)	576	522	554	466	511
Containers (tons)	3,444	3,254	3,412	3,153	3,326
General cargo (tons)	203	178	173	187	208
Dry bulk (tons)	1,807	1,801	1,706	1,819	1,811
Liquid bulk (tons)	1,621	1,527	1,609	1,682	1,929
Vehicles (tons)[a]	-	-	-	-	-
Total (tons)	7,075	6,761	6,900	6,841	7,273

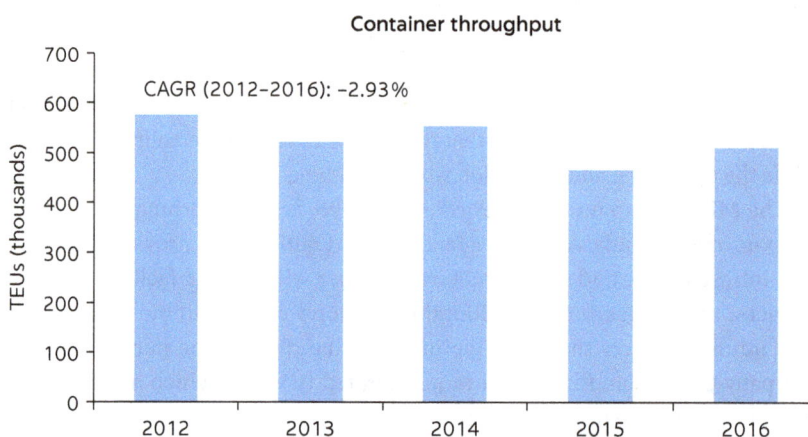

Container throughput

CAGR (2012–2016): –2.93%

Source: Mauritius Ports Authority.
Note: CAGR = compound annual growth rate; TEU = twenty-foot equivalent unit.
a. Included in general cargo.

Nacala

The port of Nacala is a regional port located in the Nampula province in the northern part of Mozambique (map 3.11). It is the largest natural deep-water port on the eastern coast of Africa. The port has no restrictions in terms of ship movements or ship size and is the primary node in the "Nacala Corridor," which connects the countries of Malawi and Zambia.

The first phase of a major rehabilitation project was completed in September 2015, and consisted of repairing berths 3 and 4, upgrading the liquid bulk terminal, and upgrading container operations with rubber-tired gantry cranes (RTGs). The second phase started in 2017 and comprises the extension of a dedicated container berth, installation of two ship-to-shore (STS) gantry cranes, and six additional RTGs. Other developments include the construction of a new coal-handling port, situated across from the port of Nacala, which is fully dedicated to the exports of coal to markets in Asia, Europe, and Brazil. This port falls outside the concession granted to Portos do Norte. While container volumes handled at Nacala have fluctuated in recent years, those of dry bulk have increased steeply (table 3.10).

The port of Nacala, and the connecting railway line, are concessioned to Corredor de Desenvolvimento do Norte (CDN); however, a management contract was signed on March 15, 2013, transferring management of the port and railway line to Portos do Norte SA. CDN retains management and operations of pilotage, berthing operations, and general cargo operations. Portos e Caminhos

MAP 3.11
Location of Nacala port

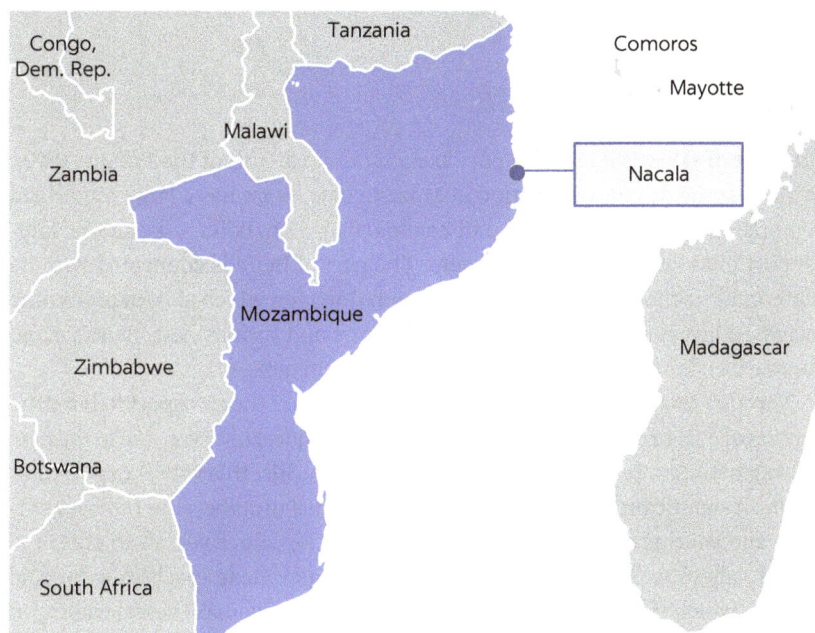

Source: World Bank.

TABLE 3.10 **Traffic composition and volume, Nacala, 2012–16**

UNIT (thousands)	2012	2013	2014	2015	2016
Containers (TEU)	65	83	97	79	71
Containers (tons)[a]	652	828	971	794	711
General cargo (tons)	418	648	717	551	552
Dry bulk (tons)	280	434	480	369	6,670
Liquid bulk (tons)	319	339	422	386	511
Vehicles (tons)	2	3	3	2	2
Total (tons)	**1,670**	**2,252**	**2,592**	**2,102**	**8,446**

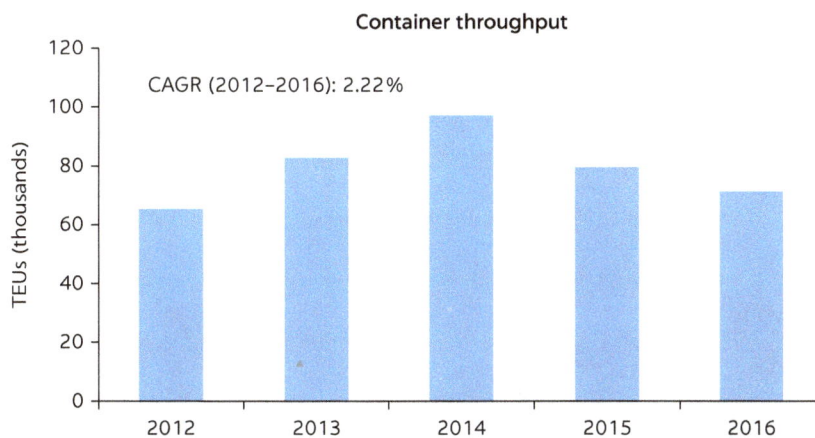

Container throughput

CAGR (2012–2016): 2.22%

Source: Portos do Norte.
Note: CAGR = compound annual growth rate; TEU = twenty-foot equivalent unit.
a. Estimated.

de Ferro de Moçambique (Ports and Railways of Mozambique, CFM) operates the liquid bulk terminal, whereas Vale owns and operates the coal terminal opposite the port of Nacala.

Beira

The port of Beira is a regional port located on the mouth of the Pungue River. With its strategic central location in Mozambique, Beira has a large hinterland comprising Zimbabwe, Malawi, and Zambia (map 3.12). Beira is the second largest port in Mozambique after Maputo. The port of Beira is connected with its hinterland via the Beira Agricultural Growth Corridor, which aims at promoting increased investment in commercial agriculture and agribusiness. Beira's cargo volume trends and composition are summarized in table 3.11.

Through this corridor, Beira has served formally as the transport hub for the exports of coal from the Tete province in Mozambique. However, due to the new railway between Tete province and the port of Nacala, this role is expected to diminish significantly. The port suffers from limited draft because of heavy siltation and shifting sandbanks, making it difficult for larger vessels to enter the port. To alleviate the constraint, Vale had two barges made specifically for coal exports, which would transport the coal to a larger (Panamax) vessel waiting at anchorage outside the port.

Portos e Caminhos de Ferro de Moçambique (CFM) manages the port of Beira. Cornelder de Moçambique (CdM), a joint venture between CFM (33 percent) and Cornelder Holdings BV (67 percent), was granted a 25-year concession in 1998 to operate the container and general cargo terminals in the port of Beira. CFM has retained operational management of the liquid bulk terminal in the port; the fishery port on berth 1 also falls outside of the responsibilities of CdM.

MAP 3.12

Location of Beira port

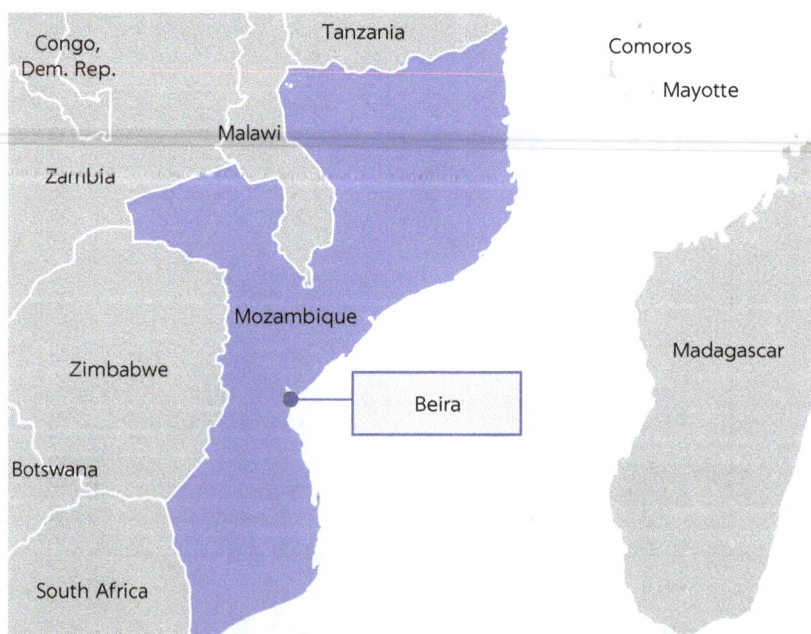

Source: World Bank.

TABLE 3.11 Traffic composition and volume, Beira, 2012–16

UNIT (thousands)	2012	2013	2014	2015	2016
Containers (TEU)	171	185	207	211	197
Containers (tons)[a]	1,707	1,845	2,072	2,114	1,972
General cargo (tons)	470	560	583	637	571
Dry bulk (tons)	3,843	5,486	6,386	6,798	4,127
Liquid bulk (tons)	1,700	2,250	2,446	2,600	2,800
Vehicles (tons)	0	0	6	29	26
Total (tons)	**7,719**	**10,141**	**11,492**	**12,178**	**9,496**

Source: Cornelder de Moçambique.
Note: CAGR = compound annual growth rate; TEU = twenty-foot equivalent unit.
a. Estimated.

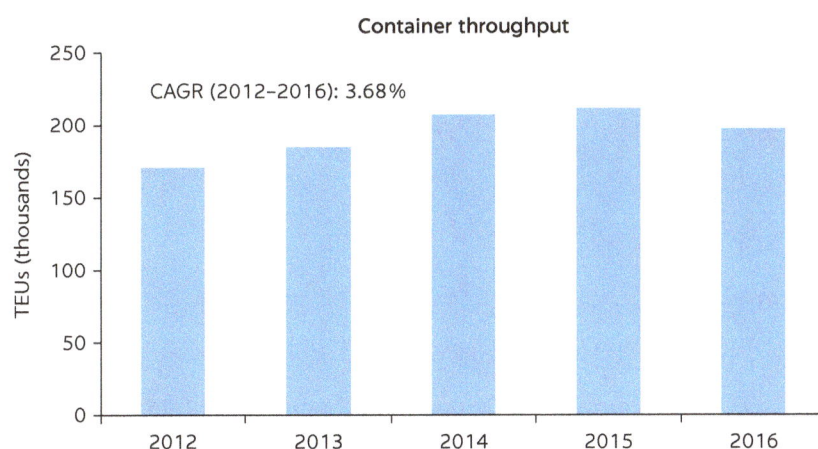

Container throughput

CAGR (2012–2016): 3.68%

Maputo

The port of Maputo is a regional port located in the southern part of Mozambique, 120 km from the South African border (map 3.13). It is the largest port in Mozambique, and the city of Maputo is the capital and most populous city in the country. The trends in volumes handled at the port are summarized in table 3.12.

The port has two main terminals: the Maputo Cargo Terminals, which includes the container terminal; and the Matola Bulk Terminals, situated 6 km further upstream in Maputo Bay, which includes a coal, grain, and aluminum terminal. Transit cargo handled by the port is mainly destined for South Africa, Botswana, and Zimbabwe. The port has experienced a large growth in throughput, with volumes having more than doubled in 5 years, from 8 million tons in 2009, to some 19 million tons in 2014. However, growth has regressed in recent years, with total throughput dropping to 15 million tons in 2016.

The port of Maputo is managed by the Maputo Port Development Company (MPDC), a Mozambican-registered joint venture. The company consists of the Mozambican Ports and Railways Authority (CFM, 49 percent stake) and Portus Indico (51 percent), which itself is a combination of Dubai Ports World (48.5 percent of Portus Indico), Grindrod (48.5 percent), and a local company Mozambique Gestores (3 percent). MPDC has a master concession that runs until 2033, with a possible 10-year extension until 2043. Under the master concession, MPDC either develops terminals under subconcession arrangements or handles its own cargoes.

MAP 3.13
Location of Maputo port

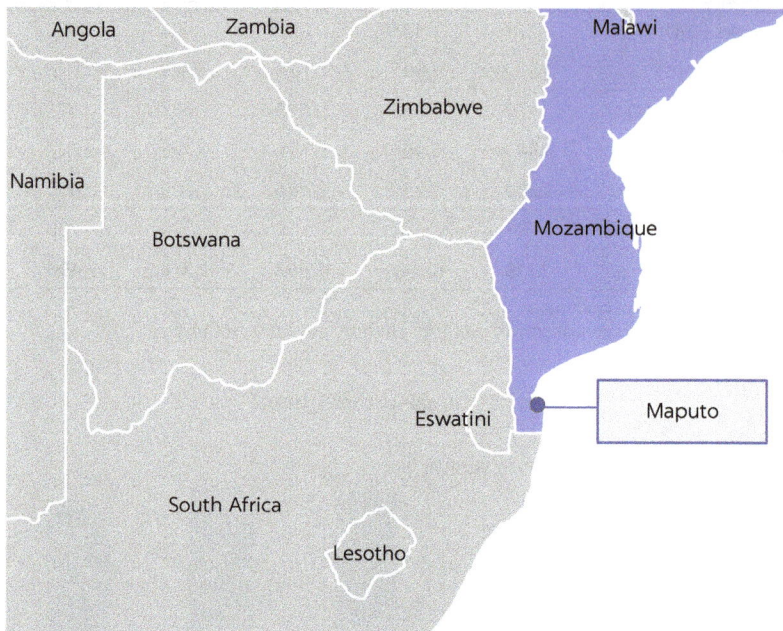

Source: World Bank.

TABLE 3.12 Traffic composition and volume, Maputo, 2012–16

UNIT (thousands)	2012	2013	2014	2015	2016
Containers (TEU)	88	111	125	123	97
Containers (tons)[a]	883	1,113	1,248	1,235	974
General cargo (tons)	571	963	269	900	498
Dry bulk (tons)	12,665	13,654	16,109	11,949	11,694
Liquid bulk (tons)	686	703	941	939	1,328
Vehicles (tons)	109	146	96	60	26
Total (tons)	**14,914**	**16,579**	**18,663**	**15,083**	**14,519**

Container throughput

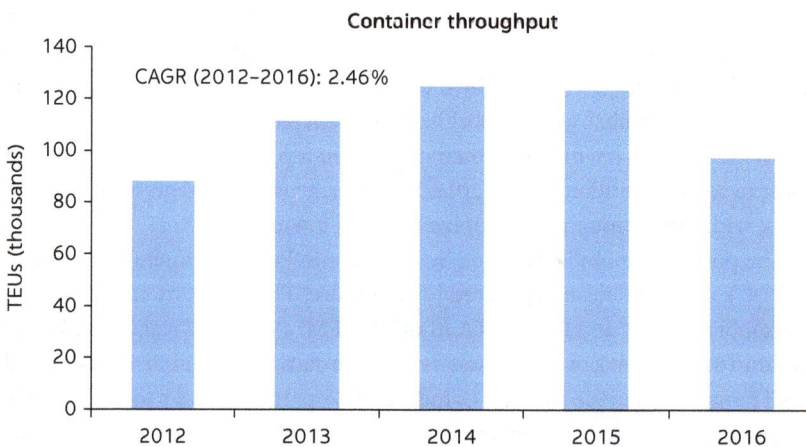

CAGR (2012–2016): 2.46%

Source: MPDC.
Note: CAGR = compound annual growth rate; TEU = twenty-foot equivalent unit.
a. Estimated.

Durban

The port of Durban is a key gateway port and transshipment hub, located along the east coast of South Africa (map 3.14). It is South Africa's main general cargo port and its premier container port, as well as the largest container port in Sub-Saharan Africa (see table 3.13 for a summary of the overall volumes handled). Only Port Said in the Arab Republic of Egypt and Tangier Med in Morocco are larger on the continent. The port is the principal port serving the KwaZulu-Natal province and the Gauteng region (Johannesburg), as well as the Southern African hinterland. It is the leading port in the Southern African Development Community (SADC) region, and is strategically positioned along the global shipping routes. The port also plays a central role in the transport and logistics chain, with 65 percent of all South Africa's containers and liquid bulks passing through the port.

Transnet National Ports Authority is the port authority of the major ports of South Africa. Transport Port Terminals operates most terminals in Durban, including the Durban Container Terminal (DCT). Furthermore, Grindrod operates a multipurpose terminal, and Vopak and Oiltanking each have a liquid bulk terminal in the port.

East London

The port of East London is located 460 kilometers south of the port of Durban, at the mouth of the Buffalo River (map 3.15). The port of East London is South Africa's only river port, and consists of a Ro-Ro terminal, South Africa's largest grain silos, a multipurpose terminal equipped to handle both general cargo and containers, and a liquid bulk terminal. Focus areas for the port are primarily Ro-Ro, grains, and vehicle-related container imports (see table 3.14). With a

MAP 3.14

Location of Durban port

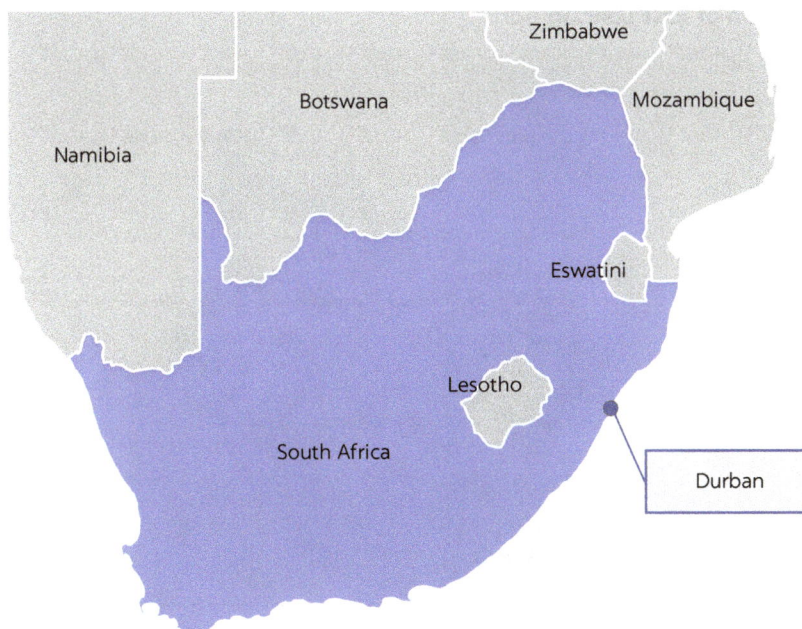

Source: World Bank.

TABLE 3.13 **Traffic composition and volume, Durban, 2012–16**

UNIT (thousands)	2012	2013	2014	2015	2016
Containers (TEU)	2,568	2,633	2,664	2,770	2,620
Containers (tons)[a]	25,681	26,325	26,643	27,703	26,200
General cargo (tons)	2,936	3,314	3,249	2,410	1,780
Dry bulk (tons)	9,293	10,378	10,682	8,811	10,241
Liquid bulk (tons)	28,558	26,644	26,876	26,813	27,947
Vehicles (tons)	694	754	702	705	661
Total (tons)	**67,162**	**67,415**	**68,152**	**66,442**	**66,829**

Container throughput

CAGR (2012–2016): 0.50%

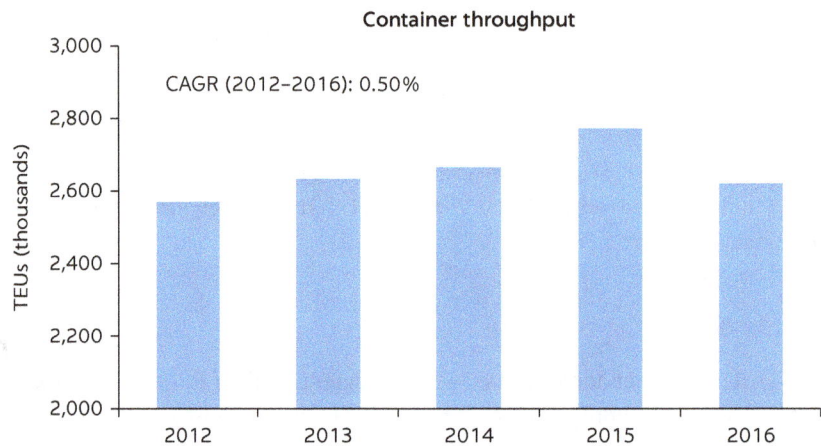

Source: TNPA.
Note: CAGR = compound annual growth rate; TEU = twenty-foot equivalent unit.
a. Estimated.

MAP 3.15
Location of East London port

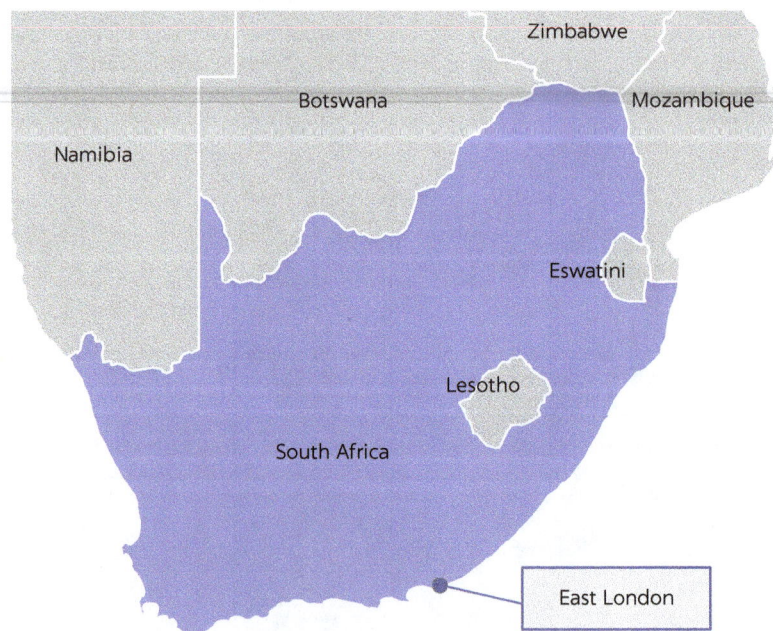

Source: World Bank.

TABLE 3.14 **Traffic composition and volume, East London, 2012–16**

UNIT (thousands)	2012	2013	2014	2015	2016
Containers (TEU)	52	44	42	66	72
Containers (tons)[a]	523	438	420	663	719
General cargo (tons)	21	77	113	48	17
Dry bulk (tons)	186	108	126	127	261
Liquid bulk (tons)	860	838	861	932	926
Vehicles (tons)	94	81	86	97	152
Total (tons)	**1,684**	**1,541**	**1,606**	**1,868**	**2,076**

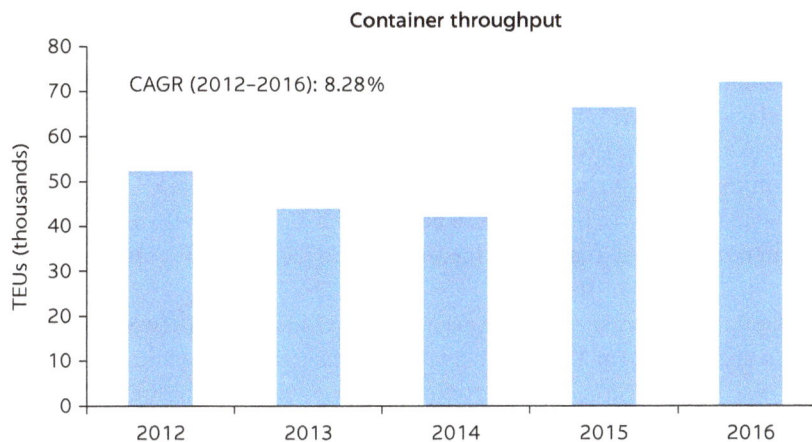

Container throughput

CAGR (2012–2016): 8.28%

Source: TNPA East London.
Note: CAGR = compound annual growth rate; TEU = twenty-foot equivalent unit.
a. Estimated.

dedicated road, the two Ro-Ro berths are connected to the adjacent Daimler factory which fabricates Mercedes-Benz models, and has led to a significant increase in volumes through the port.

The port's dependency on Daimler is represented by the fluctuating throughput in the port surrounding the launch of a new model, which occurs every 8 years. The container berth has a capacity of 90,000 TEU and handles primarily volumes related to the motor industry. As the port is not equipped with cranes, ships are required to have their own gear. With equipment investments in straddle carriers, mobile cranes, and forklifts, the port of East London has ample capacity and ability to attract additional volumes across varying cargo segments.

Transnet Port Terminals (TPT) is responsible for the commercial operations in the port of East London. All terminals, except for the liquid bulk terminal, are operated by TPT, which has a concession contract with Transnet National Ports Authority (TNPA). The liquid bulk terminal has four subconcessionaires: BP, Engen, Total, and Chevron. Operations and transport of the liquid bulks to the nearby tank farms are done by Engen.

REGIONAL TRENDS IN TRAFFIC

The number of containers, expressed in terms of TEUs, on aggregate, loaded or unloaded in the ESA ports, increased from 4.6 million in 2010 to 5.6 million in 2016. Containers now represent the largest share, by volume, of all traffic through the ESA ports. This growth equates to a CAGR of 3.4 percent, but masks wide disparities between individual ports: The largest increase in container volumes was observed in the port of Berbera, at 25.9 percent per year, followed by the port of Zanzibar with 12 percent, and the port of Djibouti with 11.8 percent. Container volumes through the port of Durban represented the largest share, accounting for 39 percent of total TEUs in 2016. However, Durban, along with Maputo, were the only ports that saw container volumes decrease between 2010 and 2016, at a CAGR of -1.2 percent and -2.8 percent respectively.

The volume of dry bulk throughput in the region's ports increased from 26.1 million tons in 2010 to 52.0 million tons in 2016, equal to a CAGR of 12.2 percent. The largest increase in dry-bulk volumes was observed in Mozambique, reflecting the significant increase in the export of coal from the Moatize mines, and in Madagascar, which increased the export of refined nickel and cobalt via the port of Toamasina. The combined volumes of dry bulk recorded in the Mozambican ports increased from 7.4 million tons to 22.5 million tons, primarily driven by the coal via Nacala, with volumes growing at CAGRs of between 11.0 percent and 83.2 percent. Total volumes through the port of Toamasina increased from just 0.1 million tons in 2010 to 2.4 million tons in 2016.

The only ports which recorded negative growth in dry bulk between 2010 and 2016 were the ports of Moroni and Port Louis, though the absolute drop in volume was negligible in each case (2,000 and 8,000 tons respectively). In all cases, it is important to note the asymmetric nature of the flows, with 60 percent of the total dry-bulk volumes in 2016 being exports of natural resources.

The volume of liquid bulk (including, among other things, petrol, diesel, and cooking oils, and hence primarily imports) throughput in the ESA ports increased from 43.4 million tons in 2010 to 53.5 million tons in 2016, equal to a CAGR of 3.5 percent. The largest increase in liquid bulk volumes was recorded in the port of Berbera, at 16.3 percent per year, followed by the port of Beira with 14.3 percent and the port of Nacala with 13.5 percent. Liquid bulk volume through the port of Durban represents more than half of the total volumes recorded in all ESA ports. And all the ports, except Moroni because of the economic crisis, and East London because of specialization, have seen an increase in liquid bulk volumes handled between 2010 and 2016.

General cargo volumes through the ESA ports increased from 7.7 million tons in 2010 to 9.1 million tons in 2016, equal to a CAGR of 2.9 percent. The growth observed between 2010 and 2016 was influenced primarily by the volumes recorded in the ports of Djibouti, Mombasa, and Durban. The port of Djibouti and the port of Mombasa recorded the highest absolute general cargo volumes in 2016, with 2.0 million tons and 1.8 million tons respectively. With a CAGR of 13.2 percent between 2010 and 2016, the port of Djibouti recorded the highest growth rate of all ports.

By contrast, in the port of Durban, general cargo volumes decreased from 2.8 million tons in 2010 to 1.8 million tons in 2016. This resulted in a 2010–16 CAGR of -7.2 percent. Another sharp decrease was observed for the port of Maputo in 2014, with volumes decreasing by 70 percent from 2013 to 2014. Despite a recovery in 2015 to 0.9 million tons, the CAGR for the port of Maputo was -2.8 percent between 2010 and 2016. In addition to the ports of Durban and Maputo, the port of Moroni saw general cargo volumes decrease between 2010 and 2016, with a CAGR of -2.9 percent.

ONGOING AND PLANNED DEVELOPMENT

Given the growth in recent years, all the ports are either implementing or planning significant capacity enhancements, primarily relying on public investment. In addition to development plans for the existing ports, there are also plans, at various stages of preparation and implementation, to develop new greenfield ports in a number of countries. These plans are summarized here.

Djibouti

Several development projects are either ongoing or are planned for the port of Djibouti. The Djibouti Liquefied Natural Gas (LNG) Port project intends to construct an LNG terminal in Damerjog, including a liquefaction plant and a pipeline, which will enable the export of 3 million cubic meters of gas from Ethiopia in phase I and 10 million cubic meters in phase II. Ground breaking was expected in 2018 (Reuters 2017). A second major project is the construction of the Djibouti International Container Terminal with a design capacity of 3 million TEU. The terminal will be built by China Merchant Group; construction was expected to start in 2018 (Capital Ethiopia 2017).

Somalia

At the Port of Berbera, a concession agreement was signed between the authorities and DP World (a leading international terminal operator) in late 2016. Under the terms of this agreement, DP World plans a US$442 million investment package. The first phase of this development focuses on operational improvements and acquisition of terminal equipment, while the second phase involves the construction of a 400-meter quay wall with a 250,000 m² container yard and an adjacent free-trade zone. The ground breaking for the construction of the new 400-meter quay wall was held in October 2018. At a national level, the Ministry of Maritime Ports and Transport, with the support of the World Bank, initiated the procurement for consultants to work on the Somalia Port Modernization Study in 2016 (Government of Somalia 2016).

Kenya

The Kenya Ports Authority (KPA) has recently completed a new master plan for the port of Mombasa: One of the key projects is the Kipevu Container Terminal, whose Phase 2 construction was set to begin in 2018, with financial support from the Japan International Cooperation Agency (JICA). This involves the construction of a new berth (berth 22), measuring 320 m in length, with a draft at the berth of –15.0 m below CD. This will increase capacity by 450,000 TEU, nearly doubling the existing capacity of 550,000 TEU in the Kipevu Container Terminal. Phase 3 envisions increasing capacity by a further 500,000 TEU, by constructing another berth (berth 23) of 230 m in length, and a draft at the quay of –12.0 m CD. After completion of all three phases, planned for 2023, the Kipevu Container Terminal will have a total capacity of 1.5 million TEU (Kenya Ports Authority 2017). In addition, the Kipevu Oil Terminal is being planned, designed to handle vessels of up to 200,000 DWT. The terminal is intended to focus on the import of crude oil, heavy fuel oil, and certain types of white oil products (IHS Fairplay 2016).

The port of Lamu is part of the larger Lamu Port–South Sudan–Ethiopia Transport (LAPSSET) project which consists of several infrastructure development projects in northern Kenya (LAPSSET 2017). With the first three berths expected to be operational in 2020, the plan is to continue to expand the port by constructing an additional 29 deep sea berths. The first berth, capable of handling vessels up to 100,000 DWT, is scheduled to be completed by the end of 2018. Combined, the three berths have an envisioned annual handling capacity of 1.2 million TEU (World Cargo News 2017a). The additional 29 berths (with a depth of −18.0 m below chart datum—able to take the largest vessels) are estimated to cost US$4.3 billion, and are expected to be financed, constructed, and operated by the private sector.

Tanzania

The National Port Master Plan, published by TPA (Tanzania Ports Authority 2009), covers the maritime ports and inland lake ports. This plan is being updated by TPA. The master plan notes that while Dar es Salaam is the main gateway port in Tanzania, with the current growth pace the port will reach full capacity in the next decade, even with the following redevelopment: The Dar es Salaam Maritime Gateway Project (DSMGP)[4] is supporting the dredging and widening of the entrance channel and turning basin (turning basin to −15.5 m CD) and strengthening and deepening the quay of berths 1–11 to −14.5 m below CD, together with the development of a new multipurpose berth on reclaimed land at Gerezani Creek. Phase 2 of the DSMGP, which is yet to be agreed upon, envisions the construction of berths 13 and 14 to expand container-handling capacity and demolishment and relocation of the Kurasini Oil Terminal. The overall objective is to increase the ports' cargo-handling capacity from 15 million tons to 25 million tons before 2024, and to allow the port to serve larger vessels.

TPA also plans to develop a new inland container depot (ICD) at Ruvu to supplement storage capacity for containers inside the port of Dar es Salaam. The new ICD is expected to be linked to the existing lines of Tanzania Railway Limited (TRL), the Tanzania-Zambia Railway (TAZARA), and the new standard gauge line. Increased attention is also being given to revitalizing maritime transport on Lakes Victoria and Tanganyika and improving landside access to further strengthen the position of Dar es Salaam port as a key maritime gateway for the subregion.

The development of a new port at Mbegani-Bagamoyo has been proposed under a public-private partnership (PPP) scheme to cope with the growing cargo traffic. The project involves the development of an entirely new port, and an adjoining Export Processing Zone, near the town of Bagamoyo, north of Dar es Salaam, close to Zanzibar Island. It is envisaged, although discussions are ongoing, that TPA will be responsible for investments in the dredging of the port, while the port operations will be transferred to the private sector, with TPA retaining a role in the marine services (pilotage, towage, and mooring).

Zanzibar

The government of Tanzania published the Zanzibar Transport Master Plan in 2007, which includes a proposed new port in Zanzibar (Maruhubi port), located 3 km north of the port of Zanzibar. With an annual handling capacity of 200,000 TEU and 250,000 tons of general cargo, the port is expected to alleviate congestion in the port of Zanzibar (Nathan Associates 2014). The new port is designed to have one 300-meter quay designed for container handling, and one 70-meter quay for general cargo. Construction of the port commenced in September 2015 and completion was expected in late 2018. Construction was being managed by the China Harbour Engineering Company (CHEC), with financing from China Exim Bank.

The port of Zanzibar is managed, operated, and developed by the Zanzibar Ports Corporation (ZPC), a parastatal organization established under the ZPC Act No.1 of 1997. It is currently unclear what the role of ZPC in the new port will be. According to ZPC, it is likely that they will continue to manage and operate the existing port of Zanzibar, and that a new entity will manage and operate Maruhubi port.

Additional developments in the port of Zanzibar, or under the auspices of ZPC, include the installation of a new weigh bridge and the construction of a liquid bulk terminal through a PPP concession. The latter is planned to be constructed in northern Zanzibar and have a 30,000-ton tank farm. The initial plans were drafted in September 2017.

The Comoros

The Comoros developed a port master plan in 2014 (European Union External Action 2014). The master plan contained numerous proposals to facilitate the accessibility of deep-sea container vessels and improve inter-island passenger transport. These include the reconstruction of the current general cargo quay and extending it by 145 meters; extending the container quay by 275 meters; dredging the port area to −10 m below CD to accommodate larger vessels, the construction of a roll-on/roll-off passenger (RoPax) terminal, and the creation of an economic zone inside the port of Moroni.

In addition, a greenfield deep-water port is planned for development in Sereheni, 2–3 km south of Moroni. This will cater to vessels of up to 30,000 gross tons.[5] However, as there is currently no road connecting Moroni to Sereheni, and as the majority of any cargo being loaded or unloaded at Sereheni will still have to travel to Moroni, the proposed development in its current form does not solve one of the existing port's principal bottlenecks: inner-city congestion.

Madagascar

In Madagascar, the Autonomous Port Authority of Toamasina (SPAT) has drafted a development plan which includes near-term projects for the port of Toamasina (SPAT 2017). This agreement was signed in March 2017 and includes the following projects: a 345-meter breakwater extension; the construction of a new container berth; and dredging works (JICA 2017). The envisioned completion date of the works is 2026. Over the longer term, there are plans to construct a combined passenger-car terminal.

The port of Mahajanga does not have a specific master plan for the development of the port. A national master plan is currently being developed by the APMF. The Mahajanga Port Rehabilitation and Development project includes the construction of new docks and the dredging of the port to increase its capacity and improve its efficiency. The project remains under preparation; expected project completion dates have not been specified (EDBM 2016).

Mauritius

The master plan of the Mauritius Ports Authority (MPA) was updated in August 2016 and provides an overview of market developments up to 2040 (Mauritius Ports Authority 2016). Several development plans have been proposed by the MPA, including the increase of container handling capacity to 1 million TEU by 2025, of which 750,000 TEU would be transshipment, the construction of a new 2 km breakwater, a new 60-hectare container terminal on reclaimed land with throughput capacity of 1.5 million TEU, and dredging of the entrance channel to −18.0 meters below CD. Technical, financial, and social-environmental studies were ongoing as of 2018 (Mauritius Ports Authority 2018). Finally, the MPA is proceeding with the construction of a new cruise-terminal building, comprising a passenger terminal, commercial areas, and office space. The preliminary design has been completed, and the project was expected to start in June 2018, and be completed before the end of 2019 (Mauritius Ports Authority 2018).

Mozambique

Each of the main ports of Mozambique has a strategic master plan: Master Plan 2035 for Beira; Strategic Master Plan on Strengthening of the Nacala Corridor; and Master Plan of the port of Maputo.

There are several development projects underway at the port of Nacala. Phase 2 of the Nacala Rehabilitation Project began in 2017 and includes dredging berth 1 to −14.0 meters below CD and dedicating it to container handling; the construction of a new access road for general cargo trucks; and the reclamation of 6 hectares of land to upgrade storage facilities. With the implementation of this project, the capacity of the port will increase threefold. Phase 3 of the project is planned to include an additional container storage yard, equipment, and dredging works. This is predicted to increase container capacity at the port to 287,000 TEU per year by 2020 (Portos do Norte 2017).

The port of Beira's 2035 Master Plan was finalized in mid-2014 and aims to develop several dedicated terminals in the port, including a sugar terminal, a fertilizer terminal, a mineral terminal, a car terminal, a sulphur terminal, and a biofuel terminal. A crucial element in realizing these terminals is the involvement of companies that are willing to guarantee volumes. Absent these conditions, Cornelder de Moçambique (CdM) does not want to risk dedicating an entire berth to a single commodity, given the volatility of dry bulk volumes.

In 2017, CdM initiated several development projects at Beira, aimed at improving productivity and efficiency inside the port area. These developments include the construction of a new multilane entrance gate, demolition of several warehouses to improve the container storage capacity of the port (scheduled for 2018 and 2019), and transformation of an adjacent old school building into additional office space. CdM is also widening and deepening the entrance channel to between 135 m and 250 m, and a depth of at least −8.0 m CD, and dredging the general cargo berths to −9.5 m below CD and the container berths to −12.0 m below CD. A separate maintenance dredging contract is planned to tackle the ongoing silting of the entrance channel and berths in the port (World Cargo News 2017b).

A 30-year concession agreement between Essar Ports and the government of Mozambique was signed in 2017 for the development and operation of a new coal terminal in the port of Beira. The new coal terminal is part of a design, build, own, operate, and transfer (DBOOT) concession through a subsidiary New Coal Terminal Beira S.A. The coal terminal will be developed in two phases, adding a 10-million ton coal handling capacity in each. Phase I will entail developing dedicated berths, along with mechanized and environment-friendly systems that will be operational as of the first quarter of 2020 (Essar 2017).

Lastly, the Macuse Deep Water Port project entails the construction of a deep-water port in Macuse, including a railway line between Moatize and the Sopinho region in Mozambique. The project is aimed at developing the Zambezi Integrated Development Corridor and providing an additional connection from the coal mines in the Tete region to the Mozambican coastline. A concession agreement was signed in 2013 for both the port and railway, and construction was scheduled to start in late 2018 (Club of Mozambique 2017a, 2017b).

There are several development projects at the port of Maputo. The port's master plan envisions expanding the bulk terminal; expanding the capacity of the Grindrod coal terminal from 6 million tons to 20 million tons per year; constructing new roads, rail, and berths; and further dredging of the access channel to a draft of –14.0 m below CD. The MPDC has the ambition to handle 40 million tons by 2020, and ultimately wants to reach an annual throughput of 50 million tons. There are also developments ongoing in the port's container terminal. These include the introduction of the RTGs, refurbishment of 15 hectares of yard, the addition of 1.5 km of rail sliding, and expansion of the container terminal, increasing the total port's container handling capacity to 600,000 TEU.[6]

In addition, a reconstruction program is planned for three berths at the port to allow vessels with a draft of –14.0 meters below CD to moor. The current draft at these quays is between 9.0 m and 11.0 m below CD, hindering the berthing of larger vessels (Port Technology 2014). Other short-term development projects include the construction of additional warehouses, establishing a dedicated area for wood chips and ferro minerals, and deepening the coal terminal to –15.6 m below CD. If the existing port of Maputo and Matola terminal become congested, there are future plans to develop another port area on the southern side of the bay of Maputo, the Catembe Terminal.[7]

South Africa

In the case of Durban and East London, the Transnet Long-term Planning Framework (TLPF) is an annually published document that aims to guide strategic investment decisions and provide an outlook on capacity requirements for the next 30 years. Together with the Corporate Plan and the Market Demand Strategy plan, they stipulate the needs and requirements for the South African ports. On a national level, the Comprehensive Maritime Transport Policy (CMTP), which was published in 2017 by the Department of Transport, aims to implement policies that will create the required infrastructure and facilities to handle much larger ships efficiently, and contribute to more effective logistics chains.

Although Durban is a mature port with increasingly congested operations, there is potential to improve throughput capacity by reconfiguring and rationalizing the existing terminals of Durban Container Terminal, Point, Maydon Wharf, and Island View. The relocation of the Durban International Airport to La Mercy in 2010 has also provided the opportunity for Transnet to secure the unique old airport site for a new dig-out port. In the past years, plans were made to develop the Durban Dig-Out Port (DDOP) at the former airport site. However, because of the slowdown in South Africa's economy, the project was put on hold. The goal was to develop a port with the following facilities: container terminals with 16 berths, capable of handling 18,000 TEU vessels; a 4-berth automotive terminal adjacent to the auto industries; a 4-berth liquid terminal with capacity to berth ultra-large container carrier (ULCC) vessels, currently restricted to offshore moorings; new rail and road access and infrastructure, in line with the 2050 Vision for the Durban–Gauteng freight corridor project; and expanded back-of-port logistics areas (Transnet National Ports Authority 2015).

Committed and planned expansion plans in the short and medium term in the port of Durban include the expansion of Durban Container Terminal (DCT) Pier 1, through the purchase of a portion of Salisbury Island, and the development of an additional 1.4 million TEU capacity, which will result from the expanded landside area, combined with two new deep-water berths (−16.5 m below CD). This extension project is set to begin in 2022 and must be preceded by the rationalization of the South Africa Naval Base. In the near term, Pier 2 of the terminal will see three of its berths extended and deepened from −12.6 m to −16.5 m below CD, allowing three super post-Panamax ships of 14,000 TEU to be berthed simultaneously, regardless of the tide. Construction was scheduled to commence in October 2018 and will ensure an additional 500,000 TEU of container-handling capacity. Also, a feasibility study for the development of a cruise liner terminal and associated commercial development at A and B berths is proceeding. Additional medium-term projects include the stack reconfiguration of the DCT and berth deepening and channel widening of Maydon Wharf. For the long term, the DDOP remains an option, but according to recent Transnet statements, this is unlikely before 2030.[7]

Transnet has voiced its commitment to advancing infrastructure and capacity development at the port of East London. The Authority's Port Development Framework Plans set out planned expansion of the port's automotive terminal, maritime engineering, and maritime commercial activities in the medium (2023–2045) to long term (beyond 2045). There is potential to grow volumes and expand business at the port, but this hinges on the ability to accommodate larger vessels through deepening and widening of the entrance channel and berths. This would better enable the port to support the city's positioning as a light manufacturing hub anchored by its strong automotive sector. The automotive demand forecast shows that the installed capacity will be exceeded in the short term (2017–2022); therefore, there is a project underway to reconfigure the terminal for 1,000 additional parking bays. Expansion of the car terminal would help the port to meet the needs of its anchor client, Mercedes Benz South Africa (East London's car terminal is shown in photo 3.1).

Additional initiatives at East London are underway to increase the movement of grain and agricultural products through the port with a number of projects in the pipeline to support volume throughput. Ship repair remains an important aspect of the port's strategy. Under the Operation Phakisa initiative various refurbishments are underway at the port's dry dock. Finally, another

PHOTO 3.1
Port of East London car terminal

Source: © Transnet National Ports Authority. Used with permission; further permission required for use.

development plan of Transnet is the proposed creation of a privately operated waterfront and yacht marina, which the city feels would be a major asset for the region.

China's involvement in the port sector in ESA

Over the last decade, there has been a significant increase in foreign direct investment from China in the African port sector. China's influence on the African continent has rapidly increased in recent years, with multiple state-owned enterprises involved in large-scale infrastructure projects. Not only does China offer finance, it has the required engineering knowledge and labor to rapidly execute these projects across the entire continent (Financial Times 2017). The recently inaugurated Doraleh Multipurpose Port in Djibouti was built in a record time of just 30 months, which included the entire process from land reclamation to installing the superstructure. Examples of large-scale projects constructed with Chinese investment along the African coast include the following:

- China Railway Group (CRG) and China Civil Engineering Construction Company (CCECC) constructed the recently commissioned 756 km electrified railway from Djibouti to Addis Ababa at a cost of US$4.0 billion. The project was funded by China's Exim Bank, the Development Bank of China, and the Industrial and Commercial Bank of China (2011–17);
- China State Construction Engineering Corporation (CSCEC) and CCECC constructed the Doraleh Multipurpose Port (DMP), with financing of the US$590 million Djibouti port project arising from China Merchants Port Holdings (CMPH; 2015–17);
- The recently constructed Ghoubet salt-export port in Djibouti (US$64 million) was funded by China's Exim Bank (2016–17);
- China constructed its first overseas naval base in Djibouti (2016–17);

- China Communications Construction Company (CCCC) constructed the 609 km standard gauge railway between Mombasa and Nairobi. This US$3.8 billion railway is financed for 90 percent by China Exim Bank (2015–17);
- Construction of the first three berths of the port of Lamu is currently carried out by CCCC. The costs of this first phase are estimated at US$480 million (2017).

Planned projects that involve Chinese firms include the following:

- Investment of US$4.0 billion in a natural gas facility in Djibouti by Chinese consortium POLY-GCL Group;
- Construction of the Djibouti International Container Terminal by CMPH. The US$1.0 billion project is scheduled to be completed in a 24-month period, with construction having started in 2018;
- Construction of the port of Bagamoyo by CMPH and its partner, the State General Reserve Fund of Oman, to include dredging of the navigational channel, construction of four marine berths, and the development of a portside industrial free zone (Bagamoyo Special Economic Zone);
- Construction of a deep-water port and railway line between the Moatize mines and Macuse for US$2.7 billion by a consortium consisting of CCECC and Mota-Engil; operations should commence in 2021;
- Construction of the Tamatave Deep-water Port Project near Toamasina, at US$1.0 billion, by CHEC.

CONCLUSIONS

This chapter summarizes the demand growth by commodity for each of the 15 ports in this study. In terms of containers, expressed in terms of TEUs, in aggregate, the number loaded or unloaded in the ESA ports increased from 4.6 million in 2010 to 5.6 million in 2016. This growth equates to a CAGR of 3.4 percent.

The volume of dry bulk throughput in the region's ports increased from 26.1 million tons in 2010 to 52.0 million tons in 2016, equal to a CAGR of 12.2 percent. The volume of liquid bulk throughput in the ESA ports (including, among other things, petrol, diesel, and cooking oils—hence primarily imports) increased from 43.4 million tons in 2010 to 53.5 million tons in 2016, equal to a CAGR of 3.5 percent. Finally, general cargo volumes through the ESA ports increased from 7.7 million tons in 2010 to 9.1 million tons in 2016, equal to a CAGR of 2.9 percent.

As a result, all the ports in the study have expansion plans that are at different stages of preparation and implementation. But these plans need to reflect the potential roles of both existing and new competing ports. And improving the way ports are managed, operated, and laid out is as important, if not more important, as enhancing existing port capacity. The next chapter reviews the current performance of the ESA ports, using a number of metrics to provide an indication of their comparative spatial and operating efficiencies.

NOTES

1. More detailed information on each of the 15 ports is provided in the second volume of the study.

2. The twenty-foot equivalent unit (TEU) is an inexact unit of cargo capacity often used to describe the capacity of container ships and container terminals.

3. A *chart datum* is the level of water from which charted depths displayed on a nautical chart are measured. A chart datum is generally a tidal datum; that is, a datum derived from some phase of the tide. Common chart datums are *lowest astronomical tide*, as used in the United Kingdom, and *mean lower low water*.

4. The project is funded by the World Bank (US$345 million), UKAID (US$12 million), and the government of Tanzania itself (US$64 million) (World Bank 2017).

5. Gross tons of a vessel is the gross weight, excluding cargo.

6. Information provided by MPDC management.

7. Information provided by TNPA HQ in Durban.

REFERENCES

Capital Ethiopia. 2017. "Djibouti's Logistics Push Continues." http://capitalethiopia .com/2017/05/29/djiboutis-logistics-push-continues/.

Club of Mozambique. 2017a. "Moatize Macuse Project to Begin in Late 2018—Govt." http:// clubofmozambique.com/news/moatize-macuse-project-to-begin-in-late-2018-govt/.

———. 2017b. "Portuguese Company to Build Railway from Moatize to New Macuse Deep Water Port." http://clubofmozambique.com/news/portuguese-company-build-railway-moatize -new-macuse-deep-war-port/.

DPFZA (Djibouti Ports & Free Zones Authority). 2017. *About Us.* http://dpfza.gov.dj/?q=about-us.

EDBM (Economic Development Board of Madagascar). 2016. "Investment Opportunities in Madagascar." http://www.edbm.gov.mg/.

Essar. 2017. "Essar Ports Signs Concession Agreement with Mozambique Government to Develop New 20 MTPA Coal Terminal in Beira Port." http://www.essar.com/article .aspx?cont_id=2Xw5icDbYKA=.

European Union External Action. 2014. "Sustainable Development of Transport Sector Support Program." http://eeas.europa.eu/archives/delegations/mauritius/eu_comoros /development_cooperation/infrastructure_transport/index_en.htm.

Financial Times. 2017. "Chinese Investment in Africa: Beijing's Testing Ground." https://www .ft.com/content/0f534aa4-4549-11e7-8519-9f94ee97d996.

Government of Somalia. 2016. "Consulting Services for Somali Port Modernization." http://mof .gov.so/en/consulting-services-for-somali-port-modernization percentE2 percent80 percent8F/.

IHS Fairplay. 2016. "Mombasa Vows to Rebuild Transhipment Volumes." http://fairplay.ihs.com /ports/article/4276436/mombasa-vows-to-rebuild-transshipment-volumes.

JICA (Japan International Cooperation Agency). 2017. "Madagascar, 411 Million US$ for the Toamasina Port Development Project." https://www.jica.go.jp/english/our_work /evaluation/oda_loan/economic_cooperation/c8h0vm000001rdjt-att/madagascar_170323 _01.pdf.

Kenya Ports Authority. 2017. Kipevu Container Terminal. Available at: https://www.kpa.co.ke /OurBusiness/pages/kipevu-container-terminal.aspx.

LAPSSET (Lamu Port–South Sudan–Ethiopia Transport). 2017. *Lamu Port.* http://www.lapsset .go.ke/projects/lamu-port/.

Mauritius Ports Authority. 2016. *Port Louis Masterplan 2016 Extract.* http://www.mauport.com /sites/default/files/public/port-master-plan-extract-1-2016.pdf.

———. 2018. *Port Development Strategy.* Port Louis: MPA.

Nathan Associates. 2014. *Zanzibar Multipurpose Port Development.* http://www.tzdpg.or.tz /fileadmin/documents/dpg_internal/dpg_working_groups_clusters/cluster_1/Energy _and_Minerals/Meeting_Notes___Workshops/2014/Revised_Preliminary_PPP_Analysis _Port_Development_Zanzibar-_clean.docx

Port Technology. 2014. "Mozambique in $3 Billion Port-Rail Plan." https://www.porttechnology .org/news/mozambique_in_3_billion_port_rail_plan.

Portos do Norte. 2017. "Rehabilitation of the Port of Nacala in 2017." http://www.portosdonorte .co.mz/rehabilitation-of-the-port-of-nacala-in-2017/.

Reuters. 2017. "Djibouti Signs Preliminary Deal with China's POLY-GCL for $4 Bln Gas Project." https://uk.reuters.com/article/china-djibouti-gas/djibouti-signs-preliminary-deal-with -chinas-poly-gcl-for-4-bln-gas-project-idUKL8N1NM2BV.

SPAT (Société du Port à Gestion Autonome de Toamasina). 2017. *Perspective et Projects*. http:// www.port-toamasina.com/la-spat/perspective-et-projets.

Tanzania Ports Authority. 2009. *Tanzania Ports Master Plan*. s.l.: s.n.

Transnet National Ports Authority. 2015. *National Port Plans 2015*.https://www .transnetnationalportsauthority.net/Infrastructure%20and%20Port%20Planning /Documents/National%20Port%20Plans%202015.pdf.

World Bank. 2017. *New Financing to Improve Efficiency and Improve Capacity at Port of Dar es Salaam*. http://www.worldbank.org/en/news/press-release/2017/07/02/new-financing -to-improve-efficiency-and-improve-capacity-at-port-of-dar-es-salaam.

World Cargo News. 2017a. *Infrastructure Boom for East African Cargo Flows*. MTBS Database.

——. 2017b. "Dredging under Way in Beira." http://www.worldcargonews.com/htm/w20171211 .473117.htm.

4 The Performance of the Individual Ports

This chapter evaluates the recent performance and status of the East and Southern Africa (ESA) ports from several perspectives, benchmarking ports against one another and against global comparators to the extent possible. The study uses three broad sets of indicators to provide an indication of the current performance and status of ESA ports. The indicators are explained below:

1. **Spatial and operating efficiency**: average ship turnaround time (in days), quay productivity (in twenty-foot equivalent units [TEU] per meter of container quay), port area container dwell time (average number of days containers are in the port), and truck turnaround time (truck time from gate in to gate out);

2. **Maritime access and connectivity:** maximum draft (in meters) at the berths, maximum length of vessel that can be berthed, length overall (LOA) in meters, the number of shipping lines calling at each port, formal indicators of maritime connectivity, ratio of berth and depth capacity usage;

3. **Technical efficiency:** an estimate of the efficiency of a port calculated by measuring the difference between observed production and theoretical or potential production, the latter based on the practices of the better-performing ports in the sample.

SPATIAL AND OPERATIONAL EFFICIENCY

In terms of average vessel turnaround time, the data show that, in relation to container ships, Maputo is the best performer, turning a container vessel around in under 1 day (0.81), whereas Zanzibar is the worst performer, with a mean ship turnaround time for containers in 4.19 days. The regional average is 2.33 days. By contrast, the best-performing container handling ports will turn a container vessel around in less than half a day (UNCTAD 2017). Figure 4.1 provides the average vessel turnaround time, by commodity group, by port, for 2016 in days.

FIGURE 4.1

Average vessel turnaround time in days, 2016

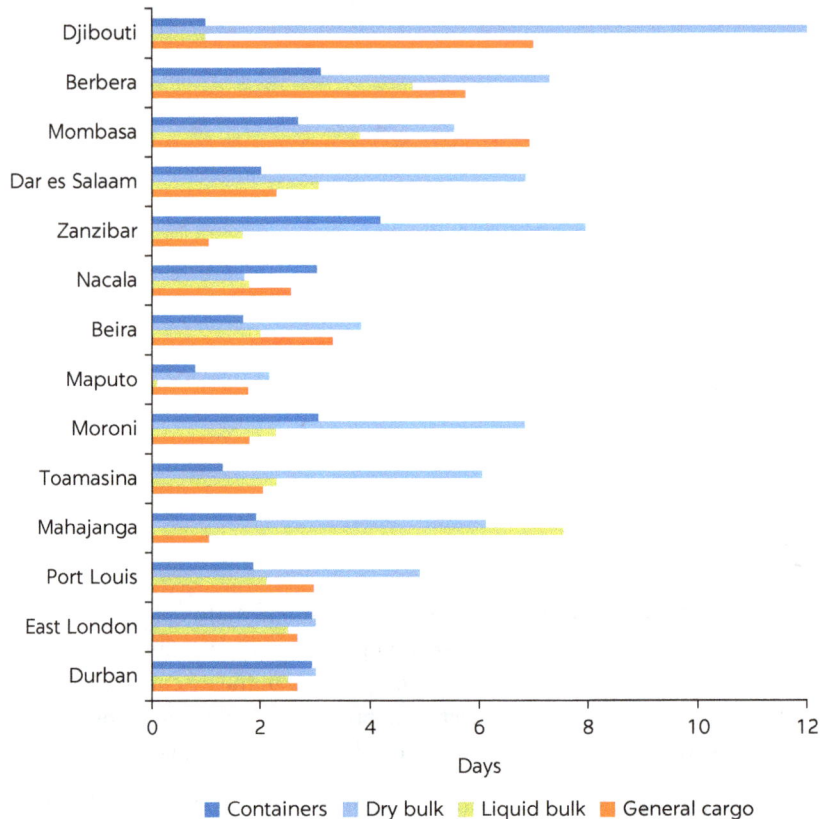

Source: World Bank analysis.

The average port area productivity in the study area ports is about 90,500 tons per hectare, but varies significantly, from less than 40,000 tons/ha at the Ports of Mahajanga, Beira, and Moroni to over 150,000 tons/ha in Zanzibar and Dar es Salaam.

In terms of quay productivity for general cargo (see figure 4.2), measured in tons per meter of quay, Dar es Salaam and Mombasa are the most efficient users of the available space, followed by Durban, Beira, and Nacala. This reflects specialization at the terminal in the case of Durban and Mombasa, and the physical constraints in Dar es Salaam which have necessitated a good use of the available space.

In terms of the handling containers given the space, the most efficient ports would appear to be Toamasina and Durban, followed by Djibouti, Port Louis, and Dar es Salaam. By contrast, the least efficient by this indicator are Mahajanga, Nacala, and Moroni (see figure 4.3). The average for the region is 466 TEU/m quay, with Toamasina's exceptional performance driven by the number of containers, the spatial constraints, and the performance of the specialist terminal operator. The global average is just over 1,100 TEU per meter of quay, and the best-performing port globally has a value of 3,000 TEU per meter of quay (Shanghai).

Dwell times for containers and average truck turnaround times for containers are not available for all ports, but average just under 9 days, and just under

FIGURE 4.2

Average quay productivity (tons/m), 2016

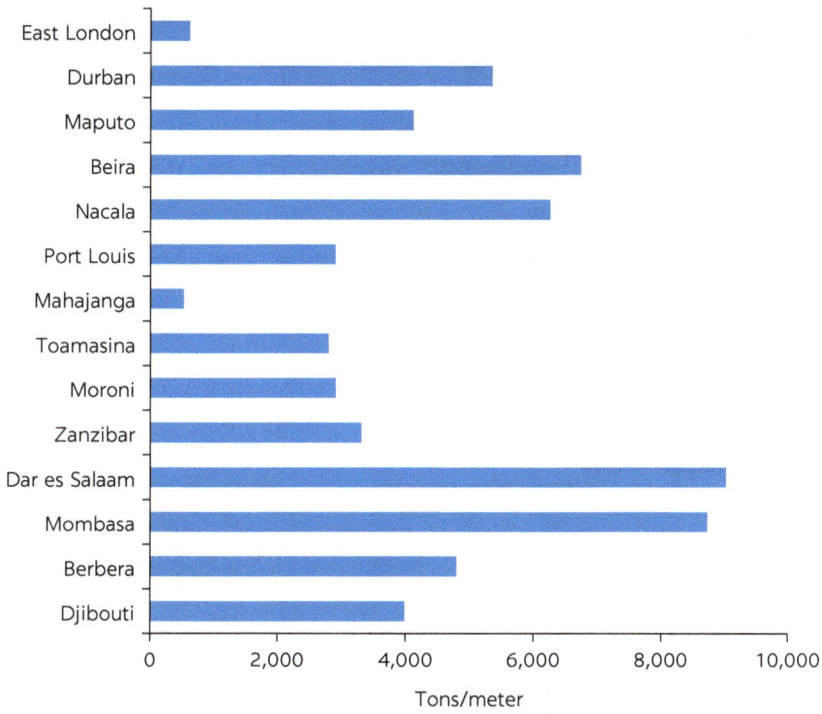

Source: World Bank analysis.

FIGURE 4.3

Average quay productivity (TEU/m), 2016

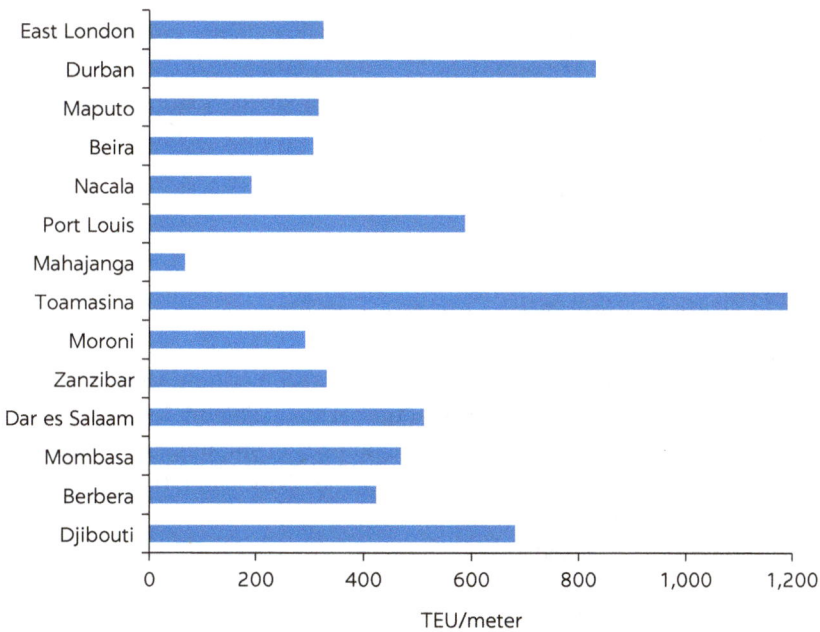

Source: World Bank analysis.
Note: TEU = twenty-foot equivalent unit.

FIGURE 4.4

Dwell time and truck turnaround time for containers, 2016[a]

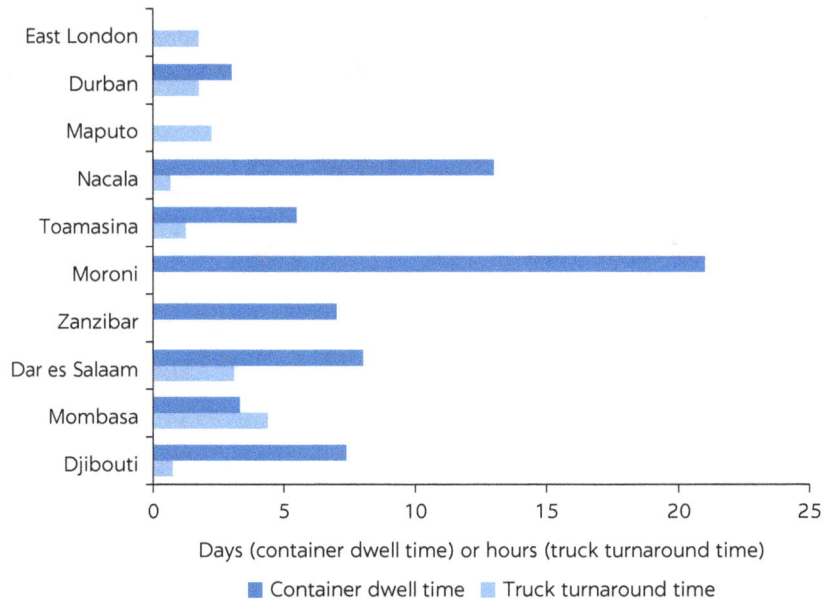

Days (container dwell time) or hours (truck turnaround time)

■ Container dwell time ■ Truck turnaround time

Source: World Bank analysis.
a. Compared to this study's relatively favorable assessment, the Ports of Mombasa and Dar es Salaam were found to be much more congested by a recent study by PwC (PwC 2018). That study found that Dar es Salaam and Mombasa port volumes exceed their actual throughput capacities by a factor of more than two, implying considerable delay (especially during busy periods).

2 hours, respectively, for those ports where the data were available (see figure 4.4)—with Durban, Djibouti, and Maputo the best performing in terms of dwell times, and Durban and Mombasa in terms of average truck turnaround times. Again, the best-performing global container ports will have a dwell time of less than 48 hours (UNCTAD 2017). One note of caution: the definition of dwell time in this study is that used by the port authorities, as the actual time the container spends in the port. As a recent study showed, this is a subset of actual dwell time, as it excludes the time expended in extensions to the port, such as inland container depots (World Bank 2012).

MARITIME ACCESS AND CONNECTIVITY

The following indicators are employed to illustrate maritime access and connectivity: maximum draft (in meters) at the berths, maximum length of vessels that can be berthed, LOA in meters, the number of shipping lines calling at each port, formal indicators of maritime connectivity, and ratio of berth and depth capacity usage.

In terms of the initial indicators, table 4.1 presents the data for each port. The data reveal that the ports with the largest draft are Djibouti, Port Louis, and Durban, and they are also the ports that can accommodate the larger vessels in terms of LOA. In terms of the ports with the most calls by shipping line, Durban, Mombasa, and Djibouti represent the top three, whereas the small island ports are the least served.

TABLE 4.1 **Maritime access indicators, 2016**

	DRAFT (M)	MAX LENGTH OVERALL (M)	NO. OF SHIPPING LINES CALLING
Djibouti	18.0	300	26
Berbera	8.8	165	8
Lamu	22.0	300	0
Mombasa	15.0	300	33
Dar es Salaam	12.5	250	24
Zanzibar	10.0	200	4
Nacala	15.0	200	10
Beira	12.0	183	9
Maputo	14.0	250	11
Moroni	4.5	80	4
Toamasina	14.0	230	8
Mahajanga	4.5	80	3
Port Louis	16.5	110	20
East London	10.4	245	1
Durban	16.5	350	42

Source: World Bank analysis.

Maritime indices

An index displays the variation between countries in terms of their maritime connectivity and illustrates their accessibility to global trade. Higher values or scores of the index indicate greater access to high-capacity and high-frequency global maritime freight transport systems—and more effective participation in international trade. An appropriately designed index can be considered a measure of connectivity to global maritime networks, and also a measure of trade facilitation.

Possibly the most well-known index of this type is the Liner Shipping Bilateral Connectivity Index (LSBCI) (Fugazza and Hoffmann 2016). The LSBCI was designed to identify the role of maritime connectivity in trade flows between pairs of countries for container traffic. One recent study (Fugazza, Hoffman, and Razafinombana 2015) found that the absence of a direct connection between two countries is associated with a reduction in export value of between 42 and 55 percent, and each additional transshipment is associated with a reduction in export value of between 20 and 25 percent.

In this study, two sources are used to estimate the maritime connectivity of the ports of ESA: the LSBCI data and the ship movement database.[1] The LSBCI captures connectivity at the country level, and the ship movement data allow an estimate to be calculated at the level of individual ports.

In terms of the former, the LSBCI comprises five components (Fugazza and Hoffman 2017): (1) the theoretical minimum number of transshipments required to move a container between country j and country k; (2) the number of common direct connections between any two countries in each country pair, thus the total number of countries that have a direct connection to both origin country j and destination country k in the pair; (3) the geometric mean of the number of direct connections, which reflects the centrality of a country pair in the network of liner-shipping connections; (4) the level of prevailing competition between each country pair; and (5) the size of the largest ship on the thinnest route. Maximum ship size is an indication of the level of infrastructure in the trading countries, as well as the countries through which they transship. Vessel size is also an indicator of economies of scale on the sea leg. The LSBCI is computed by taking the simple average of the five normalized components. As a consequence, the LSBCI can only take values between 0 and 1, with the higher values indicating better connectivity.

The LSBCI for the ESA countries is provided in map 4.1. In general terms, the figure indicates that South Africa, Djibouti, and Mauritius are the best-connected countries, with the Comoros, Madagascar, the Seychelles, and Somalia the least connected. Kenya, Mozambique, and Tanzania fall somewhere in the middle. Djibouti and South Africa require the least number of transshipments (typically none or one). The remaining countries typically require more than one transshipment to transport cargo to their bilateral trade partners.

MAP 4.1

The LSBCI for the ESA countries, 2016

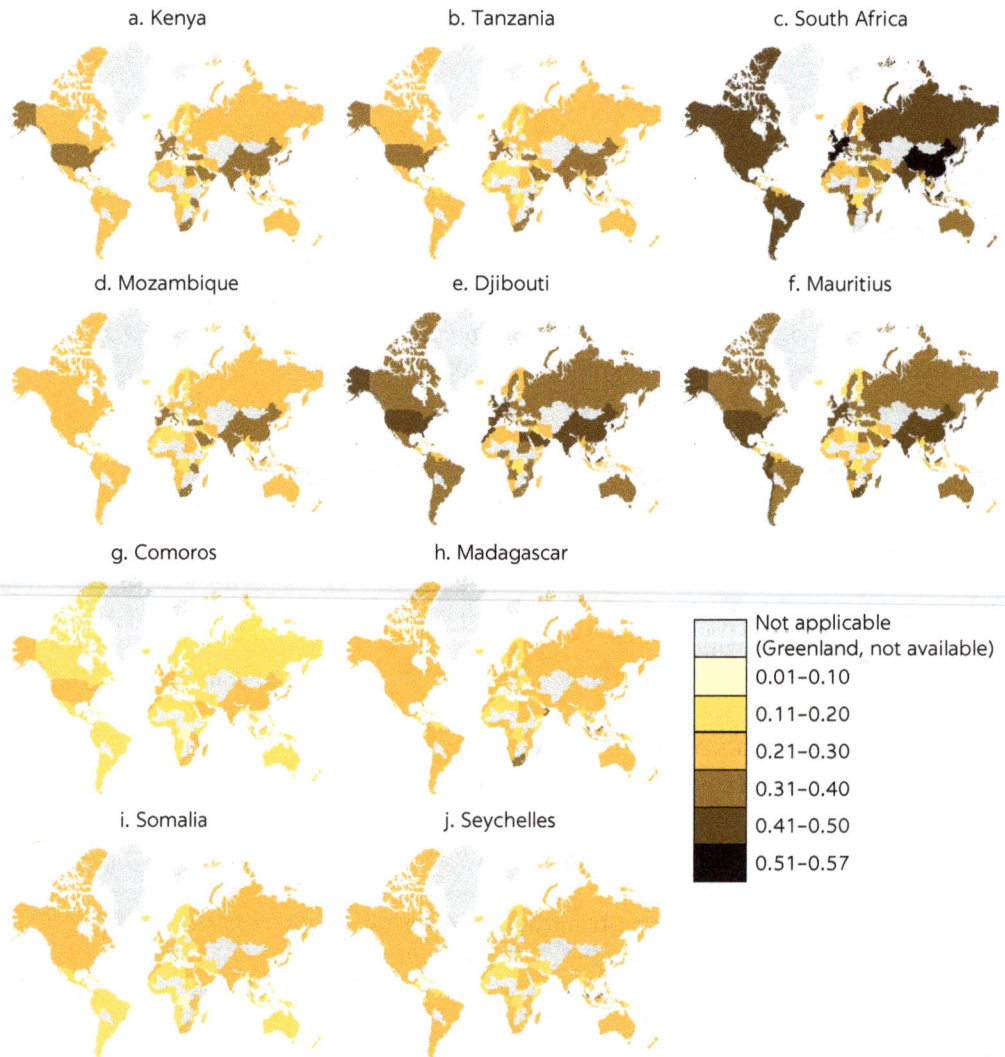

a. Kenya   b. Tanzania   c. South Africa

d. Mozambique   e. Djibouti   f. Mauritius

g. Comoros   h. Madagascar

i. Somalia   j. Seychelles

Not applicable (Greenland, not available)
0.01–0.10
0.11–0.20
0.21–0.30
0.31–0.40
0.41–0.50
0.51–0.57

Source: World Bank.
Note: ESA = East and Southern Africa; LSBCI = Liner Shipping Bilateral Connectivity Index.

In terms of connecting to other regions, ESA countries are connected most closely with other African countries and with Asia. Regarding the level of competition in maritime services, there is a clear polarization among ESA countries, with extremely limited competition in shipping to the small island states, and significant competition to Djibouti, Mauritius, and South Africa. The cases of Kenya and Tanzania also reflect a relatively high degree of competition.

The size of the largest ship on the weakest route, another component of the LBSCI, can be considered an indication of the level of infrastructure available in the country pair. South Africa, Djibouti, and Mauritius again show the highest levels of connectivity; the rest of the coastal Eastern African countries constitute an intermediate group; and the other island states show the lowest performance.

A more compact and comparable measure of connectivity is the average of the LSBCI for each ESA country across all its bilateral country pairs, weighted by the value of trade flows. Again, South Africa emerges as the most connected, followed by Djibouti and Mauritius, and somewhat more distantly by Kenya and Tanzania. The Comoros, Somalia, and Madagascar again rank the lowest, with connectivity indices at about half that of South Africa's (figure 4.5).

There are only minor differences between the indices, some weighted by the value of imports and some that use the value of exports. South Africa shows a higher level of connectivity for its exports, while Mauritius, Kenya, Djibouti, and the Comoros show the opposite. Comparing the connectivity levels across time (2010–16), there is no clear pattern across the entire region. All countries except the Comoros had higher levels of LSBCI in 2016 than in 2010; however, only South Africa, Mauritius, the Seychelles, and Somalia show a clear and significant positive trend, with some countries slipping back in 2016, reflecting the consolidation of lines and services.

FIGURE 4.5

LSBCI by country (exports and imports, weighted by value)

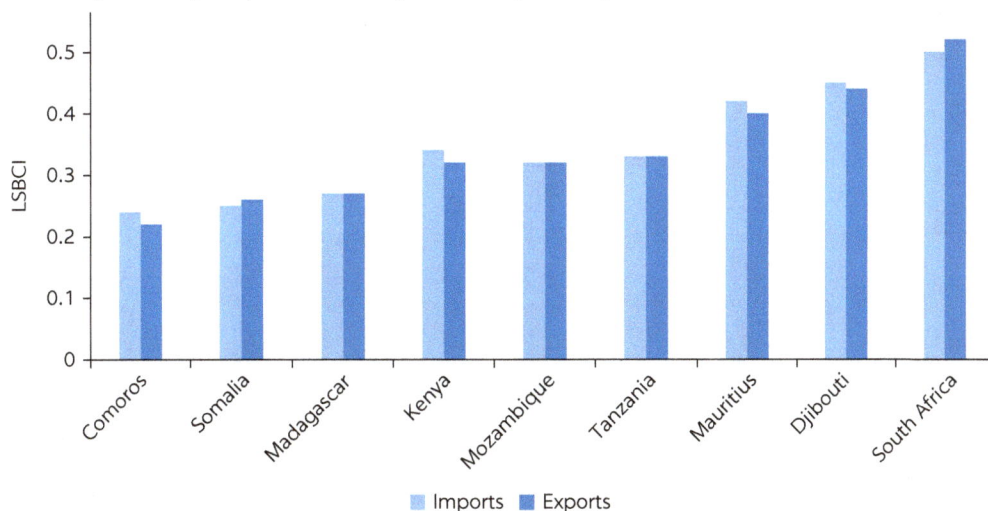

Source: Trade value data from COMTRADE and as reported by ESA's trade partner countries.
Note: LSBCI = Liner Shipping Bilateral Connectivity Index.

For comparative purposes, the study also calculated the port-level maritime connectivity using the ship movement data set, which contains information on over 3.6 million movements of container vessels in 2013–15. A bilateral connectivity index similar to the LSBCI was constructed for each pair of ports, in terms of both incoming and outgoing flows, as the simple average of the normalized values of distance, number of movements, average gross weight of the vessels on the route, their age, and their length. The results for incoming services for direct routes are presented in figure 4.6.

The average index in 2015 for direct incoming routes was the highest in Djibouti, followed by Durban, Port Louis, and Nacala. It was the lowest for the ports of Moroni, East London, and Berbera. With respect to direct outgoing routes, Port Louis was at the top of the ranking, followed by Maputo, Durban, and Toamasina; while Moroni, East London, and Berbera were again the least connected.

Next, ship movement data were used to derive a bilateral connectivity index that also considers indirect routes between country pairs. The index was again constructed for each pair of ports as the simple average of the normalized values of the number of stopovers, the time in port, the sailing time, and number of movements. In this case, the ranking of the ports is quite different compared with an index based only on direct connectivity. The results for incoming services for indirect routes are presented in figure 4.7.

In terms of incoming indirect routes, Djibouti and Port Louis remain among the best connected; however, Durban declines in the ranking to fifth place, behind Mombasa and Cape Town and on par with Berbera. Considering outgoing indirect routes, Durban appears to be the best connected, along with Cape Town and Port Elizabeth, while Port Louis and Maputo—the two highest-ranking ports in terms of the connectivity of direct outgoing routes—move significantly down the ranking, below Dar es Salaam, Mombasa, Nacala, and Toamasina. Richards Bay, Zanzibar, and East London appear to be the least connected in terms of indirect incoming routes, while outgoing indirect connectivity is also particularly low in Berbera and Beira.

FIGURE 4.6

Average LSBCI by port ordered by incoming routes for direct routes, 2015

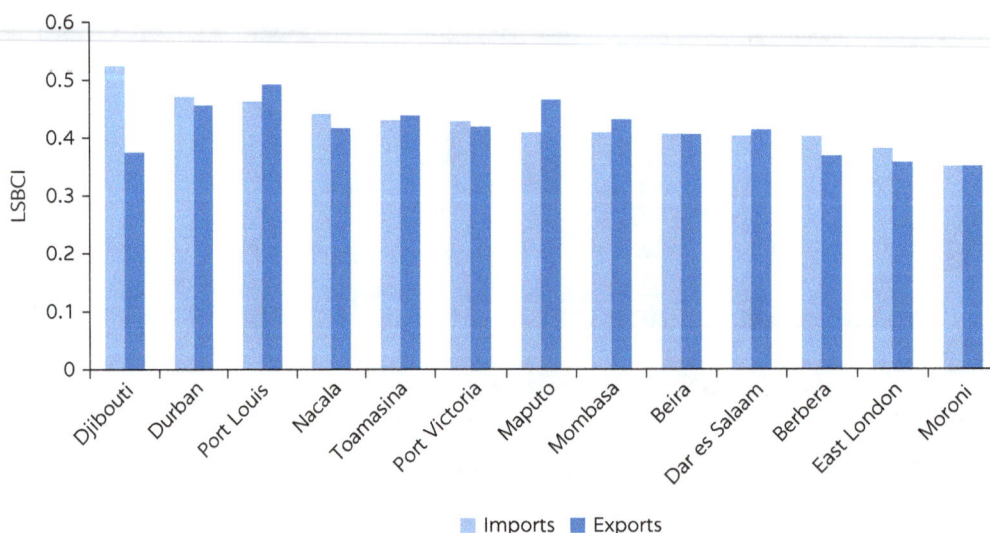

Source: World Bank analysis.
Note: LSBCI = Liner Shipping Bilateral Connectivity Index.

FIGURE 4.7
Average LSBCI by port ordered by incoming services for indirect routes, 2015

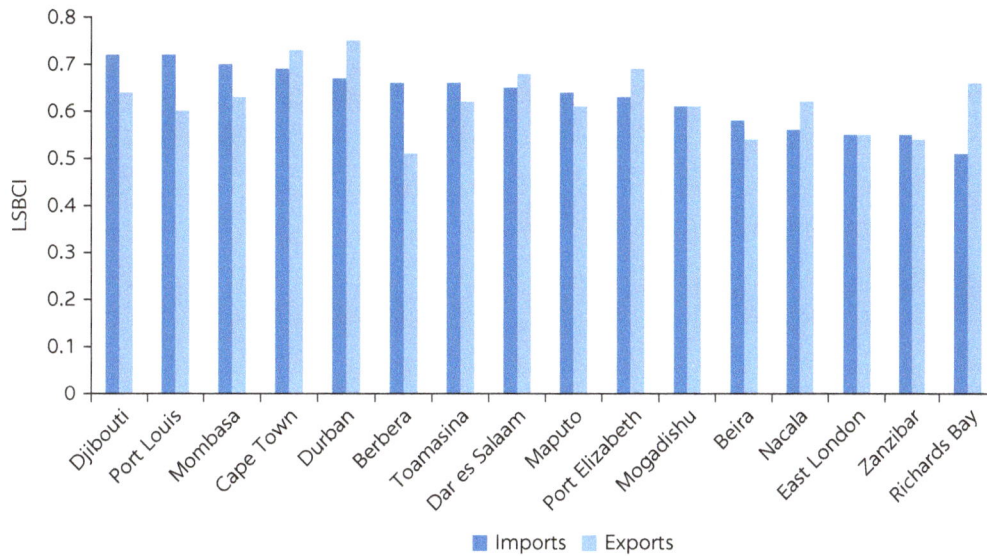

Source: World Bank analysis.
Note: LSBCI = Liner Shipping Bilateral Connectivity Index.

Average waiting and berthing times

As a complementary measure of operational performance, the ship-movement data were also used to calculate the average berthing and waiting times of the vessels that dock in the ESA ports. The competitiveness of any port can be significantly diminished by high vessel waiting times. The study calculated an effective average waiting time by multiplying the average observed waiting time by the probability of a ship waiting at an anchorage. This probability was calculated as the ratio of the number of waiting movements over the number of total berthing movements in a port.

Figure 4.8 shows the average waiting time at anchorage prior to berthing, for ships in the named ports. Among the ports in this study, the highest waiting times were found in Djibouti and Dar es Salaam, and the lowest non-zero waiting times in Port Louis, Maputo, and Beira; Nacala and East London showed no waiting time. As an example, the average waiting time in Dar es Salaam—across all container vessels that were required to wait—was approximately 24 hours, adding the cost of an additional vessel day to consignment costs.

The "effective" average waiting time should reflect the reality that not all ships berthed in the ports had to wait at anchorage. Accordingly, the study calculated effective average waiting time by multiplying the average waiting time by the ratio of the number of waiting movements over the number of total berthing movements in a port. The results are presented in figure 4.9.

The average waiting probability in 2015 was 50 percent, and Toamasina, Maputo, Djibouti, and Mombasa had waiting probabilities lower than the average. The highest effective average waiting times were recorded in Port Elizabeth and Durban, followed by Dar es Salaam, Cape Town, and Djibouti. Beira, Nacala, and East London appeared to have no waiting times.

FIGURE 4.8

Average waiting time, 2015

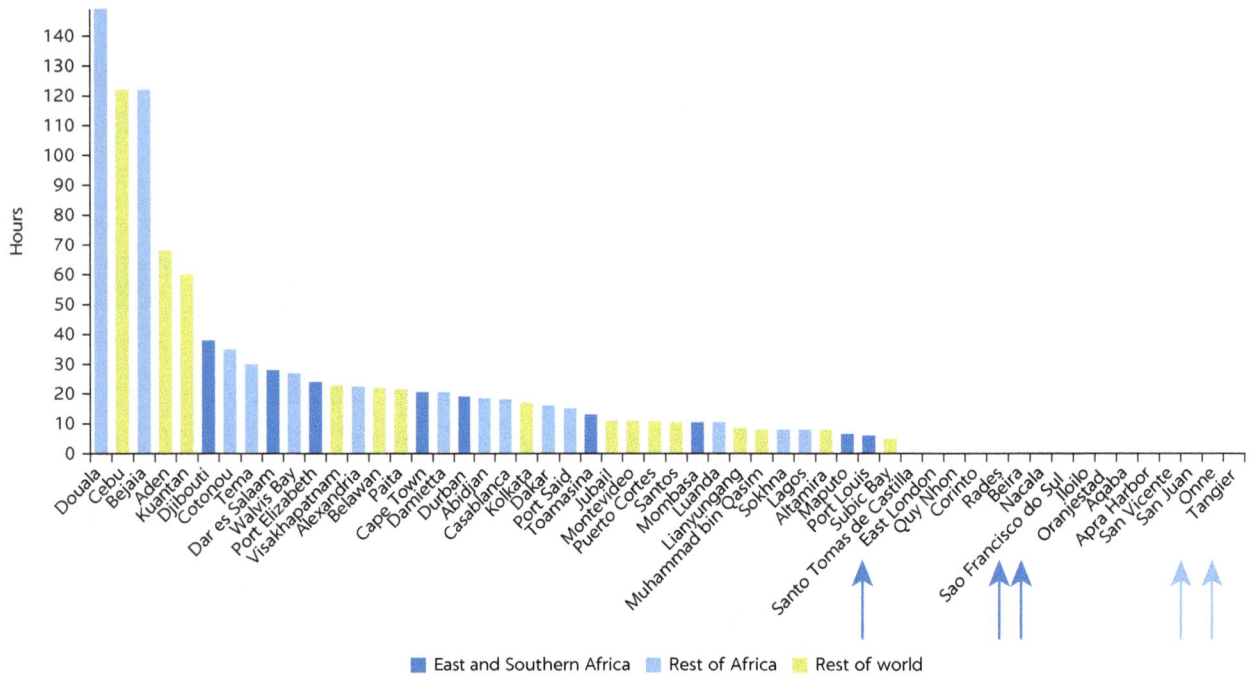

FIGURE 4.9

Effective average waiting time, 2015

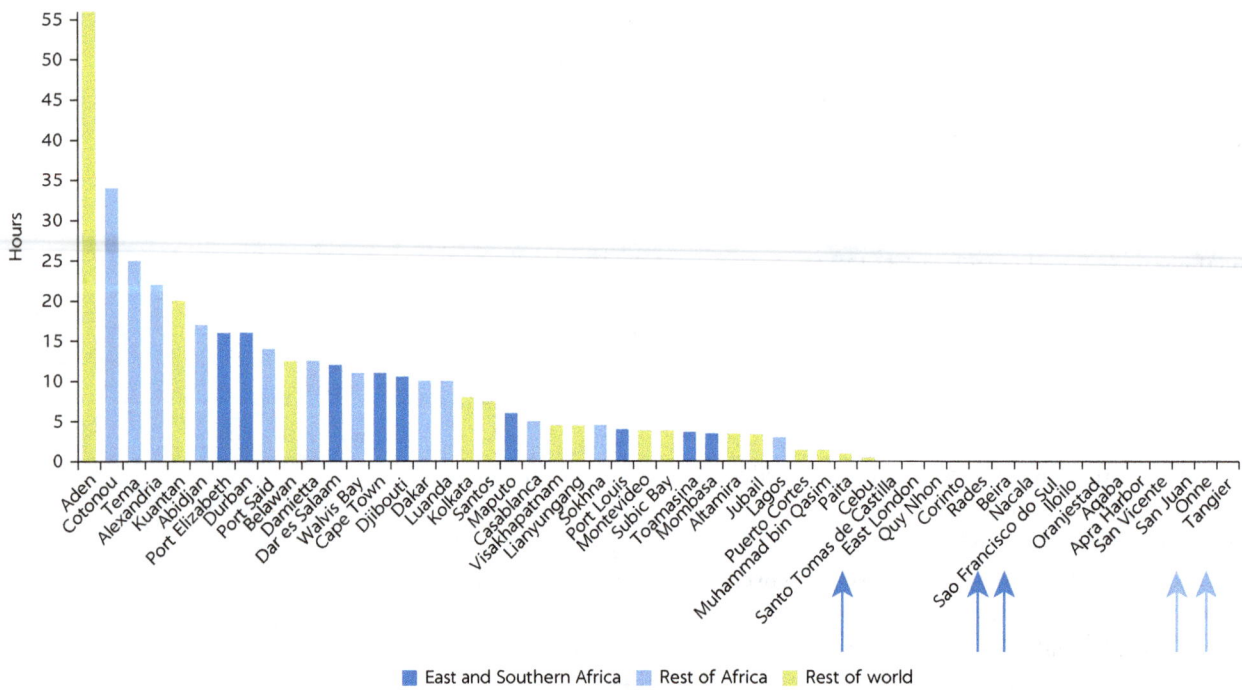

The exact vessel loading or unloading time is not available in the database; therefore, berthing time is used as an approximation. While higher waiting times always reduce the competitiveness of a port, the same is not necessarily true for the average berthing time, since high berthing times can also be attributed to larger-size ships and a larger number of containers unloaded. Among the ports studied, the best performers in terms of average berthing times in 2015 were Toamasina, Maputo, and Port Louis, with berthing times averaging about 10 hours. The worst performers were East London, Mombasa, and Dar es Salaam, where average berthing times exceeded 30 hours.

Theoretically—other port characteristics being equal—lower berthing times should be accompanied by lower waiting times; however, this is not the case in the ESA ports, where there is no clear correlation between the two measures. Ports like Beira and Durban, with similar berthing times, display quite different waiting times. The same can be observed in the cases of Maputo and Toamasina. Average total times—waiting plus berthing—are the lowest in Toamasina, Port Louis, and Maputo, and the highest are in the larger ports—Durban, Mombasa, and Dar es Salaam.

Generally, higher port throughput (in TEUs) is accompanied by lower effective waiting times. This negative relationship is stronger in Africa than in other regions, but it is weaker in ESA than in other parts of the continent. The relationship between throughput and berthing time shows a completely different pattern. While in ESA higher port throughput is associated with higher berthing times, this is not the case in other ports. Presumably, the higher throughput in ESA is because of bigger ships and greater average amounts of containers that need to be unloaded, which tends to increase the berthing times. Higher waiting times seem to be positively correlated with berthing times across all regions; however, the relationship is particularly strong in ESA.

Use of existing capacity

The study estimated an indicative measure of the maximum capacity of a port, in terms of container berths, by looking at the maximum depth available and the maximum length of the container vessels it currently berths. The ship movement database provides the average draft and length of all the container vessels that docked in a port. The ratio between the average vessel length and draft, and the maximum length of berth, and depth, respectively, provides an indication of how close the container berths are to operating at their respective capacity limits. The results are illustrated in figure 4.10.

The results, which reflect 2014 data, indicate that a significant number of ESA ports lay near or slightly above the total estimated available capacity for their container berths: Port Louis, Mombasa, Port Elizabeth, and Durban all lay close to the estimated capacity, while Dar es Salaam, Djibouti, Beira, and Toamasina seemed to be above capacity, and hence under stress at that time, clearly indicating the need for additional capacity.

Figure 4.11 presents a similar calculation of the ratio of vessel size and average port depth, again using 2014 data. Again, a significant number of the ESA ports appeared to operate close to maximum capacity at that time, while a number (Durban, Dar es Salaam, Toamasina, and Mombasa) were under stress.

FIGURE 4.10

Ratio of container berth capacity usage, 2014

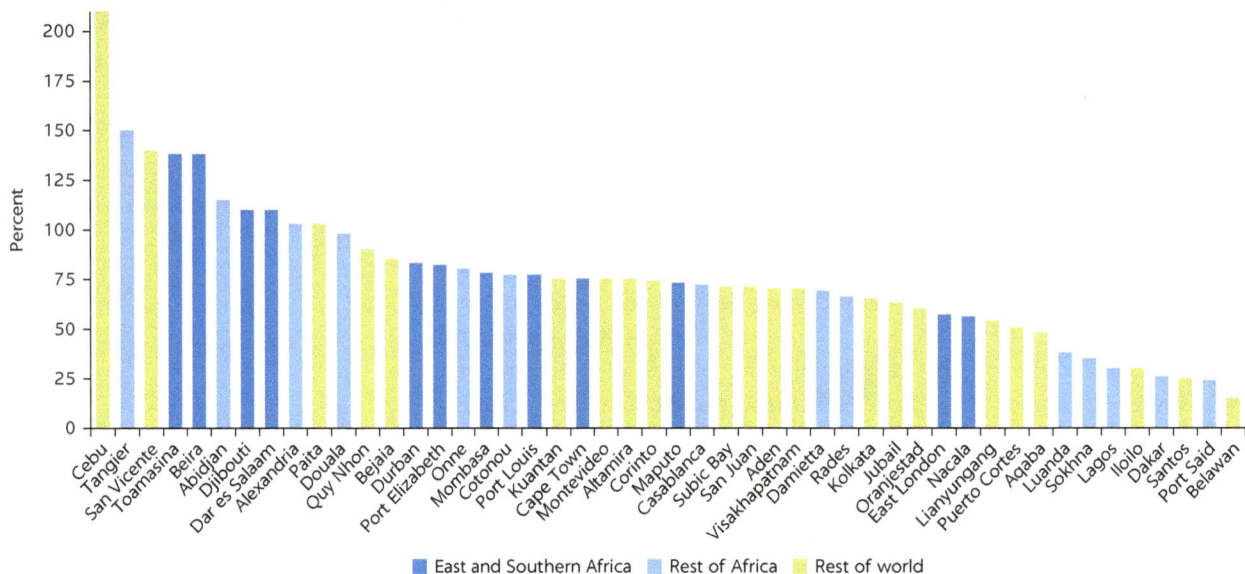

FIGURE 4.11

Ratio of depth capacity usage, 2014

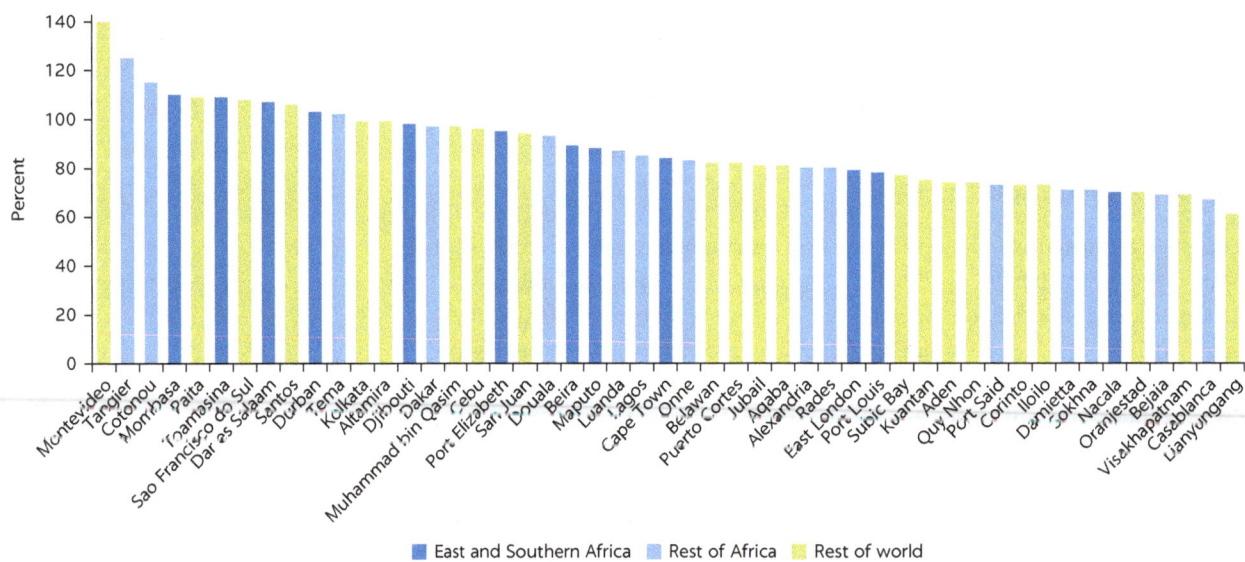

TECHNICAL EFFICIENCY

Since the 1990s, there has been a proliferation of research on the efficiency of ports; much of it supports the unsurprising premise that increased efficiency reduces transport costs (Herrera-Dappe, Jooste, and Suárez-Alemán 2017; Nordås and Piermartini 2009). The technical efficiency of port infrastructure has also been identified as a key contributor to overall port competitiveness

(Clark, Dollar, and Micco 2004). Technical efficiency is defined here as the difference between observed production and theoretical potential production, the latter based on the practices of the "better-performing" ports.

In this section, the technical efficiency of a subset of the 15 ESA ports is estimated using data from two data sets (2000–10 and 2008–17), focusing specifically on container terminals. The objective is not only to establish a ranking of the ports according to their efficiency, but also to identify the factors that influence the estimate of efficiency or inefficiency.

The literature on efficiency in the port industry emerged about three decades after Farrell proposed the concept of "technical efficiency" (Farrell 1957). However, research on the efficiency of African ports dates only to the beginning of the 21st century. Two approaches have been developed to estimate the technical efficiency frontier: linear programming techniques, mainly data envelopment analysis (DEA), and econometric (stochastic) approaches. As Cullinane and Song (2006), among others, show, the results obtained using the two approaches are reasonably correlated. Only a few studies to date have analyzed the technical efficiency specific to African ports' container terminals. Focusing on the period between 1998 and 2007 and covering 37 African ports, Trujillo, González, and Jiménez (2013) found that, on average, landlord ports—specifically those that were commercializing all their operations, promoting decentralization, and encouraging private sector participation—were the most technically efficient.

The current study measures port efficiency using a stochastic frontier production function. The production frontier shows the maximum output quantity that can be obtained with a given combination of inputs. The efficiency of a port is calculated by measuring the difference between observed production and theoretical potential production, the latter based on the practices of the "better-performing" ports in the sample of similar ports. The logic of using a matched sample of similar ports[2] is that larger ports will reach levels of technical efficiency that are unattainable by ports of the scale of the ESA ports. The estimation used in the study is based on a model first proposed by Battese and Coelli (1995).

The results, however, need to be interpreted with a note of caution: in one example, a port under stress may appear an exemplar in comparison, as the pressure forces an improvement in the utilization of space and improvement in operational practices. By contrast, a port under less stress may not face the same pressures, and in some cases may encourage higher dwell time for revenue maximization. The picture is obviously nuanced, and the key message is that the different metrics should not be taken unilaterally and need to be considered with respect to the context.

Given the challenges of data availability and reliability, the analysis was done with an existing data set, covering the years 2000–10, and a new data set collected for this exercise, covering the period 2008–17. The analysis considered three main input variables: the sum of the length of all container and multipurpose berths in the port, the total container terminal area of the port, and the combined capacity of the cranes, including ship-to-shore (STS) gantry cranes, and any mobile lifting capacity in the port with a capacity of more than 15 tons. Also, several "environmental variables" were defined to ensure that other key contextual factors were reflected in the analysis. These included a dummy variable if there is at least one privately operated terminal, a dummy variable if the port has railway access, and a connectivity index.[3]

A time trend was included to reflect the effect of technological change. Other variables that have been included are a dummy variable for the port being an international or regional hub, to try and capture the importance of transshipment for the port; a dummy variable for the port being a landlord port or a service port; the arithmetic mean of the time that a container ship is in the dock; the number of container operators in the container terminals; the port area; and the number of trade agreements signed by the country where the port is located, as they offer a larger market for a country and generate more port traffic.

Results of the analysis

The analysis shows that the average technical efficiency of container terminal operations in the 10 ESA ports (Beira, Dar es Salaam, Durban, East London, Maputo, Mombasa, Nacala, Port Louis, Djibouti, Toamasina) falls in a range of 44–53 percent for the 2000–10 data set. The ranking is constant, more or less, across the different models: Durban, Mombasa, Dar es Salaam, and Port Sudan are the most efficient ports, in terms of container handling, while Beira, East London, and Nacala are the least efficient. Globally, the port of Mombasa, based on this data, is the most technically efficient port, and ranks as the 43rd most efficient container port in the global sample. Dar es Salaam and Durban follow at 64th and 70th positions respectively.

The analysis also reveals that the main factors that drive higher efficiency in container terminal operations in the port are (1) the presence of a specialist terminal operator(s) (2) the existence of a rail connection to the port; (3) the existence of transshipment traffic; (4) a higher score on the LSBCI; and (5) reduced time at berth.

The 2008–17 data set provides broadly similar findings: Mombasa, Durban, and Dar es Salaam are again the most efficient ports for container handling, with Djibouti replacing Port Sudan.[4] Beira, Nacala, and East London remain the least efficient. Again the main factors that drive higher efficiency are found to be the presence of a specialist terminal operator(s), the existence of a rail connection to the port, the existence of transshipment traffic, a higher score on the connectivity index, and reduced time at berth. The benchmarking results of the model run only on the sample of ESA ports are again similar; they are shown in figure 4.12.

While the analysis provides insights at the level of container handling in the ports in aggregate, ideally the analysis should be undertaken at the level of individual terminals; future data permitting, additional ports—such as Richards Bay in South Africa—could also be added among the ESA ports being benchmarked.

Assuming the availability of reliable disaggregated container traffic data, technical efficiency can vary significantly across terminals, modes of operation (public or private, port authority vs. specialist), and contexts.

Overall, the analysis presented in this chapter illustrates the somewhat uneven performance of the ESA ports, depending on the indicators against which they are evaluated. In terms of *spatial and operational efficiency*, while the ports of Maputo and Djibouti appear more efficient when evaluated on vessel turnaround times, the productivity of port equipment is significantly higher in Mombasa, Dar es Salaam, Durban, and Toamasina. In the port of Djibouti, vessel turnaround times vary significantly depending on the type of cargo, perhaps reflecting the port's focus on containerized shipments. With respect to *maritime access and connectivity*, Durban, Djibouti, and Mombasa

FIGURE 4.12

Average technical efficiency, by port, among ESA ports, 2008–17

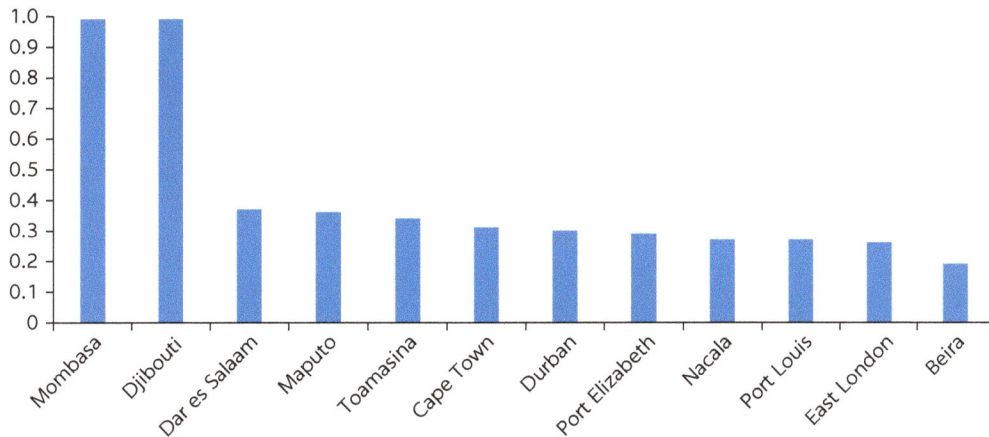

again perform among the best, but in this case are rivaled or even outperformed by the well-connected port of Port Louis. The Mozambican ports of Beira and Nacala, on the other hand, stand out as having exceptionally low average waiting and effective waiting times at anchorage. Finally, the current de facto regional hubs, Mombasa, Durban, and Djibouti (along with Dar es Salaam) emerge as the best performers in terms of *technical efficiency*. Yet, compared with the global benchmarks, even these best performers still have significant potential to make more efficient use of the infrastructure and to cost-effectively reduce transport and trade costs.

The next chapter summarizes some of the challenges faced by the port sector in ESA.

NOTES

1. Purchased from IHS Markit.
2. The matched sample contains 35 African ports, 18 ports in Latin America and the Caribbean, and 29 ports in Asia.
3. The index, similarly to the LSBCI mentioned in the previous section, is generated using five components: (1) the number of ships; (2) the total container-carrying capacity of those ships; (3) the maximum vessel size (LOA); (4) the number of services; and (5) the number of companies that deploy container ships on services from and to a country's ports.
4. Port Sudan was omitted from the second data set due to concerns over the reliability of the data.

REFERENCES

Battese, G. E., and T. J. Coelli. 1995. "A Model for Technical Inefficiency in a Stochastic Frontier Production Function for Panel Data." *Empirical Economics* 20: 325–32.

Clark, X., D. Dollar, and A. Micco. 2004. "Port Efficiency, Maritime Transport Costs, and Bilateral Trade." *Journal of Development Economics* 75 (2): 417–50.

Cullinane, K., and D. W. Song. 2006. "Estimating the Relative Efficiency of European Container Ports: A Stochastic Frontier Analysis." *Research in Transportation Economics* 16: 85–115.

Farrell, M. J. 1957. "The Measurement of Productive Efficiency." *Journal of the Royal Statistical Society, Series A* 120 (3): 253–67.

Fugazza, M., and J. Hoffman. 2016. *Bilateral Liner Shipping Connectivity Since 2006*. UNCTAD Research Series.

——. 2017. "Liner Shipping Connectivity as Determinant of Trade." *Journal of Shipping and Trade* 2 (1): 1. https://doi.org/10.1186/s41072-017-0019-5.

Fugazza, M., J. Hoffman, and R. Razafinombana. 2015. "Building a Dataset for Bilateral Maritime Connectivity." *Region et Developpement* 41: 101–24.

Herrera-Dappe, M., C. Jooste, and A. Suárez-Alemán. 2017. "How Does Port Efficiency Affect Maritime Transport Costs and Trade? Evidence from Indian and Western Pacific Ocean Countries." Policy Research Working Paper 8204, World Bank.

Nordås, H. K. and R. Piermartini. 2009. "Infrastructure and Trade." World Trade Organization Working Paper. World Trade Organization.

PwC. 2018. *Strengthening Africa's Gateways to Trade: An Analysis of Port Development in Sub-Saharan Africa*. Price Waterhouse Coopers.

Trujillo, L., M. M. González, and J. L. Jiménez. 2013. "An Overview on the Reform Process of African Ports." *Utilities Policy* 25: 12–22. doi:10.1016/j.jup.2013.01.002.

UNCTAD (United Nations Conference on Trade and Development). 2017. *Review of Maritime Transport*. UNCTAD.

World Bank. 2012. *Why Does Cargo Spend Weeks in Sub-Saharan African Ports*. Directions in Development Series. Washington, DC.

5 The Challenges Facing the Ports in ESA

The ports in the region face numerous challenges, not least substantial demand growth. However, the latter is a benefit as well as a challenge for the ports and will be discussed in the next chapter. This section focuses on the main external and internal challenges that are confronting the East and Southern Africa (ESA) ports.

TRENDS IN THE SHIPPING INDUSTRY

One of the key challenges facing the ESA ports is the need to adapt to global trends in the shipping industry—trends that are, if anything, accelerating. Understanding and responding to these trends is important if a port is to maintain its competitiveness, let alone improve it. These trends are broadly categorized as follows:

- Changes in the pattern of ship calls (types and size of vessels, the frequency of calls, establishment of feeder services, reducing turnaround time in port, etc.)
- Changes in shipping industry structure affecting the ESA port sector (economic conditions, changes in shipping line ownership and alliances, consolidation of services)

The primary driver underpinning these trends for all shipping lines has been the need to improve efficiency of operations and reduce costs. The higher bunker costs, which have led slow steaming (the practice of operating cargo ships at significantly less than their maximum speed, to save fuel and reduce costs per unit) to become the norm, has accelerated the movement toward improved efficiency.

Cost efficiency as a driver

Containers

These trends are possibly most pronounced in the container market, which is a highly competitive segment with low (and declining) margins. Container ships are divided into small feeder, feeder, feedermax, Panamax, Post-Panamax, New Panamax, and the so-called ultra-large container carriers (ULCCs). This movement toward larger vessels has been underway for some time, but the pace has increased in recent years. Over the last 15 years, container ship sizes have tripled.

The pursuit of greater economies of scale has led ship owners to continually order larger vessels, with vessels up to 21,413 twenty-foot equivalent units (TEU) now sailing around the world (for example, OOCL Hong Kong). One major shipping line, CMA CGM, recently announced that it has placed an order for nine liquefied natural gas (LNG)–fueled 22,000 TEU vessels, scheduled for delivery in 2020. Meanwhile, MSC recently announced the purchase of eleven 23,000 TEU vessels (World Maritime News 2018). As of December 2017, there were 423 container ships that could carry 10,000 TEU or more.

The ULCCs (18,000+ TEU), such as the Triple E class of Maersk, are deployed almost exclusively on the main East–West trade routes. This is the main arterial trade route for global containerized traffic, on which the most cost efficiencies can be gained. However, with these new giant vessels entering the main East–West trade, smaller ships are then redeployed to the remaining shipping routes, including the ones servicing ports in Africa. This effect has been named the "cascade" effect and entails the deployment of increasingly larger container vessels on trade routes around the world.

A good example of this accelerating trend is the introduction of the West African Maximum class vessels (WAFmax) by Maersk Line in 2011 and 2012 for their service (FEW-2), between West Africa, the Far East, and calling at the port of Walvis Bay. The WAFmax vessel was uniquely designed for West African ports, with a design that fully utilized the available draft and access characteristics of the regional ports at the time the vessels were commissioned.

The result was a unique class of container ships, able to carry up to 4,500 TEU, a length overall (LOA) of 250 m, and a draft of 13.5 m. The WAFmax vessels, as well as being more efficient in terms of fuel consumption, carried twice as much cargo than the vessels calling previously at West African ports. This increased overall port productivity by facilitating a greater utilization of cranes, faster turnaround times for the vessels, and hence lower unit costs.

However, the changes in the container sector in recent years have been so rapid that now the WAFmax class vessels themselves are becoming something of an anachronism. Now vessels that can carry 13,000 TEU are already calling at the port of Lomé, and 8,000–9,000 TEU ships have been deployed on services calling at the port of Pointe-Noire. These vessels have significantly larger dimensions, with their LOA exceeding 300 m.

The impact of the ultra-long container ships (ULCSs) on their ports of call has been substantial. Higher and heavier ship-to-shore (STS) gantry cranes are required to reach and handle the container cargo. Consequently, the quay wall has to be reinforced or, in some cases, the terminals must be entirely rebuilt. Often, with ships measuring up to 300 or 400 meters, quays also have to be lengthened and deepened, and access infrastructure improved, requiring significant capital investment.

Similarly, the cascading of vessels places demands on the smaller ports to allow them to service increasingly larger vessels. Though the vessels currently calling in most ESA ports have a capacity of between 2,900 and 5,500 TEU, this will change, necessitating investment in many of the same areas:

- Additional port investments in equipment to efficiently service larger vessels
- Dredging, quay wall extensions, and berth extensions
- Improved access infrastructure and transportation facilities to handle peak demands

The magnitude of the impact of this trend will obviously be larger for the ports of Durban, Djibouti, Mombasa, or Port Louis, compared with the small regional ports like Moroni, Mahajanga, or Berbera.

Shipping line consolidation and links with global terminal operators

Container shipping joint services, vessel sharing agreements, alliances, and consolidations are as old as container shipping itself. However, what happened in 2016 and 2017 in this regard was unprecedented, with a corresponding impact on port and terminal operators. In those two years, multiple traditional shipping lines have ceased operations.

The East–West container routes are dominated by the so-called East–West Alliances. There were more than six alliances several years ago, then four, now the number has fallen to three, uniting 10 Alliance members, as illustrated in figure 5.1.[1]

FIGURE 5.1

Far East–Europe capacity share by alliance

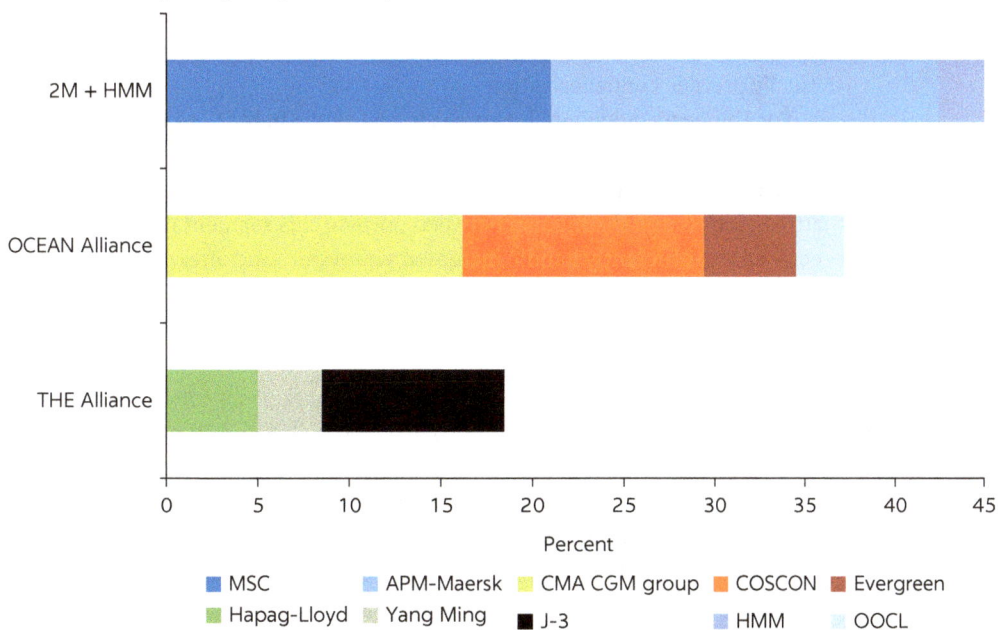

Note: APM-Maersk = A.P. Moller-Maersk; CMA-CGM = Compagnie Méridionale d'Affrètement–Compagnie Maritime Générale; COSCON = China Ocean Shipping Company Container Lines Company Limited; HMM = Hyundai Merchant Marine; MSC = Mediterranean Shipping Company S.A.; OOCL = Orient Overseas Container Line.

There is also a stronger relationship between the shipping lines and the global port and terminal operators than in the past. Many shipping lines have a network of terminals. For example, the AP Møller group owns APM Terminals and Maersk Line, CMA CGM owns Terminal Link, and COSCO Container Lines Company Limited (COSCON) owns Cosco Pacific terminal group. Next to the shipping line terminal operators are independent terminal operators such as PSA, DP World, Eurogate, and International Container Terminal Services Inc. (ICTSI).

This consolidation will allow shipping lines to put more pressure on the ESA ports to upgrade port facilities, invest in new equipment, and accept larger ships, while simultaneously bargaining for lower port charges. Failure to respond to these demands could result in non-shipping-line-related terminal operators, and thus ports, being excluded from the larger service loops. Consequently, having to accept smaller, less-efficient feeder services is unlikely to significantly reduce, if at all, the cost of imports and exports.

General cargo

General cargo is a type characterized by a wide variety of different cargo loads and comprises all cargo that does not belong to bulk, containers, or vehicles. General cargo shipping is following two main trends: First, general cargo operators are moving toward larger vessels, driven by the same desire to lower unit costs; and second, the industry is moving toward containerizing or palletizing as much general cargo as feasible, for similar reasons.

In the former case, general cargo is often shipped in other vessel types, such as dry bulk vessels, that have become obsolete in their original markets. These vessels are usually larger than the typical general cargo vessels and are sometimes slightly adjusted to carry specific loads of general cargo.

In the latter case, the industry is continuously seeing more general cargo being palletized and containerized. Containerized cargo is easier to handle, and overall port efficiency is enhanced if the size and shape of the cargo being handled is as uniform as possible. In less mature markets, palletizing of cargo will usually precede containerization.

For the ports, adequate berth space and the capability to handle general cargo (heavy lifting capacity) are the main requirements to attract and retain general cargo. Greater specialization and optimization can enhance relative attractiveness and distinguish between ports in this segment. In other words, ports able to efficiently handle increased vessel sizes and offer good, if not specialized, services will be expected to capture the largest market shares.

Dry bulk and liquid bulk

Shipping lines in the dry bulk and liquid bulk markets also focus on cost efficiency. The main global trend in the bulk shipping business is again to increase the size of vessels to realize economies of scale, and hence cost savings, for shipping lines. The bulk shipping business has a slightly different structure compared with the container shipping business. Bulk carrier operators have less influence on the port of call, since the port of call in the bulk market is usually determined by the origin of the commodity, and the end user.

The port from which these commodities are exported depends primarily on the available infrastructure to transport the product to the coast, and then ship it out. Therefore, the bulk carrier operators have little influence on the decision for the ports of call. An example of this is the export of coal from Nacala in

Mozambique—the closest deep-water port to the mine in Tete province in Mozambique, connected by a dedicated railway.

Companies owning bulk carrier ships earn revenue via two main channels: the spot and the charter market. In the spot market, the bulk vessels are contracted for a short time period at the prevailing market rate. In the charter market, the bulk vessels are contracted at fixed rates over a longer period, usually a couple of years, and often include renewal options of the contract.

Ro-Ro

In the roll on–roll off (Ro-Ro) sector, a distinction is made between two main types of deep-sea Ro-Ro vessels: conventional Ro-Ro vessels and Ro-Ro carriers. Conventional Ro-Ro vessels combine different cargo types. Examples are the Ro-Ro multipurpose carriers that carry general cargo in addition to Ro-Ro, and the container Ro-Ro vessels, also called the "ConRo" category.

The worldwide export of vehicles increased significantly at the end of the last decade, hence the demand for Ro-Ro vessels also increased. However, the global automobile market had collapsed after the economic crisis in 2008, which led to the scrappage of Ro-Ro vessels on a large scale. Since 2009, the compound annual growth rate (CAGR) of conventional Ro-Ro vessel fleets has been minus 6 percent. In contrast to the shrinking conventional Ro-Ro fleet, the Ro-Ro carrier fleet has increased by 85 vessels. It is expected that the Ro-Ro carrier type will ultimately, or at least largely, take over the conventional Ro-Ro type of vessel. This is also reflected by the total amount of conventional Ro-Ro vessels on order, which is much lower compared with the amount of Ro-Ro carrier vessels.

The Ro-Ro industry also follows the trend of increasing economies of scale. The average Ro-Ro vessels increased substantially over time, in both size and capacity. However, unlike the other cargo segments, the impact on port infrastructure in this business is less substantial. This can be mainly explained by the method of unloading Ro-Ro vessels, which is done by a ramp positioned on the quay. Hence, the Ro-Ro cargo segment does not require expensive quay cranes that need to constantly improve in size and performance. The maximum vessel size in terms of draft and length is also limited in this industry, to about 12.3 meters (draft) and 265 meters (LOA), respectively. The global Ro-Ro or Ro-Ro car carrier market is controlled by a small number of carriers. The top five Ro-Ro carrier operators combined represent a vessel share of about 80 percent of the top 15 carriers' capacity, and about 75 percent of the total Ro-Ro carrier market.

Changes in ship calls

A further major global trend of shipping lines is to reduce the number of calls in a loop—service from origin to destination—and to call at more efficient ports. To compete with existing ports, new greenfield ports like the port of Lamu need to provide a superior proposition for container shipping lines. This proposition must be tailored to the new trends and the key factors that influence the decision making of shipping lines. The proposition of a new greenfield transshipment port must include the following critical factors:

- Favorable location regarding the main trade lanes (minimal deviation from East–West route)
- Superior infrastructure supply (berth depth, quay length, berth availability)
- Superior service (speed of handling)

Unless these attributes are substantially better than the current ports of call, the probability of the greenfield port developing into a major transshipment port is constrained.

An extensive database containing the vessel calls in all 15 ESA ports, obtained from Marine Traffic, was used to analyze changes in shipping patterns over 2013–16 with respect to the shipping calls' average LOA, average deadweight tonnage (DWT), average TEU capacity (for container vessels), and average vehicle capacity (for Ro-Ro vessels). The region's ports are categorized into groups, depending on their size, for each cargo type.

Containers

As mentioned in the previous section, one of the most important patterns in the container market is the cascading effect. The implication is that ports need to accommodate larger and larger vessels at berth, as containers are shipped on increasingly larger vessels.

The ESA ports in this study have been divided into two groups based on their historical container throughput. This split is made as the lower TEU volumes recorded in these ports are expected to be correlated with the vessel size: ports that recorded lower TEU volumes are expected to receive smaller vessels, either because of their limited hinterland demand or their limited berthing capacity.

The ports in group 1 recorded a TEU throughput above 100,000 TEU in the most recent year for which statistics are available. These include Djibouti, Mombasa, Dar es Salaam, Beira, Durban, Toamasina, Port Louis, and Maputo. The second group of ports—with a throughput of less than 100,000 TEU— include Berbera, Zanzibar, Nacala, East London, Mahajanga, and Moroni.

For both groups, the study has graphed the trend in average TEU capacity and average LOA of container vessel calls. The results of this exercise are presented in figure 5.2, which clearly indicates the upward trend in average TEU capacity and average LOA of container vessel calls for group 1 ports.

FIGURE 5.2

Shipping call pattern (containers), 2013–16, group 1

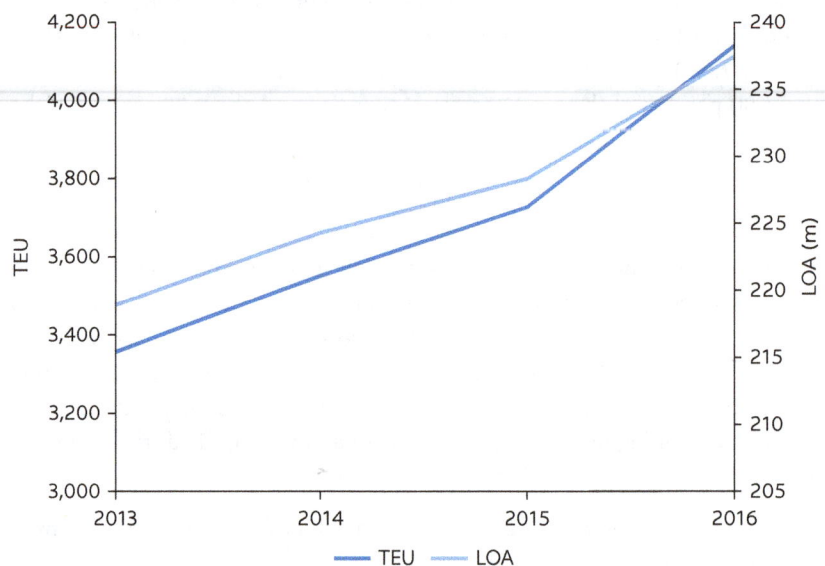

Source: World Bank analysis based on data from MarineTraffic.
Note: LOA = length overall; TEU = twenty-foot equivalent unit.

FIGURE 5.3

Shipping call pattern (containers), 2013–16, group 2

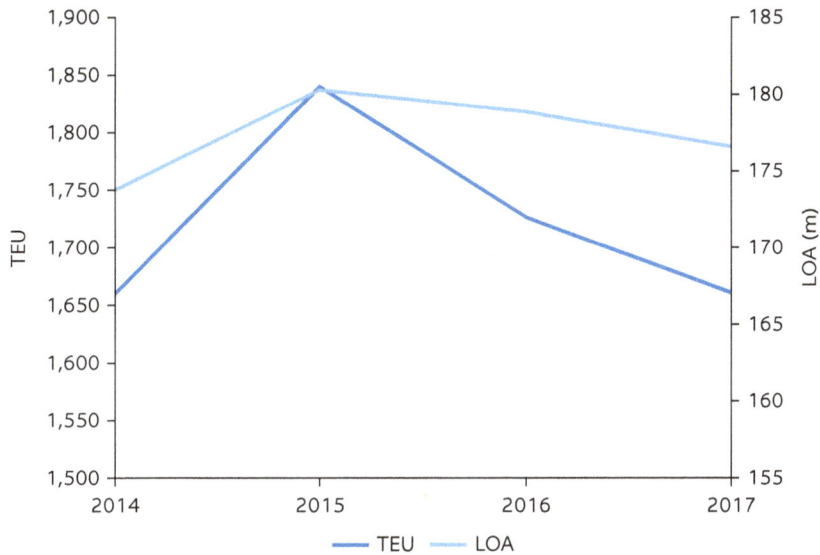

Source: World Bank analysis based on data from MarineTraffic.
Note: LOA = length overall; TEU = twenty-foot equivalent unit.

Based on the vessel calls recorded between 2013 and 2016, the average TEU capacity of the ships deployed to call at the group 1 ports increased from 3,350 TEU in 2013 to 4,140 TEU in 2016. This represents an increase in TEU capacity of almost 25 percent in four years. Furthermore, the average LOA of the container vessel calls at the same ports increased from 219 meters to 237 meters, equal to a vessel-size increase of 8.5 percent.

For the group 2 ports, figure 5.3 reveals that the average container vessel size has remained broadly stable over the same period, with a TEU capacity of 1,650 and a LOA of 175 m. More precisely, average TEU capacity increased 1.6 percent over four years, and the average LOA increased just 0.1 percent. This is explained primarily by the limited berthing capacities available in the smaller ports (for example, the port of Mahajanga has a depth at berth of just 4.5 meters). The potential cascading effect—the use of larger vessels to make these calls—and realization of potentially significant reductions in unit costs is constrained by the available infrastructure.

General cargo

An important global trend related to general cargo shipping is the containerization of goods, mentioned earlier. Given the fact that general cargo comprises such a variety of different types, it is difficult to identify an accurate driver for categorizing the different ports without analyzing the actual cargo that is loaded or discharged. Also, the absolute general cargo volumes handled do not differ significantly across the ESA ports. As the available database does not specify the characteristics of the cargo loaded onto the ships, and the absolute difference in general cargo volumes is limited, the analysis is performed for all ports jointly.

Both the average DWT and the average LOA remained stable in the period between 2013 and 2017 (figure 5.4). This is not surprising, given that an increasing amount of cargo is transported via containers. However, both the increasing

FIGURE 5.4

Shipping call pattern (general cargo)

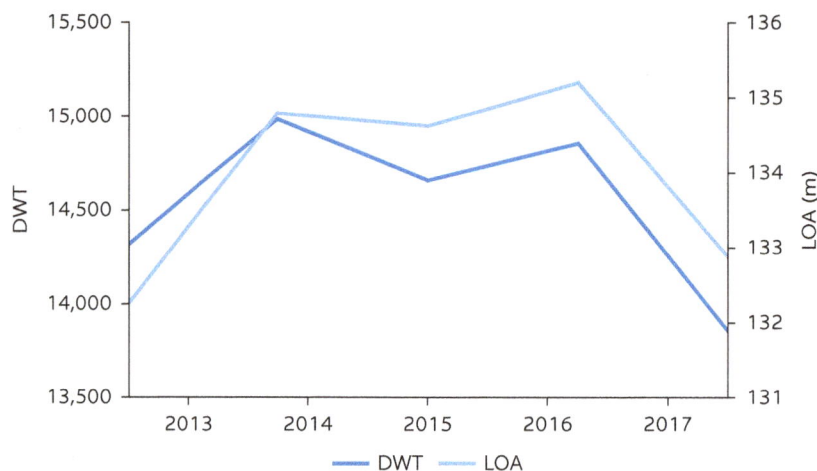

Source: World Bank analysis based on data from MarineTraffic.
Note: DWT = deadweight tonnage; LOA = length overall.

container vessel call trend and the decreasing general cargo vessel call trend might be explained by factors other than the containerization of goods, such as a simple increase or decrease in the hinterland demand of actual containers or general cargo goods. Without reliable disaggregated information from each of the ports, the real reasons remain unclear.

Dry bulk

The main trend in the dry bulk market is also an increase in vessel size, to realize economies of scale and transport cost savings for the shipping lines. In this market, the end users rather than the bulk carrier operators determine the port of call, because of the required infrastructure to transport large quantities of dry bulk commodities from and to the ports.

Given the large distinction in historical dry bulk volumes across the different ports, the analysis is conducted for three different port groups, defined based on the historical dry bulk throughput recorded. The ports in group 1 have recorded annual dry bulk volumes larger than 6 million tons in the most recent year for which statistics are available—these include Durban, Maputo, Beira, and Mombasa. The ports in group 2 recorded annual dry bulk volumes between 1 million tons and 6 million tons, and include Djibouti, Dar es Salaam, Toamasina, and Port Louis. Finally, the ports in group 3 have a yearly dry bulk throughput lower than 1 million tons, and include East London, Moroni, Mahajanga, Zanzibar, Nacala, and Berbera.

For group 1, the average LOA remained stable between 2013 and 2017, while the average DWT increased slightly, from approximately 47,500 tons to 52,700 tons. This is explained by the beam (width) of ships increasing rather than the length. Because of stability factors and steel thickness requirements, to increase the capacity of the largest ships it is easier to increase the beam than to increase the length (Marine Insight 2017). For the second group, the average vessel size in terms of DWT increased from 44,000 tons in 2013 to 52,000 tons in 2017, while average LOA increased from 183 m to 190 m. A similar pattern of ships increasing the beam rather than the length explains this result.

In the low throughput group 3 ports, both the average DWT and the average LOA increased between 2014 and 2017, primarily from the large increase in 2016 in the port of Nacala, related to the start of the Nacala-a-Velha coal terminal operations. Though the actual dry bulk volumes recorded in Nacala are limited, the vessel call size increased significantly with the start of coal exporting operations. In fact, at the port of Nacala separately, the average LOA increased by 9.7 percent, while the average DWT increased by nearly 33 percent. Nacala, given the growth in volumes of coal, would now be considered a group 1 port.

Liquid bulk

Given the large variation in liquid bulk volumes across the different ports, the analysis is again conducted for three different port groups, divided based on the historical liquid bulk throughput. The only port in group 1 is the port of Durban, which recorded a liquid bulk throughput of 25.5 million tons in 2016. At the port of Durban, there was no significant change in the typical liquid bulk vessel between 2013 and 2017. The average LOA increased slightly from 165 meters to 170 meters, and the average DWT increased from 36,000 tons in 2013 to 37,000 tons in 2017.

The ports in group 2 recorded significantly smaller annual liquid bulk volumes, ranging between 0.5 million and 7.5 million tons. These include Dar es Salaam, Beira, Toamasina, Port Louis, Djibouti, Nacala, Mombasa, and Maputo.

For the second group, the trend was very different (figure 5.5): Both average vessel size in terms of DWT and average vessel size in terms of LOA decreased between 2013 and 2017.[2] More specifically, the average DWT decreased by nearly 22 percent, while average LOA decreased by almost 10 percent. The explanation is not entirely clear, but the suggestion is that the liquid bulk market is also starting to be increasingly served by a hub-and-spoke system. Liquid bulk volumes are transported to the larger hub ports, from which smaller volumes and vessels feed the remaining spoke ports.

FIGURE 5.5

Shipping call pattern (liquid bulk), group 2

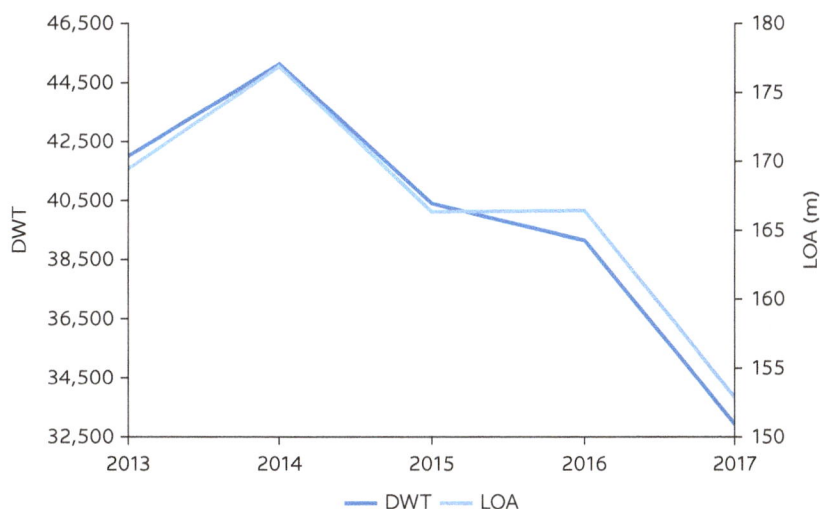

Source: World Bank analysis based on data from MarineTraffic.
Note: DWT = deadweight tonnage; LOA = length overall.

FIGURE 5.6

Shipping call pattern (liquid bulk), group 3

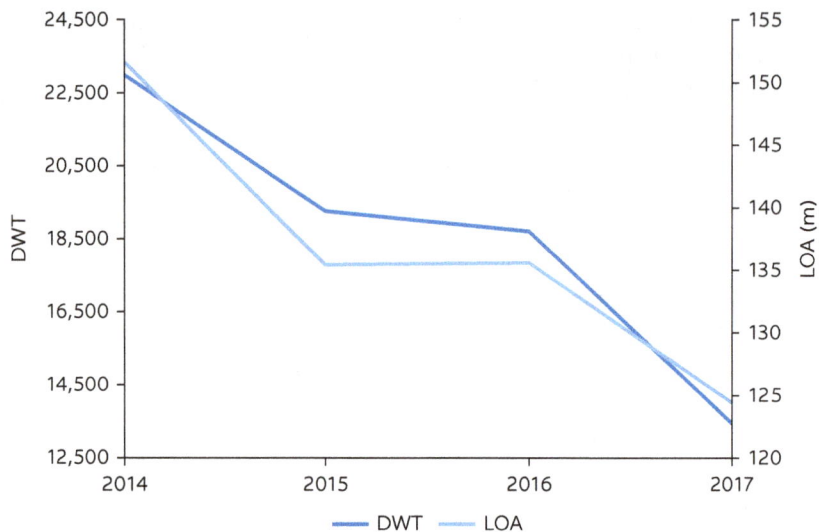

Source: World Bank analysis based on data from MarineTraffic.
Note: DWT = deadweight tonnage; LOA = length overall.

Lastly, the five ports classified in group 3—East London, Moroni, Mahajanga, Zanzibar, and Berbera—have an annual liquid bulk throughput of less than 0.5 million tons. The earlier interpretation is supported by a similar decreasing trend in vessel size in the low-throughput ports. The average DWT and the average LOA decreased from 23,000 to 13,500 tons and from 152 to 124 meters, respectively (figure 5.6). The average DWT decrease was approximately twice as large as the average LOA decrease.

Ro-Ro

In the Ro-Ro segment, the most important indicator is the vessel's vehicle capacity. The Marine Traffic database does not record Ro-Ro vessel calls for the ports of Moroni, Zanzibar, or Mahajanga, which are therefore excluded from the analysis, so the ports are delineated into two groups: Ports in group 1 are those that recorded a vehicle throughput larger than 100,000 tons in the most recent year for which data are available. These include Dar es Salaam, Durban, East London, Maputo, Mombasa, and Djibouti.

The ports in group 2 (<100,000 tons) include Nacala, Beira, Berbera, Port Louis, and Toamasina. For group 1, the average LOA remained roughly stable between 2013 and 2017, at approximately 200 meters, whereas the average vehicle capacity decreased from 5,800 to 5,500 (-3.8 percent) (figure 5.7). A similar pattern is observed for the ports in group 2 (figure 5.8) as in group 1, with the average LOA remaining at approximately 180 meters, and the average vehicle capacity decreasing by about 300 units.

Changes in shipping patterns

This section elaborates on other trends affecting shipping patterns in ESA, and hence cost drivers for investment.

FIGURE 5.7

Shipping call pattern (Ro-Ro), group 1

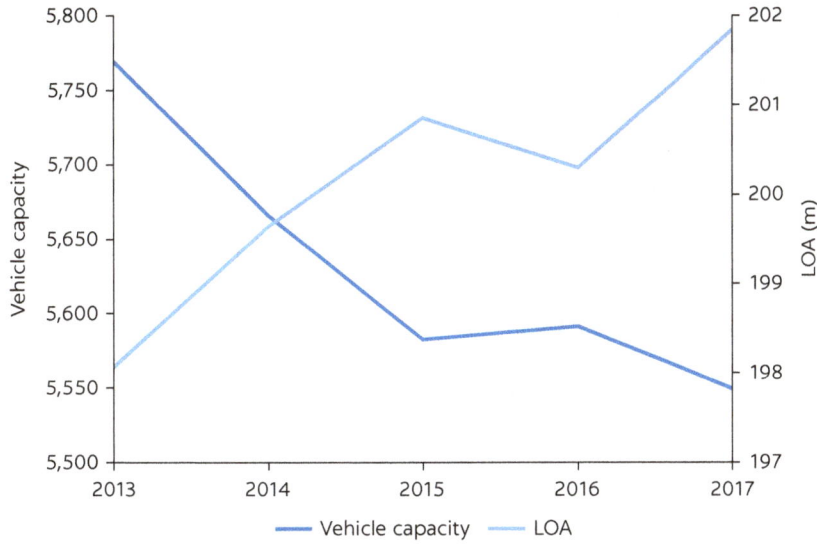

Source: World Bank analysis based on data from MarineTraffic.
Note: LOA = length overall.

FIGURE 5.8

Shipping call pattern (Ro-Ro), group 2

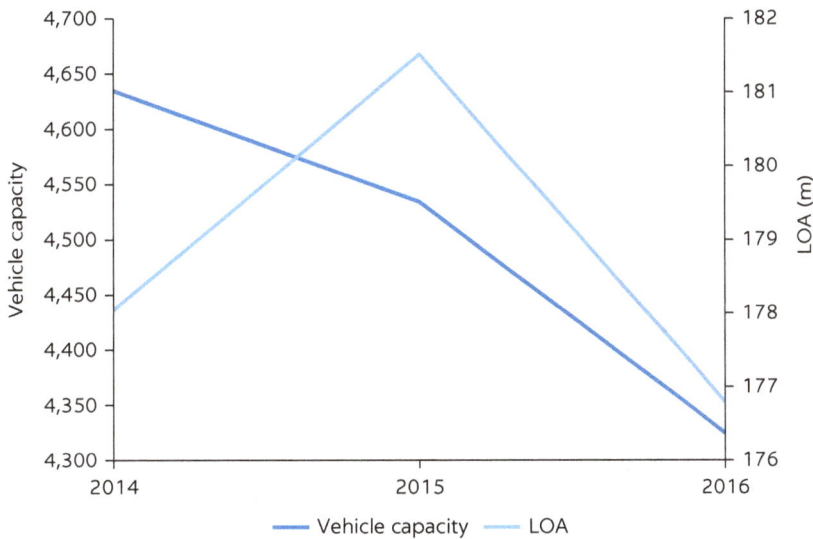

Source: World Bank analysis based on data from MarineTraffic.
Note: LOA = length overall.

Trend 1: Emergence of hub ports and development of the hub-and-spoke system

Since the unit costs of cargo handling generally decline as the volume of traffic increases, the hub-and-spoke system has received stronger focus over the years. Rather than calling at all ports with a larger vessel, the hub-and-spoke system uses main hub ports served by the largest vessels to discharge large volumes, which are transshipped and subsequently transported on smaller vessels to feeder ports. In West Africa, the hub-and-spoke system is already used for Asian trade, with MSC using the ports of Lomé and San Pedro, and other shipping lines using hub ports like Abidjan or Pointe-Noire frequently.

Even though most African countries are either developing or planning to develop new larger greenfield ports (Lamu, Bagamoyo, Techobanine), it is likely that only one or two dominant ports will eventually develop as large-scale regional hubs. A similar trend is observed in Asia (Singapore and Shanghai), Europe (Rotterdam and Antwerp), and North America (Los Angeles, New York, and New Jersey). In Africa, one recent study predicted these ports would be Durban in the South, Abidjan in the West, and Mombasa in the East (PwC 2018). The justification for the latter is that Mombasa has an advantage, with established warehousing and trading facilities offered in addition to its shipping line connectivity and the size of the port's hinterland. This is sufficient to offset the disadvantage of being further from the main shipping lines and being constrained in terms of draft, at least currently. The development of the port of Lamu complicates the assessment slightly, as when fully developed, it will offer superior draft, multimodality, and modern port infrastructure.

Based on the analysis undertaken in this study, and the ongoing port and hinterland developments, a more likely scenario for ESA is for Durban and Djibouti to emerge as the regional hubs. This conclusion is based on the assessment of current shipping patterns, with both close to the main shipping lines, the infrastructure provided, and sufficient draft.

But the development of any port as a hub port in ESA faces several additional challenges: First, many of the ports serve only one transport corridor, so diversion from other corridors is difficult; second, there is slow progress in changing the maritime trade routes in east and southern Africa, which at present do not fully employ a hub-and-spoke system; third, infrastructure investments focus on less-viable port facilities; and fourth, many of the ports lack the attributes and efficiencies sought by shipping lines. As a result, distant hubs are emerging as African transshipment centers because of inefficiencies in the African ports (one example is the US$974 million majority stake bought by CMH in the port of Hambantota, Sri Lanka, with the intention of developing it to serve as hub for East Africa).

Trend 2: Development of purpose-built bulk ports

Given the region's dependence on commodity exports, the development of dedicated bulk ports can facilitate more favorable terms of trade in the global market through increased efficiency and larger handling capacities than those associated with the traditional ports. Examples of such dedicated ports and facilities include the Nacala-a-Velha Coal Terminal (Mozambique), the Djibouti LNG port (Djibouti), and the Palma LNG port (Mozambique).

Ideally, these purpose-built facilities need to be connected to the rail network, preferably dedicated, to ensure optimal functionality. The construction of the Nacala-a-Velha coal terminal and the new line to Tete is an illustrative example of how this trend can affect shipping patterns along the African coastline with the transfer of coal shipments from Beira to Nacala. Rather than continuing to use existing terminals in current ESA ports, a rise in both liquid and dry bulk exports from this region could induce a shift of significant bulk volumes to new purpose-built bulk facilities along the coast. The development of the Uganda–Tanzania oil pipeline to the port of Tanga is another development of this type.

Trend 3: Changing balance of imports and exports

For most of the countries in the study area, imports consist primarily of containerized cargo or liquid bulk, whereas exports comprise agricultural products or commodities typically shipped as bulk cargo. The asymmetry between the volume and method of transport of imported goods versus exported goods presents major challenges to costs of both imports and exports. For example, without return cargo, the charge for all import containers reflects the expectation that they will return to the maritime gateway empty.

If export processing was expanded, some of the cargo currently transported as bulk could be containerized, preventing some of the containers from returning empty. This would be beneficial to both cargo streams, as exporters would benefit from containers potentially available at marginal cost, whereas import costs would fall as the backhaul would be excluded. Improving their trade position and expanding trade in higher-value exports would also improve the balance of containerized trade and lead to lower costs for both imports and exports.

What the overall trends mean for ESA ports

The trends described above are global trends. They are likely to impact some ports in the ESA region more than others. The first trend, the emergence of the hub-and-spoke system, is primarily relevant for the ports on the African mainland and the port of Port Louis, as the smaller ports on the islands located in the Indian Ocean are already feeder ports or regional ports. Regional hubs are likely to arise in Djibouti, Durban, and maybe Port Louis and Lamu. The remaining ports on the African mainland are more likely to become feeder ports in the hub-and-spoke system.

The development of purpose-built bulk ports is only a threat to those ports that currently serve as large bulk ports or are situated in countries that have a vast amount of natural resources. In South Africa, the effects of this trend are expected to be low, mainly because the ports of Durban and East London do not focus on dry bulks. Moreover, the probability of Durban being replaced as the main port for liquid bulks is low. However, Mozambican ports are more at risk of losing significant cargo volumes, particularly related to coal. This trend could pose a risk to the port of Maputo, which is currently handling large volumes of magnetite as well.

The increase in vessel sizes is expected to impact all ports, as the cascading effect will influence nearly all shipping routes. This will require all ports to adapt their port infrastructure to larger vessels calling in the future. However, the impact is expected to be more prevalent for regional hubs (such as Djibouti) than for feeder ports (such as Beira) and even less for smaller regional ports (such as Mahajanga).

Similarly, the impact of shipping-line consolidation is expected to be higher for the ports of Djibouti, Mombasa, Lamu, Dar es Salaam, Durban, and Port Louis than for the remaining ports. This is because competition for transshipment volumes is more influenced by shipping lines than competition for feeder ports or regional ports. As feeder ports serve a specific hinterland, shipping lines have fewer options to redirect their cargo via other ports while at the same time assuring cost-efficient transportation.

LIMITED VERTICAL OR HORIZONTAL INTEGRATION

The global port industry has for some time been impacted by vertical and horizontal integration among producers (port operators and port authorities), terminal operators, shipping lines, and land transport.

Horizontal integration is a strategy where an organization acquires or takes control over other organizations at the same level of the value chain in similar or different industries. This implies that the organization acquires a related business either within the same geographical market or in a new geographical market. The main reasons for pursuing a horizontal integration strategy relate to growing, increasing product differentiation, achieving economies of scale, reducing competition, or getting access to new markets (Strategic Management Insight 2013).

Vertical integration is a strategy in which a firm or organization acquires or takes control over other parts of the value chain either through involvement in the supply of raw materials and semi-finished products or through involvement in distribution activities in the chain. By doing so it assumes (more) control over its value chain. Some examples of vertically integrated structures in the port sector (Van de Voorde and Vanelslander 2009) include, for example, terminal operators that serve hinterland destinations as an "extended gate," and logistics service providers that offer clients a vertically integrated transport product from origin to destination.

Vertical and horizontal integration trends in the port sector are relevant in the ESA port sector because of the potential of the following:

- Improved landside connectivity through vertically integrated structures (Van de Voorde and Vanelslander 2009)
- Offering vertically integrated solutions through dedicated terminals, while preserving a competitive port sector (Álvarez-SanJaime et al. 2013)
- Offering efficient and cost-effective transport solutions through port authorities (PAs) that take on roles as cluster managers (Baccelli, Percoco, and Tedeschi 2008)
- Specialization of PAs by setting up regional port authorities
- Attracting private operators in new business segments, such as the DP World–operated logistics center in Kigali
- Increased port efficiency through horizontal integration by private operators and logistics service providers

Horizontal integration

From a public perspective, the horizontal integration of ports has several benefits, including lower costs and increased products and services offerings. However, the reduced number of market players could result in monopoly pricing by the integrated organization. Government measures to prevent this are then required, such as tariff or price regulation, and implementation of quality standards. In the port sector, this occurs if a single terminal operator is responsible for all cargo being handled in a country or region, especially if this operator is also present in competitive ports and can have a monopoly over certain regions (for example, DP World, serving as the operator of the main container terminal in Djibouti and as the port operator in Berbera, was handling about 90 percent of Ethiopian-bound containers).

The degree of horizontal integration is relatively high in the ports of Djibouti, Mahajanga, Maputo, and the two South African ports. In the case of Djibouti, for example, there is presence of an international operator that is also present in other regional ports (DP World). The Port de Djibouti S.A. (PDSA) is a nationwide port authority that is also responsible for developments of other ports in the country. The logistics services providers in the port are also active in other ports in the region. Horizontal integration is relatively strong also in the port of Moroni. Autorité Portuaire de Comoros (APC, Comoros Ports Authority) is the national ports authority of the country, and terminal operator Bolloré is also present throughout the region. In the port of Maputo, DP World and Grindrod are present as port and terminal operators in multiple ports in the region, and Portos e Caminhos de Ferro de Moçambique (CFM, Ports and Railways of Mozambique) as a national PA is also involved in the other ports in Mozambique in different public-private partnership (PPP) structures. In Durban and East London, Transnet National Ports Authority (TNPA) is the national PA of South Africa and Transnet Port Terminals (TPT) serves as the main operator of container, general cargo, and RoRo terminals in the country. Private operators Bidfreight and Grindrod serving Durban are large South African general cargo terminal operators that are also active in other ports on the continent. Liquid bulk storage operator Vopak is also providing its services on a global level. Furthermore, Shell, Total, and BP are present as liquid bulk storage operators in the port. The logistics services providers at Durban are also active in other ports in the region.

The degree of horizontal integration is less advanced in Mombasa and Dar es Salaam. In the case of Mombasa, Kenya Ports Authority (KPA) is a nationwide PA also responsible for developments of other ports in the country (for example, Lamu). In Dar es Salaam, Tanzania Ports Authority (TPA) is a nationwide PA that is also responsible for the development of ports in the country (Bagamoyo). But the specialization that would be expected from horizontal integration is not yet visible.

Vertical integration

An example of vertical integration by public-sector entities in the port sector concerns the role of PAs as cluster managers. In this role, PAs are involved in the development of hinterland links (rail and road), logistics platforms, and port terminals to offer efficient and reliable transport services to shippers, thereby ensuring sufficient flows of goods through the port (Baccelli, Percoco, and Tedeschi 2008).

The move toward vertical integration in the port sector is to a large extent fueled by the drive for increased efficiency and for more complete control of the transport chain. In the ESA port sector, this vertical integration trend is visible, but to a lesser extent than it is in the more economically developed countries. Furthermore, the vertical integration trend in many of the countries in the project region is driven by public sector authorities, while the vertical integration trend in western countries is usually driven by the private sector, or through PPPs.

The degree of vertical integration is strong in the ports of Djibouti, Mombasa, Toamasina, Port Louis, Durban, and the three Mozambican ports. In Djibouti, logistics services are provided through a network of container depots and inland container depots (ICDs) in both Djibouti and Ethiopia, and the logistics services for hinterland transport are largely in control of a single entity: Ethiopian state-owned Ethiopian Shipping & Logistics Services Enterprise

(ESLSE) can be regarded as a fourth-party logistics (4PL) provider that uses different service providers in Djibouti and asset-based Ethiopian trucking companies to provide their services to Ethiopian importers and exporters. At Mombasa, logistics services are provided through a network of container depots and ICDs in Mombasa and the hinterland (Nairobi). In Port Louis, the logistics services for hinterland transport are provided by local second-party logistics (2PL) and third-party logistics (3PL) providers. In Beira, Cornelder de Moçambique (CdM)—the operator—also offers ICD services at a depot in the Zimbabwean border town of Mutare.

There is limited vertical integration in the port of Dar es Salaam, excepting the ICDs and container freight stations (CFSs) that are available, operated by TPA and by private logistics operators. The amount of systemic organization between terminal operations and landside transport is negligible. There is also no effective gate management system.

Vertical integration is also absent in the port of Berbera; however, this is expected to change with the involvement of DP World. Similarly, there is almost no degree of vertical integration in the ports of Moroni and Mahajanga. In Moroni, Bolloré operates an in-house developed terminal system, but no other systems are used. So far, there is almost no degree of vertical integration in the port.

THE PROBLEM OF LANDSIDE ACCESS

One challenge faced by all ESA ports, almost without exception, is the need to improve landside access. In many cases, the issue of landside access is as important, if not more important, as improving maritime access and capacity. One recent report that forecast global trade to 2050 found that current and planned port capacity in ESA will be close to exhaustion by 2030, and a significant increase in the capacity of hinterland connectivity will be required (OECD 2016). There are three main constraints in landside access: (1) limited intermodality; (2) poor quality road connectivity and delays at the border crossing points; and (3) congestion at the port-city interface.

Limited intermodality

Current connectivity from ESA's ports to hinterland destinations in nearly all the countries still largely depends on a road network of variable quality and coverage. A significant part of the ESA railway network is in a poor state, and most lines are single track and not electrified, the exception being South Africa, where the rail network is mostly electrified and double tracked. Road transport moves the majority of cargo to and from the region's ports: More than 70 percent of all cargo to or from the ports is carried by road transport. If one excludes South Africa, the figure increases to 90 percent. Where rail exists, it is important to ensure it is utilized for appropriate traffic by incentivizing the switch, rather than mandating it (the example of the Port of Rotterdam in this regard is briefly summarized in box 5.1).

Djibouti

Because of Djibouti's function as a transit port to Ethiopia, the port is well connected by road. However, the condition of the road network has deteriorated in recent years. At the end of 2017, a new 756 km electrified railway became operational, linking the port of Djibouti to Ethiopia. The new railway is not only expected to connect to Ethiopia's capital Addis Ababa, but also to other land-locked east African countries such as Uganda and South Sudan (DPFZA 2017). The new railway is expected to cut transport time from Djibouti to Addis Ababa from 7 days to just 10 hours (Xinhua 2016).

Kenya

To improve intermodality, several investments and policy initiatives have been undertaken in recent years or are ongoing. In early 2018, the first freight train departed from Mombasa on the new standard gauge railway (SGR) connecting Mombasa to Nairobi. The government of Kenya has mandated that at least 40 percent of cargo transported between Mombasa and Nairobi is to be transported via the SGR. The Kenya Revenue Authority is mandated to ensure compliance (World Cargo News 2018). There are also plans for a standard-gauge Lamu Port–South Sudan–Ethiopia Transport (LAPSSET) Corridor Railway line from Lamu to Isiolo, from where rail connections to Nakodok (South Sudanese border), Juba (South Sudan), Moyale (Ethiopian border), and Addis Ababa (Ethiopia) are to be constructed. However, all rail investment is dependent on the future cargo volumes being handled by Lamu port. Thus, in the short to medium term, only road transport is envisioned.

Madagascar

Currently all cargo to and from Toamasina is carried by road transport. In the past, around 5–10 percent of containers were transported by rail, but the rail operator has difficulties with the differential in height between Toamasina and Antananarivo (1,300 meters).

The Comoros

There are no railway links or intermodal solutions provided by the port of Moroni; all import consignments are picked up in the port by importers, using road haulage.

Mozambique

The National Transport Policy of Mozambique has a special focus on railway transport, and specifically on the development of various corridors to improve the connection of ports with their hinterlands. The advantage of a corridor concept is that it facilitates the integrated planning of road, rail, and port developments at once.

The port of Maputo has a functioning rail service at the Matola terminals and the Maputo cargo terminals, and connects into the Mozambican railway system, with links to South Africa, Swaziland, and northern Mozambique. About 80 percent of the cargo handled in Maputo is moved via road, and 20 percent via rail. The Matola coal and magnetite terminal is 100 percent serviced by rail.

The port of Beira is also relatively well-connected by rail, as it has two rail connections: one to Machipanda at the Zimbabwean border and one to Moatize, the mining region in the Tete province.

> **BOX 5.1**
>
> ## Facilitating modal switching in the port of Rotterdam
>
> The Port Authority of Rotterdam was the first port authority to introduce a new instrument, within the boundaries of the port, to realize a modal shift from roads. This included modal split obligations in the concession contracts of the specialist terminal operating companies, to realize a modal shift toward rail and inland waterways.

In Nacala, there are rail connections to the multipurpose port and to the coal terminal, but currently only the coal terminal is served by rail. There is a railway connection to Blantyre/Lilongwe in Malawi that could be used for a block-train service for Malawian consignments, but there is no operator available that can perform these services. The existing rail operator is only interested in serving the demand from the coal mines.

The government of Mozambique plans to rehabilitate and improve the existing railway network infrastructure that connects to the port, and where necessary to expand and construct new infrastructure. The Moatize–Nacala Railway Project was inaugurated in May 2017; stretching over 900 km, this new railway facilitates the exports of coal from the Moatize mine in north Mozambique via the coal terminal located on the opposite side of the bay the in port of Nacala. With the new railway connection, coal exports in Mozambique were expected to increase from 8.7 million tons in 2016 to 18 million tons in 2018, overtaking aluminum as Mozambique's largest source of export revenues. In September 2017, the governments of Mozambique and Malawi signed an agreement to expand this corridor with an additional US$2.5 billion investment to "foster economic growth by promoting and coordinating economically viable businesses in the transportation, agriculture, trade, mining, and tourism sectors," according to the Mozambican government.

Also, the Nacala–Chipata Railway Project involves the construction of a new railway between Chipata (in eastern Zambia) and Serenje (in the central part of Zambia), providing part of a trade route from the landlocked areas of the region to the eastern coast, and specifically the port of Nacala (Portos do Norte 2017).

South Africa

In South Africa, landside connectivity and, especially, intermodality for freight transport, has received special focus on the policy side, including the South African National Transport Policy White Paper. Similarly, the National Transport Master Plan 2050 has an explicit objective to encourage the transfer of cargo from road to rail: "to rectify the unbalanced 89–11 percent modal split between road and rail freight" and "to keep the expansion of the current road network to a minimum." The 2015–20 Strategic Plan presents a focus on integrated transport, including landside facilities, with the objective "to develop and implement strategies to enhance seamless movement of freight and passengers across all modes of transport."

However, the policy objectives have not led to a significant change in modal split—as only 12 percent of containers through the port of Durban, destined for the Gauteng region, currently move by rail. This is despite the substantial railway capacity available for block trains to the hinterland. The axle loads of the existing Cape-gauge railway system need upgrading, as it would allow reducing the unit cost of transport and increasing the rail share from the current 12 percent to closer to 30 percent. In the port of East London, a limited share of cargo is currently moved by rail, as almost all cargo is originating from, or destined for, the Mercedes-Benz factory adjacent to the port. A proposed coal export project expects to use dedicated rail services to transport the coal to the port.

Tanzania

In recent years, less than one percent of the cargo from the port of Dar es Salaam to the hinterland is moved by rail, despite the port being served by two railway lines: the meter-gauge railway along the central corridor and the Cape-gauge railway along the Tanzania-Zambia Railway (TAZARA). In the past, the percentage of freight moved via rail was higher, but the deterioration in the quality and reliability of the service, and the improvement in the road infrastructure, has led to a significant diversion to roads.

To address this issue, the government of Tanzania is investing in the construction of a new 2,561 km SGR. In the first phase, 1,216 km of railway will be constructed, linking the port of Dar es Salaam to Dodoma, prior to continuing to Mwanza on the southern shores of Lake Victoria, enabling more efficient transport between the port of Dar es Salaam and transit countries Rwanda, Burundi, the Democratic Republic of Congo, and Uganda. The construction of the first 205 km of this stretch began in March 2017 and was scheduled to last for 30 months (World Cargo News 2017). There are also plans to construct a new inland container/clearance depot at Ruvu, linked to the port by rail, and connecting with the existing lines of Tanzania Railway Limited (TRL) and the TAZARA.

Roads and borders

Overall, the core regional road network on the main trading corridors is in good to fair condition. There are some sections in poor condition, notably in Zimbabwe, Zambia, Malawi, and Mozambique (Nathan Associates 2011), and there are some missing links in the Democratic Republic of Congo and Angola.

A major issue across the region is the efficiency and scope of maintenance of the road network. Despite the substantial investments made in road infrastructure in the past, limitations in management, inadequate enforcement of axle-load restrictions, and inadequate maintenance, coupled with inadequate funding, have led to premature deterioration of the roads and increased transport costs in many countries.

Also, the border crossing points (BCPs), despite improvements in many locations, remain a significant point of delay and additional cost: An analysis of the road corridor on the Southern North-South Corridor revealed that border posts were responsible for 15 percent of the total monetary costs (comprising one percent, one percent, and 13 percent for Beitbridge, Chirundu, and Kasumbalesa, respectively) and 37 percent of the total travel time (comprising 13 percent, 11 percent, and 13 percent for Beitbridge, Chirundu, and Kasumbalesa, respectively) for the movement of a consignment (Nathan Associates 2011).

The analysis also revealed mean processing times of 39 hours at Chirundu, 48 hours at Beitbridge, and 49 hours at Kasumbalesa, adding five and a half days to the total corridor journey time. Transport costs along the corridors in the Southern African Development Community (SADC) region are some of the highest in the world, requiring almost eight days for the 2,000 km trip by road (carrying one TEU from Durban port to Lusaka in Zambia, and costing almost US$5,000).

Djibouti

Because of Djibouti's function as a transit port to Ethiopia, the port is very well-connected by road. But the condition of the road network has deteriorated in recent years.

In addition to the development of the SGR, potential infrastructure investments identified in the Djibouti Development Plan for Infrastructure 2017–22 include widening and upgrading the quality of the road corridor to Addis Ababa, and potentially constructing a toll road from the port of Djibouti to Ethiopia.

Somalia

Somalia's ports are connected to their hinterlands by roads, but almost all the main roads are in poor condition from lack of proper maintenance and repairs as a result of the long period of civil unrest. There are five major roads in the country: two from the port of Mogadishu, one from the port of Berbera, and single routes from both Bosaso and Kismayo.

Kenya

Kenya's major trade corridor, the Northern Corridor, connects the port of Mombasa by both rail and road to Nairobi, Kisumu, and Kampala. Current road conditions and severe congestion underline the need for improvement, which the government of Kenya has heeded. Ongoing projects include the upgrade of the Lesseru–Nadapal road, with support from the World Bank, and the development of the Dongo–Kundu Bypass Highway to improve connectivity to Mombasa.

Also, the planned Mombasa–Mariakani Road Project will construct a dual carriage highway to ease traffic congestion in the port and city vicinities. The 41.7 km six-lane highway has a total project cost of approximately US$250 million.

The LAPSSET corridor is the largest ongoing infrastructure project in northern Kenya, developing a port and associated trade corridor with Kenya's neighboring countries via new roads, railways, and oil pipelines. Associated infrastructure projects in northern Kenya include a number of interregional highways. The Isiolo–Marsabit–Moyale (505 km) stretch is completed, with several other sections under preparation or construction, including Lamu–Garissa–Isiolo (537 km), Lamu–Witu–Garsen (112 km), and Isiolo–Lokichar–Nakodok (738 km).

The Comoros

The Comoros has approximately 800 km of roads that have received little to no maintenance over the last 20 years. The poor quality of infrastructure, especially the road network, has been identified as a significant constraining factor for the economic diversification of the country.

Madagascar

The port of Toamasina is connected to the capital of Madagascar, Antananarivo, via rail and a paved road, whereas the port of Mahajanga is connected to the capital via a paved road only. Rail transportation is conducted by Madarail, a subsidiary of African railway operator Comazar. The total road network comprises approximately 50,000 km, of which just 10 percent is paved, and the remaining 90 percent are dirt roads. Due to regular floods, heavy rainfall, and limited road maintenance, the condition of the road infrastructure is poor.

Mauritius

Infrastructure in Mauritius is well-developed, with the average quality of the roads high and almost 98 percent of them paved (OECD 2014). The National Development Plan states the requirement for developing port access roads and highways to serve the future development of the port. Furthermore, the 2002 and 2016 master plans highlight the need to develop access roads to serve the expected vehicle traffic associated with the expanded port. Finally, the Port Development Strategy 2018 document has a large section on truck-routing options for the Mauritius Container Terminal (MCT) and Island Container Terminal (ICT) container terminals.

Mozambique

The ports of Nacala, Beira, and Maputo in Mozambique each have their dedicated corridors which connect the ports to key cities and provinces in Mozambique and countries in the hinterland. Maputo is connected via road and rail to Johannesburg, and to the largest mining sites in the northern part of South Africa. The Beira Corridor provides Zimbabwe, Malawi, and Zambia with maritime access through the port of Beira. The Nacala Corridor serves the northern provinces of Mozambique as well as Malawi and Zambia.

Additional objectives of the agreement signed in September 2017 between the governments of Mozambique and Malawi included improved regulation and coordination of cross-border aspects (Macauhub 2017).

South Africa

Road and rail infrastructure in South Africa is generally in good condition. All ports have road and rail connections that stretch across the entire country and connect to Namibia, Botswana, Zimbabwe, Mozambique, and Zambia (Transnet Port Terminals 2017). Included in the current redevelopment plans for the port of East London is the construction of a new rail bridge adjacent to the current Buffalo Bridge. This bridge should facilitate the rail transportation of cargo to the port's hinterland.[3]

Border crossings and associated wait times

Besides the reliance on the road network, accessibility to the hinterland areas from ESA ports is also affected by delay, uncertainty, and additional costs along the corridors and at the BCPs. Along the road corridors themselves, there are frequent formal and informal checkpoints where trucks are required to stop, consuming time and modest amounts of money. As one example, on the North–South Corridor in Tanzania, there are 34 formal and informal police checkpoints between Dar es Salaam and the border with Zambia.

There remain issues at the BCPs on the national borders. Map 5.1 illustrates the issue, using data collected from the GPS tracking devices on trucks in spring of 2018, as part of the Southern and Eastern Africa Corridor Performance Monitoring System.[4] The map shows that median crossing times in several cases exceed 8 hours, and they exceed one or even two days on average at certain crossings, such as at Beitbridge (South Africa–Zimbabwe), Bwera/Kasindi (Uganda–Democratic Republic of Congo), Kasumulu/Songwe (Tanzania–Malawi), Kazungula (Botswana–Zambia), and Nimule (Uganda–South Sudan).

The border crossings of Malaba and Busia (both on the Kenya–Uganda border) are the two busiest crossings on the Northern Corridor, together handling more than 300,000 trucks every year (Fitzmaurice and Hartmann 2013). The same data show that, while the median border crossing times are less than two hours in either direction at Busia, trucks have to spend more than 11 hours at the Malaba border crossing point (the top 5 percent wait more than 83 hours).

MAP 5.1

Median border wait times in early 2018

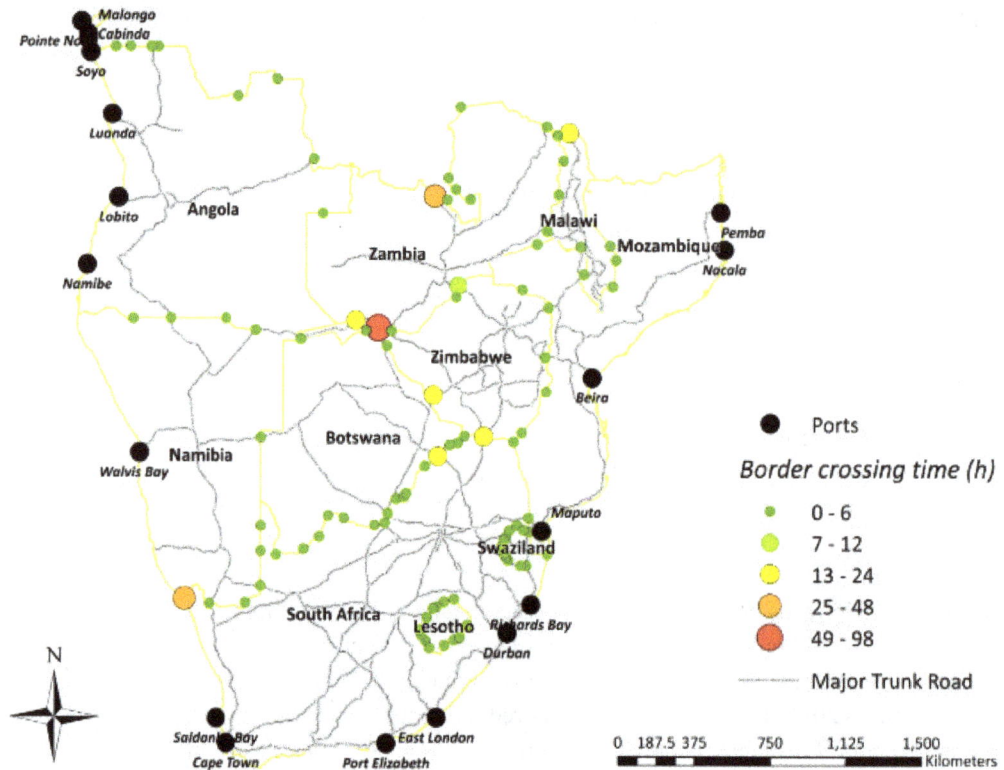

Source: World Bank analysis and map based on Crickmay & Associates 2018 data.

The impact on port competitiveness

The penalty resulting from lower-quality road infrastructure on the competitiveness of a port is illustrated in map 5.2, which displays the drive-time isochrones in different colors for each of the ports. Taking the area covered up to the 24–48-hour isochrone, the area within that isochrone for Durban is considerably larger than the comparable area for Dar es Salaam or Mombasa, providing one reason why some consignments to and from Eastern Democratic Republic of Congo, Zambia, and Malawi go via Durban.

The port-city interface

Another major challenge for many of the ESA ports is what is known as the port-city interface (box 5.2). The evolution and development of ports creates a number of benefits for their host cities and countries: First, ports and their related services and industries have created employment for local workers. As port traffic has grown, port-related labor demand has increased, usually unskilled and drawn from the immediate vicinity of the port. While increased containerization and mechanization in a port has diminished the number of unskilled cargo handlers, generally ports remain a significant local employer.

Second, ports have played a vital role in the facilitation of global trade. With ports offering efficient and cost-effective links to global markets, market access for both importers and exporters has enlarged considerably. Third, ports provide an opportunity to add value, through the economic activities performed within

MAP 5.2

Drive time isochrones to African ports

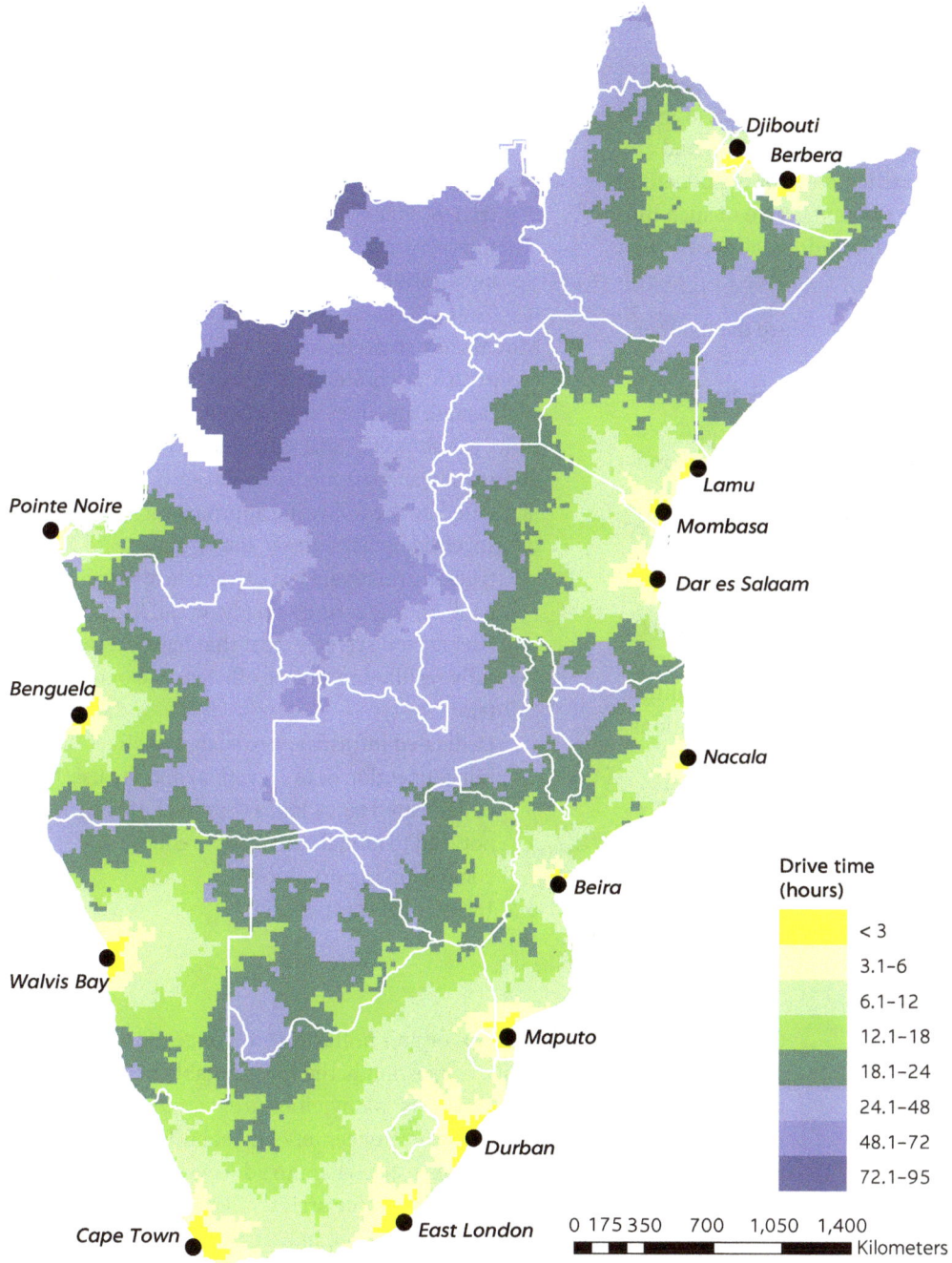

Djibouti
Berbera

Pointe Noire

Lamu
Mombasa
Dar es Salaam

Benguela

Nacala

Drive time (hours)

	< 3
	3.1–6
	6.1–12
	12.1–18
	18.1–24
	24.1–48
	48.1–72
	72.1–95

Beira

Walvis Bay

Maputo

Durban

0 175 350   700   1,050   1,400

Kilometers

Cape Town   East London

Source: World Bank analysis.

ports and through port-related firms. Finally, the evolution of ports has stimulated the creation of clusters focusing on innovation and research and development (R&D). In many cases, large port metropolises lead the shipping-related innovation and R&D, resulting in both direct and indirect spillover benefits to other sectors, and eventually the country itself.

Despite the benefits, the negative impacts of ports on cities—both direct and indirect—are substantial. These externalities range from environmental issues

BOX 5.2

Port–city interface: Road congestion reduction policies

Road congestion hinders a port's competitiveness and is a major nuisance to urban residents. Hinterland transport strategies help reduce congestion and aim to provide for smooth traffic flows, for the benefit of both the port and urban residents. Two of such hinterland strategies are applied to address road congestion:

- **Port gate strategies** aim to reduce the number of idle trucks at port gates:
  o Terminal appointment systems can be successful if all parties can access updated (web-based) shipment data 24/7; preferential treatment of trucks with an appointment using dedicated lanes can be enforced; and all logistics service providers are willing to participate in the program (USEPA 2006; Guiliano and O'Brien 2007).
  o Extending gate hours (EGHs) can redistribute truck arrival times. Market and political (environmental lobby pressure) conditions determine EGHs' likelihood of success. Market conditions beneficial for EGHs' success include large carriers that operate the terminals; cargo that belongs to large national shippers; and the number of inland port distribution centers and customer

opening hours (Spasovic, Dimitrijevic, and Rowinski 2009).
  o Virtual container yard systems are a web-based approach to match tractors with trailers as they head back to the port, rather than returning empty. However, the penetration of this strategy is likely to be low (5–10 percent).

- **Modal shift strategies** aim to shift to other (non-trucking) hinterland transport modes, such as rail, pipelines, inland waterways, and short-sea shipping. Still, trucking remains the dominant transport mode. Modal shift can be facilitated by the following approaches:
  o Incentive schemes that aim to make trucking relatively less attractive by levying a toll on trucks or a subsidy on rail/barges. Various toll systems exist that have successfully resulted in a more efficient use of truck trips.
  o Dedicated infrastructure such as a direct rail connection at the terminal and the use of dedicated truck lanes (however, this will not lead to modal shift); both reduce congestion in port cities.
  o Intermodal competition.

(air emissions, water pollution, or soil pollution) to congestion issues and safety risks. Port-induced city congestion is the most notable negative externality that is present in the ESA ports. Many cities grew around the existing port, with roads running through the city centers and suburbs. Box 5.2 illustrates some of the interventions taken elsewhere to address this challenge.

As one example, in the port of Durban, the arrival of large container vessels leads to a peak of trucks picking up and dropping off all the containers to and from the port to the hinterland. The 3 km port access road, Bayhead Road, is jammed truck-to-truck, causing massive congestion on the city's roads. This situation is not atypical for other port cities in ESA and elsewhere.

Also, in many port cities, the benefits and costs induced by the port are asymmetrically distributed between the port, the city, and the country. Addressing this imbalance between the costs and benefits generated by the port is the challenge of the port-city interface, which remains significant for many ESA ports and their host cities.

The one country in the ESA region that has endeavored to address the challenge is South Africa (box 5.3), where there are explicit efforts at coordination between the port and the city, the port master plan is usually embedded in the

BOX 5.3

Addressing the port–city interface: The case of Durban and East London

An illustrative example of common port-city master-planning is Durban. The eThekwini Municipality and Transnet jointly drafted a long-term development plan for the Durban-to-Gauteng Freight Corridor "Vision 2050" in 2010. It provided an integrated framework aligning the interests of the city and the port. Vision 2050 included, among other things, the development of the new Durban Dig-Out Port (DDOP) at the old airport site and the provision of an extensive road and rail corridor development plan between Durban and the Gauteng area. This co-aligned the interest of both parties, as it allowed the port to expand and move operations to the new port area, whereas the city could alleviate congestion and negative externalities induced by the large volumes originating from the current port site.

In the case of the port of East London, a five-year memorandum of understanding (MoU) was signed in March 2019 between the Buffalo City Metropolitan Municipality (BCMM), Transnet National Ports Authority (TNPA), and the East London Industrial Development Zone Company (RBIDZ). It establishes a framework for the parties to work together to promote economic growth in Buffalo City and find new ways to bring investments to the harbor.

development plan for the city, and each port city has a local Compulsory Port Consultative Committee (CPCC). This committee seats TPT, TNPA, local government, provincial government, cargo owners, terminal operators, shipping lines, and the South African Maritime Safety Association to discuss port-city issues.

Despite this, as of now, 70–80 percent of boxes handled by the port of Durban are stuffed or de-stuffed within the port's immediate vicinity, causing huge flows of container trucks from the port to the stuffing or stripping areas, and huge flows of general cargo trucks between the city and the hinterland.

WEAKNESSES IN THE INSTITUTIONAL FRAMEWORK

Numerous articles and studies have assessed the complexity and the weaknesses in the institutional framework in the port sector in the ESA region. A conclusion from many of these is that a large number of ports in the region face inefficiencies and unprofitable operations that are directly attributed to the institutional framework of the sector. This section provides an overview of the weaknesses identified in the institutional framework of each port.

International compliance

The oversight of international maritime transport is the responsibility of International Maritime Organization (IMO), of which all countries in the region are members. The objective of the IMO is to facilitate safe, secure, and efficient shipping on clean oceans, and because of the international nature of the shipping industry, improve safety in maritime operations at an international level, rather than through individual countries.

The IMO has adopted 50 conventions and protocols and more than 1,000 codes concerning maritime safety and security, the prevention of pollution, and related matters. All safety designs and standards for vessels, as well as the training and qualifications of seafarers, are determined by the IMO and its international conventions.

A table that provides an overview of the ratification of the individual countries toward 42 key IMO conventions is presented in appendix A. This overview suggests that there is substantial variation in ratification by countries. Somalia has only signed the main IMO convention and loadline convention, and it is unclear in what manner Somalia's signature of IMO conventions impacts the port of Berbera in the self-declared state of Somaliland, which is internationally recognized as an autonomous region of Somalia.

Of the other countries in the region, Djibouti, Tanzania, the Comoros, Madagascar, and Mozambique have each ratified about 20 conventions. Kenya, Mauritius, and South Africa have ratified the largest number of conventions, with 32, 29, and 29 ratifications respectively.

The national policy framework

Port policy can be described as the set of principles and guidelines that a government formulates and enforces to achieve its goals related to the port sector.[5] These goals can be broad, overarching goals, such as "an efficient port sector," or more specific, such as "reduced emissions from port operations near the city center in city *x*." This assessment focuses on port policy in the broader sense, where the long-term goals of a government or a PA are embedded in their policies.

The following list presents an overview of requirements for a substantive port policy:

- Is initiated and documented by a government entity
- Can be developed at different government levels: central, regional, or decentralized
- Generally focuses on the longer term
- Is regularly updated (at least once every two years)
- Is based on a clear timeframe and sequence for the goals to be achieved
- Presents objectives that describe what is to be achieved

At a minimum, a substantive port policy needs to cover the following:

- The sustainable development of a port in terms of its surroundings and the environment
- Corporate governance and organizational structures in the port sector
- The financing principles of the sector, that is, the role of the government
- The division of responsibilities regarding port development and port operations
- The possibilities and requirements for private sector involvement in the sector
- The criteria for investment
- The underlying principles that govern the development of relevant legislation: the way the policy is written, passed in legislation, and implemented by government bodies

An example of well-defined and clear port policy is in box 5.4, which provides a summary of the National Policy Statement for Ports of the United Kingdom. This list of requirements has been used as a template to assess the current port policies in each of the ESA countries.

BOX 5.4

National policy statement for ports (United Kingdom)

The Government seeks to:

- Encourage sustainable port development to cater for long-term forecast growth in volumes of imports and exports by sea, with a competitive and efficient port industry capable of meeting the needs of importers and exporters cost effectively, and in a timely manner, thus contributing to long-term economic growth and prosperity
- Allow judgments about when and where new developments might be proposed to be made on the basis of commercial factors by the port industry, or port developers operating within a free market environment
- Ensure all proposed developments satisfy the relevant legal, environmental, and social constraints and objectives, including those in the relevant European Directives and corresponding national regulations

In addition, in order to help meet the requirements of the Government's policies on sustainable development, new port infrastructure should also:

- Contribute to local employment, regeneration, and development;
- Ensure competition and security of supply;
- Preserve, protect, and where possible, improve marine and terrestrial biodiversity;
- Minimize emissions of greenhouse gases from port-related development;
- Be well designed, functionally and environmentally;
- Be adapted to the impacts of climate change;
- Minimize use of greenfield land;
- Provide high standards of protection for the natural environment;
- Ensure that access to and condition of heritage assets are maintained and improved where necessary; and
- Enhance access to ports and jobs, services, and social networks they create, including for the most disadvantaged.

Source: Department for Transport (U.K.) 2012.

The assessment

Of the ESA countries, South Africa performs best in terms of its port policy, performing below the required standard against only 2 of the 13 criteria identified above. Tanzania ranks second, scoring below what is required against only four of the criteria. All the other countries fall below what is required against at least 6 of the 13 criteria. Madagascar, Zanzibar in Tanzania, and the Comoros are the countries that perform below what is required against the largest number of criteria.

Generally, the four criteria that the majority of countries perform poorly against concern (1) the regular updating of policy documents; (2) the criteria for investment decisions and the financing of port investments; (3) the role of the private sector in financing and operating in ports; and (4) limited attention toward continuous policy monitoring and implementation.

A summary of the key weaknesses by country is provided below, with summary tables provided in appendix A.

Djibouti

- There is no clear national government policy on transport or ports. All current policy documents are published by the autonomous DPFZA and PDSA (a subsidiary of DPFZA).

- Little attention is paid to the environmental sustainability of the port sector.
- There are no clear guidelines as to the type, size, or nature of private-sector participation in the port sector.
- Port PPPs are developed on a case-by-case basis, and there is no clear line of reasoning why a certain structure is selected for a specific project.

Somalia

- There is a lack of an integrated policy for Somaliland's port sector.
- There is no dedicated entity involved in policy making for the port sector.
- There is a lack of consideration of environmental principles in policy goals.
- The legal and regulatory framework for the port sector remains unclear.
- The policy-making process is currently not clear from the documents.
- There is a lack of financing principles included in the policy goals.
- There are no criteria for investment decisions specified in the National Development Plan documents.

Kenya

- There is a lack of clarity over the policy mandate for two major ports: KPA is responsible for the development of Mombasa, but the LAPSSET Corridor Development Authority (LCDA) is responsible for the development of Lamu.
- There is a lack of time-based policy goals in the National Transport Policy, which contains general statements (for example: "The Government of Kenya shall expedite plans to construct a new port at Lamu").
- There is a lack of financing principles in the policy documents. It is unclear how the KPA or the government of Kenya plans to finance proposed port investments.
- Some policy and planning documents need updating: National Transport Policy (Ministry of Transport of Kenya 2009) and KPA Master Planning for Ports (Kenya Ports Authority 2012).
- There is a clear contradiction between policy statements and policy implementation on PPPs. KPA's handbook (Kenya Ports Authority 2017) states that it is not moving toward a landlord model and is focusing on improving KPA's own capabilities (such as operating terminals by itself). This is not the model proposed for developing Lamu.

Tanzania

- Some policy and planning documents need updating: The National Port Master Plan is from 2009 and does not represent the reality on the ground.
- There is a lack of financing principles included in the policy goals. The National Transport Policy document does not provide an overview of financing principles or a way in which the government plans to fund the policy goals.
- There are no criteria for investment decisions specified in the National Transport Policy document. It is unclear how investment decisions are validated by the government, and how a decision on whether to invest is made.

Zanzibar, Tanzania

- Some of the policy planning documents—such as the Master Plan for the Development of the Port Sector on Zanzibar, from 2007, and strategy plans from 2006–15—need to be updated.

- There is a lack of information on the financing principles in the policy goals.
- There are no criteria for investment decisions specified in the National Transport Policy documents or the Multipurpose Port Master Plan.
- There are no clear guidelines on the type, size, or nature of private sector investments in the nation's ports and port sector, nor have any criteria been specified.

The Comoros

- Despite infrastructure being one of the four defined axes of sustainable development, the *Stratégie de Croissance Accélérée de Développement Durable* (SCA2D, National Five-Year Plan for Accelerated and Sustainable Growth)[6] devotes very little specific attention to the port sector.
- A National Port Master Plan was prepared in 2014, but the implementation of a key recommendation—the establishment of a national port authority—has been halted.
- The SCA2D does not devote any attention specifically to the environmental considerations in rehabilitating or developing port infrastructure.
- The SCA2D does not adequately distinguish between public and private sector responsibilities in terms of management, operations, or financing.
- The SCA2D does not provide adequate guidelines on the financing mechanisms or resources available to implement the priority projects.

Madagascar
- The main shortcoming of the Malagasy port sector policy framework is the lack of a National Port Master Plan that lays out a development plan for the sector over a 20-year horizon.

Mauritius
- There is a National Port Master Plan for Port Louis, but it lacks financing principles associated with the policy goals. It is unclear how the Mauritius Ports Authority (MPA) or the government of Mauritius aim to finance the proposed port investment plans that are listed in the various policy documents.
- Some policy and planning documents need an update, such as the National Development Plan (NDP). An updated NDP, if enforced, would encompass the Port Master Plan and consider recent developments such as the Island Container Terminal development in Port Louis.
- There is a clear contradiction between policy statements and policy implementation with respect to private-sector participation. The role of the MPA as a landlord port is highlighted in most policy documents, while in practice the main cargo handling concession is granted to the public Cargo Handling Corporation Ltd., in which MPA has a 40-percent shareholding position, and the other shares are owned by the External Communications Division and the State Investment Corporation.
- Criteria for investment decisions are not clearly mentioned in the main policy documents. A clear guideline, with minimum requirements for public investment, is a necessity to ensure value for money.

Mozambique

- Some key policy and planning documents need an update: National Transport Strategy (2009, with an updated presentation in 2013) and the Maputo Port Master Plan (2011).
- There is a lack of adequate consideration of environmental sustainability in the port development plans currently envisaged.
- Corporate governance and structures of power in the port sector are unclear in the available policy documents.
- There is a lack of financing principles included in the policy goals. It is unclear how CFM or the government of Mozambique aim to finance the proposed port investment plans that are listed in the different policy documents.
- There is a lack of transparency with respect to the division of responsibilities between port development and port operations in the national policy documentation.
- The National Transport Strategy does not present clear criteria to guide investment decisions.
- There is little clarity as to the principles that guide the development of legislation, policy, and implementation in the port and transport sector.

South Africa

- Policy goals in the national policy documents (except for the 2015–20 Strategic Plan for Transport) are not time-bound.
- Criteria for investment decisions are not mentioned in the policy documents. It is unclear how investment decisions are validated by the government, and how a decision on whether or not to invest is made.

The legal and regulatory framework

The legal and regulatory framework is the system of rules, regulations, laws, and guidelines that govern, regulate, and affect the port sector.[7] An effective legal and regulatory framework is critically important for an efficient and well-functioning port sector. One study on African ports (African Development Bank 2010) found a clear link between performance and the strength of the legal and regulatory framework.

Ideally, the legal and regulatory framework for the port sector needs to

- Consider the policy objectives for the port sector, the maritime sector, and the transport sector more generally
- Be consistent over the different bills, acts, rules, regulations, and treaties
- Be consistent with international norms and agreements

It also needs to cover regulatory responsibilities and associated monitoring bodies; managerial and governance responsibilities, such as the appointment of directors; development responsibilities, related to private sector involvement; operational responsibilities; safety and environmental protection responsibilities and measures; financing principles of the port sector, as related to the role of the government; and possibilities and requirements for private sector involvement in the port sector. While a summary of the assessment is provided in appendix A, the following paragraphs present key findings.

Madagascar, Mauritius, Tanzania, and South Africa perform best in terms of the legal and regulatory framework for the port sector. All these countries have only two criteria where they are performing below what is required. Djibouti, Kenya, and Zanzibar, Tanzania have a suboptimal score on the legal and institutional evaluation. Somalia, Mozambique, and the Comoros attain the lowest scores of the ESA countries.

Djibouti, Somalia, and Mozambique all lack a port-sector regulator. Tanzania has a regulator, although responsibility has recently changed from Surface and Marine Transport Regulatory Authority (SUMATRA) to the new Tanzania Shipping Agencies Corporation (TASAC), but capacity constraints and the asymmetry of information underline the ability of the agency to fulfill the function of an independent regulator. Also, the responsibility for the designation of port safety and environmental protection responsibilities and measures are not allocated in an independent entity but are handled by TPA and TASAC. The lack of independence of a regulator able to evaluate performance and set rules is regarded as a major issue.

The financing principles of the port sector regulatory bodies are well-defined only in Kenya, Tanzania, Mauritius, and South Africa. The Kenya Maritime Authority (KMA) Act and Merchant Shipping Fees Regulation (Republic of Kenya 2012) specify clearly how the KMA shall derive its funds, namely through funds appropriated by Parliament, and through fees as approved by the Minister of Transport.

Similarly, in Tanzania, the SUMATRA Act clearly specifies that SUMATRA can charge fees on every consignment of cargo discharged or loaded at any Tanzania port. The Zanzibar Maritime Authority (ZMA) Act clearly specifies that ZMA can charge fees to compensate for the services it renders. In Mauritius, the Port Act presents the financing principles of the MPA as the main regulator in the port sector and describes the right of the MPA to levy fees and charges for its services as a regulator. In South Africa, the regulator is funded by fiscal allocation from national government.

Most of the port acts, and the laws providing the legal basis for port management, development, and operation, do not consider or enable modern PPP practices. Accordingly, the majority of the port acts in the region still prescribe that PAs are responsible for development, maintenance, and operation of ports. This is increasingly outdated, as in practice many do not operate all of the port facilities anymore.

Port sector organizations

Until the 1980s, the relevant institutions in the port sector were the port authorities, which acted as the operators of ports, under the auspices of the line ministry, generally transport. At that time, there was increasing recognition that ports worldwide, rather than facilitating global trade, had in many cases become bottlenecks in the distribution chains. There were three reasons for this: (1) restrictive labor practices, which developed in the days when ships were unloaded by hand, by teams of stevedores; (2) centralized government control and inefficient command and control structures; and (3) limited public investment in infrastructure (World Bank 2007).

In a similar manner to any other sectors, a number of countries began reconsidering the boundary line between public and private responsibilities in the 1980s. There was increasing recognition that private sector involvement could improve efficiency and service quality, and reduce the capital and recurring demands on the public purse. As a consequence, many ports around the world have adopted the landlord model of port structure, in which the public sector acts mainly as planner, facilitator, developer, and regulator, providing connectivity to the hinterland, and the private sector acts as service provider, operator, and sometimes also developer (World Bank 2007).

The Port Reform Toolkit (World Bank 2007) notes that globally, various models are used for the management of ports. These models are based on a division between public and private responsibilities of a port's roles and functions. The main regulator functions and the planning functions are a public task that should not be allocated to the private sector. The public entity should retain control over the main regulatory functions concerning safety, security, and the environment. The remaining functions can be allocated to the public or private sector, depending on the port management model.

The most common management models are summarized in table 5.1, where the landlord model is considered as a single model. However, there is a fundamental difference between three types of landlord models now existing globally, and table 5.1, which presents a total of six potential port management models.

The Port Reform Toolkit (World Bank 2007) lists the main strengths and weaknesses of the different port management models. The public service port and tool port management structures have generally fallen out of favor in the current global setting for a number of reasons, including the lack of internal competition between terminals; a lack of specialization in cargo handling; underinvestment because of government interference and dependence on government budgets; poor spatial and operating efficiency; a lack of innovation; and an overly hierarchical, centralized decision structure.

The better-performing ports, generally, are market-oriented, have financial and policy-making autonomy at the PA level, and involve specialization in terminal operation, usually private sector. The best port management structure in any country will depend on the size of the economy that the port serves, the amount and types of cargo handled, and the presence of competing ports in the region.

TABLE 5.1 **Port management models**

TYPE	REGULATION	INFRASTRUCTURE	SUPERSTRUCTURE	EQUIPMENT	LABOR	NAUTICAL SERVICES
Public service port	Public	Public	Public	Public	Public	Public
Tool port	Public	Public	Public	Public	Private	Public or private
Landlord + Public-private terminal	Public	Public	Public-private joint venture	Public-private joint venture	Public-private joint venture	Public or private
Landlord port	Public	Public	Private	Private	Private	Public or private
Landlord + DBFM[a]	Public	Public and private	Private	Private	Private	Public or private
Private port	Public or private	Private	Private	Private	Private	Private

Source: World Bank 2007.
a. Under a DBFM (design, build, finance, maintain) contract, the landlord transfers responsibilities for the design, construction, financing, and maintenance of an infrastructure asset to the private sector contractor. The contractor guarantees the availability of the infrastructure asset and receives availability payments in return.

TABLE 5.2 **Framework for the assessment of port sector functions**

FUNCTION AND RESPONSIBILITIES	PREFERRED RESPONSIBLE ENTITY
Landlord function: real estate management of port land and buildings	Port authority
Local port policy-making and planning function: develop medium- to long-term port plans	Port authority
Regulatory, supervisory, and surveillance function: ensure legal/administrative compliance of activities in the port perimeter	Port authority
Monitoring and promotion function: monitor, promote port performance	Port authority
Port training function: create a knowledge base in the port	Port authority
National policy-making and planning function: develop port policies	Ministry of Transport
Legal function: draft, implement, and monitor laws	Ministry of Transport
International relations function: representation in multilateral/bilateral agreements	Ministry of Transport
Financing function: finance basic infrastructure and assess business plans	Ministry of Transport
Port sector auditing function: independent monitoring	Ministry of Transport/ports regulator
Port sector tariff regulation function: independent tariff monitoring	Ministry of Transport/ports regulator
Cargo handling function: stevedoring and warehousing	Private operator
Terminal equipment function: acquire and maintain equipment	Private operator
Terminal development function: develop and maintain superstructure	Private operator
Terminal operations function: maintain a safe, secure, and environmentally friendly terminal	Private operator
Nautical services function: provide towage, pilotage, and mooring	Private operator

Source: World Bank 2007.

However, these main themes are considered essential to maximize the efficiency of any port in a given context.

Table 5.2 presents the key functions and responsibilities for the maritime sector, given this preferred structure. These functions and responsibilities underpin the assessment of the ESA ports for the purposes of this report.

The main findings from the assessment of port management models in the ESA countries are summarized below.

The primary weakness in the majority of ESA countries, with the singular exception of South Africa, is the lack of an independent regulator, with sufficient resources and capacity to ensure effective auditing, monitoring, and tariff regulation in the port sector. In many of the ESA countries, these functions are carried out by the PAs themselves. As an example, seven of the PAs regulate themselves in terms of tariffs (Djibouti, Kenya, Zanzibar in Tanzania, the Comoros, Madagascar, Mauritius, and Mozambique).

Second, despite many policy documents stating the desire of the respective governments to move toward the landlord port management model, in many countries in the region, port operations are still carried out in whole or in part by the PAs themselves, using their own employees (Kenya and Tanzania in part plus Zanzibar), or by publicly owned companies working as operators (Mauritius, South Africa). While neither is ideal, the latter, at least, offers the advantage of transparency with respect to the profits and costs of port operations, and avoid any implicit cross-subsidization.

Third, the national policy-making and planning function, which would normally lie with the line ministry, in practice lies with the PA in five of the ESA countries (Djibouti, Kenya, Tanzania, Madagascar, and Mauritius).

Port tariff structures and levels

Given the lack of effective oversight, and the importance of port tariffs, both for the efficient operation of a port and the financing of the port sector, an assessment was made of the scale and structure of the applicable tariffs in each of the ESA countries. The assessment involved a qualitative review of the port tariff policies in each of the ESA countries, against a good-practice benchmark of port tariff structures. The main objective was to identify and propose necessary reforms to the port tariff structures in the countries in the region.

Prior to undertaking the assessment, it is worth reviewing the logic underlining the definition of the scale and structure of applicable tariffs. The main objective for a PA in setting its tariffs should be to fully recover all port-related costs, including capital costs, together with an adequate return on capital (World Bank 2007).

The full recovery of costs will help the PA to maintain internal cost discipline, attract outside investment and establish secure long-term cash flows, stimulate innovation in the various functional areas to guarantee a long-term balance between costs and revenues, and generate internal cash flows needed to replace and expand port infra- and superstructure.

It will also allow the PA to compete according to the rules of the market system, without a distortion of competition, limit implicit cross-subsidization, and avoid dissipation of the PA's asset base to satisfy objectives of third parties (such as port users).

Finally, a proper tariff structure also encourages the efficient use of port infrastructure: the more time an entity uses port infrastructure (whether that is a quay wall, a terminal stacking area, or any other port asset), the more should be paid to the PA/terminal operator. An example would be an increasing tariff for container storage as storage time lengthens, to encourage consignees to collect containers from the port.

Globally, five broad types of port tariffs are distinguished in the Port Reform Toolkit (World Bank 2007) and illustrated in figure 5.9: port dues,

FIGURE 5.9

Relationship between port charges and locations where they are incurred

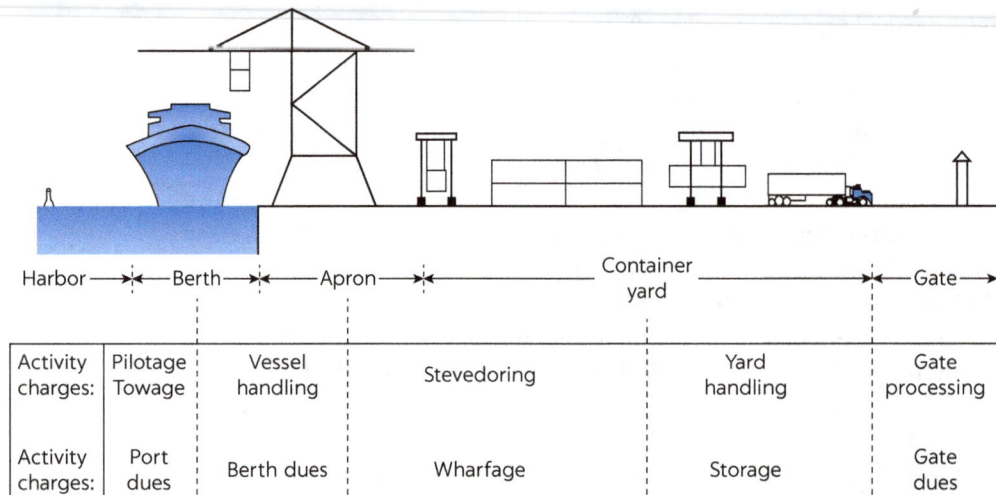

	Harbor	Berth	Apron	Container yard	Gate
Activity charges:	Pilotage Towage	Vessel handling	Stevedoring	Yard handling	Gate processing
Activity charges:	Port dues	Berth dues	Wharfage	Storage	Gate dues

Source: World Bank 2007.

vessel-handling charges, stevedoring charges, storage and warehousing charges, and other charges, such as long-term mooring dues. This delineation enables an approach in which costs can be allocated to revenue-generating activities, or what is known as activity-based costing.

The purpose of activity-based costing is to allocate all overhead and direct costs to revenue-generating activities. These revenues derive from the dues outlined in the PA's tariff book and can be globally divided into vessel-based and cargo-based dues. The guidelines outlined in the Port Reform Toolkit can be used to distinguish vessel- from cargo-based dues.

One qualification is that, while this general allocation of costs can be used as a guideline, it may conflict with PAs' strategic interests in terms of tariff strategy. For example, a PA may run a container terminal as a profit center, and assuming it has sufficient space, may charge disproportionately low storage dues to encourage the use of the available space for storage, thereby maximizing income.

Using the activity-based costing method, a port tariff scorecard (see table 5.3) was developed that assessed for each of the ports how the tariffs are structured

TABLE 5.3 Preferred port tariff structures

TARIFF ITEM	PREFERRED STRUCTURE
Port dues	***Vessel dimensions: GRT/GT***—Port infrastructure needs to be adequately constructed and maintained to enable receiving the larger vessels; the costs for these construction and maintenance works need to be recovered.
Light(house) dues	***Vessel dimensions: GRT/GT***—Similar to port dues, light dues are preferably charged based on vessel dimensions for the same reasons as mentioned for port dues.
Wharfage	***Cargo dimensions: ton/TEU/m³/unit***—General landside port infrastructure needs to be adequately constructed and maintained to enable receiving of cargo; the costs for the construction and maintenance of this port landside infrastructure need to be recovered.
Berthing dues	***Vessel dimensions per time unit: m/h, berth/h, or m/day***—The quay wall and shore facilities that are occupied by a vessel of a specific length need to be adequately constructed and maintained to enable receiving vessels; the costs for the construction and maintenance of these quay walls and shore facilities need to be recovered.
Pilotage	***Vessel dimensions per move/activity: GRT, LOA, or other vessel characteristics***—Pilotage activities need to be provided on a sufficient scale compared to the size of a vessel (e.g., longer duration of a pilot on board). The costs for the acquisition and maintenance of the pilot boats and the operational costs need to be recovered. Pilotage can also depend on the pilot's length of voyage, but this is mostly applicable in ports where each terminal is located at a different distance from open sea.
Towage	***Vessel dimensions per move/activity: GRT/GT/LOA and number of tugs***—Tugging activities need to be provided on a sufficient scale compared to the size of a vessel (i.e., more tug boats for larger vessels). The costs for the acquisition, operation, and maintenance of the different tugs need to be recovered.
Mooring	***Vessel dimensions per move/activity: GRT/GT/LOA***—Mooring activities need to be provided on a sufficient scale compared to the size of a vessel (e.g., more lines for larger vessels). The costs for the acquisition and maintenance of the mooring boats and the operational costs need to be recovered.
Cargo handling costs	***Cargo dimensions: ton/TEU/m³/unit***—There is a possible separation between a shore handling tariff for transferring the cargo between ship and quay, and a land-handling tariff for transferring the cargo between quay and the storage area. For containers, there is often a difference in cargo-handling charges for import/export/transit containers and for transshipment containers. For the latter, there is substantial competition between ports, and transshipment tariffs are often strongly reduced, compared with regular handling tariffs. Transshipment tariffs are rarely published in tariff books, as it is a highly competitive market.
Storage tariff	***Cargo dimensions per time unit: days per ton/TEU/m³/unit***
Gate handling fees	***Cargo dimensions per move: ton/TEU/m³/unit per move***

Source: World Bank 2007.
Note: GRT = gross registered tonnage; GT = gross tonnage; LOA = length overall; TEU = twenty-foot equivalent unit.

as compared to the framework. The good-practice framework for the different tariffs considers the structure of the tariffs but does not consider the magnitude of the tariffs.

To undertake the assessment, the availability of tariff books and schedules is a key starting point. The main types of tariff documents usually provided by PAs and port operators are port tariff books (which provide an overview of the dues payable to the authority), marine services tariffs (which list the pilotage, tugging, and mooring charges), and the cargo handling tariff books (which provide tariffs for the handling of cargo from vessels). These tariff books are usually available for different cargo types.

In the ESA countries, port tariff books are generally publicly available. The only gaps—documents that are non-existing or not made available—were the port tariff books and marine services tariff books for both of Madagascar's ports, as well as the separate tariff books for general cargo, RoRo, dry bulk, and liquid bulk for the ports of Mahajanga, Durban, and East London. The container tariff book is also missing in the case of Mahajanga, while the port of Lamu (not yet operational) does not yet have tariff books available.

In several cases, the tariff books provided by PAs or port operators lacked the necessary information. This was the case for the ports of Toamasina, Mahajanga, Nacala, Beira, and Maputo. Some of the tariff books obtained did not present port dues or berthing dues, some did not present marine services charges, and some did not present cargo handling and storage charges. In some cases, this was due to confidentiality considerations.

Table A.5 in appendix A presents for each of the countries in the scope of work their scoring on the criteria based on a review of their available tariff books, either from the PAs or from public/private operators. The following paragraphs present a summary of the key findings.

With respect to the main tariffs charged, most of the ports in the region use the preferred structures. In many of the ports, there are drawbacks in the tariff structures, such as charging of berthing dues based on GRT per hour instead of the preferred meters per hour. For several ports, the main drawback was that parts of the tariff books were lacking completely.

None of the ports in the region apply an incentive-based scheme that stimulates 24/7 operations on the port's landside. The land-side port tariffs (gate tariffs) in many of the ports would benefit from having a peak-pricing component, as it is understood from interviews conducted during the field visits that local logistics companies prefer to pick up their cargoes during the daytime.[8] This leads to congestion during daytime hours and underutilized assets during other hours. A mandated requirement for all shipping agents to remain open 24 hours a day—as seen in one of the countries, irrespective of whether they have a vessel arriving at the port—adds little to efficiency and raises costs unnecessarily for the customer.

The sea-side port tariffs (port/harbor dues) usually do not have a peak-pricing component, as the sea-side operations are considered a 24/7 business. Especially in modern-day container shipping, the liner schedules are based on 24/7 operations, with vessels arriving at a port at any time of the day.

The identified deficiencies in the tariff structures have an impact on both the ports' efficiency and revenues. For example, in the case of Djibouti, the fixed fees charged per volume class for pilotage, towage, and mooring services tend to overcharge small vessels and undercharge large vessels. Not only does this not adhere to the principle of activity-based costing (as large vessels require more resources) but also potentially foregone revenue.

The implications are similar in the case of the practice by the ports of Berbera and the Comoros to not charge berthing dues per time unit but, instead, per vessel call. This practice implies a potential revenue loss for the PAs when vessels use the anchorage area and are not incentivized to move.

In the port of Dar es Salaam, the wharfage charge that is included in the tariff book for noncontainerized cargoes is charged on an ad valorem basis, causing a double "tax" on the value of the cargo due to the charge of the PA as well as the customs authority charge. This is not in line with activity-based costing principles, it increases costs to port users, and raises the costs to importers and exporters.

INSUFFICIENT USE OF MODERN IT SYSTEMS

Ports and shipping today cannot operate effectively without comprehensive management information systems. These include automatic identification systems (AIS), vessel traffic management systems (VTMS) and port/terminal operating systems (P/TOS). Such systems, when combined with a port community system (PCS) acting as the hub, offer a wide range of advantages to the transport sector in the country and the region, by improving the efficiency and productivity of port and hinterland transport operations. The benefits pass not only to port operators, but also to port customers including shipping lines, freight forwarders, and shipping agents.

The use of information technology (IT) systems is in a new era of development with the introduction of smart applications, mobile apps, and the use of GPS data. This can bring advantages in terms of tracking and tracing of cargoes and shipments; truck (re)routing and avoidance of congestion; and on-demand arrival of trucks (reducing waiting times at gate). Therefore, in addition to raising the quality and skills profiles of their staff and the efficiency of core port planning processes, PAs should be focusing on digital information platforms such as port community systems, paperless customs, digital bill of ladings (not only in container shipping but also in bulk shipping), and digital orders in the transport chain (container release orders, pickup orders, etc.)

Port/terminal operating systems

Despite these advantages, in a number of the ports, the current modus operandi in the terminals is characterized by operational and administrative procedures for which approval and information exchange is carried out on paper, in offices at multiple locations inside the port operations area. Agents, truck drivers, and customs officers walk between offices, resulting in operational delays. Also, import cargo is subject to customs inspection, with many trucks and cars also inside the operations area, causing safety and security risks as well as obstructing efficient cargo and equipment flow.

A P/TOS, ideally of a standardized design compatible with new operational and administrative practices, would be a major step forward. An improved P/TOS combined with modified organizational set-ups are prerequisites for the introduction of efficient operating procedures and an efficient implementation of the capacity-building program. The combined effect of these measures is likely a significant increase in the capacity of the terminal or the port. The P/TOS then provides the foundation for the PCS.

Port community systems

The provision of a PCS and P/TOS is crucial for the efficient operation of a port. A PCS is an electronic platform that connects multiple systems operated by various organizations that operate in a seaport or inland port community. It is shared, in the sense that it is used by all stakeholders in the sector—in this case, the port community. A PCS provides electronic exchange of information among all port- and logistics sector users and is recognized as the most advanced method for the exchange of information within a single or national port community infrastructure.

A PCS can integrate with a National Single Window, should one be introduced by the respective revenue authority. A PCS is crucial for reducing duplication of data input through an efficient electronic exchange of information. The main advantages of using a PCS are faster cargo flows (benefitting the utilization of infrastructure, modalities, and assets), and time and efficiency gains for players throughout the entire supply chain. PCSs also have a clear positive impact on sustainability, transparency, reliability, safety, and security (Port of Rotterdam Authority 2013).

The implementation of PCSs, either in individual ports or as national systems, is widespread across the globe. Portbase, established in 2009, offers a range of services and allows for an easy exchange of information among all participants of the logistics chain (box 5.5).

In Hamburg, Singapore, and Busan, the respective PAs played a key role in the creation and setting up of the PCS (Keceli 2014).

Although many ports in the ESA region provide services that could be part of a PCS (e.g., single-window, tracking-tracing, automatic data interchanges, or truck appointment systems), there are only three that operate a full PCS similar to that of the Portbase system: Port Louis, Durban, and East London. The port of Djibouti is in the final phase of implementing its PCS by connecting private sector entities to the current public system. In the port of Maputo, Maputo Port Development Company (MPDC) and CFM jointly made investments in IT and systems, such as the MCNET single-window system and terminal operating systems (Zodiac and CommTracTM).

Kenya's KPA and its partners (KENTRADE), and the government of Madagascar have made substantial investments in IT and systems such as single windows and terminal operating systems. In some cases, the private operators invested in terminal operating systems and gate management systems.

In other ports, there is little movement toward a substantive PCS, with some terminals, operated by the port authority, still running inefficient paper-based P/TOS systems; the publicly operated berths in Dar es Salaam port being one example.

Blockchain technology in ports

Blockchain is a new, distributed ledger technology that has not yet been fully defined or understood. A blockchain is a distributed database (with multiple

BOX 5.5

The port community system (PCS) in the Netherlands—Portbase

The Portbase PCS as it functions in the ports of the Netherlands was developed jointly by the port authorities of Rotterdam and Amsterdam. Portbase was created by a merger between Rotterdam's Port infolink (est. 2002) and Amsterdam's PortNET (est. 2000). The new organization was set up in 2009 by the Port of Rotterdam Authority and Port of Amsterdam and enjoys wide support among the port business community (Portbase 2018).

Portbase offers more than 40 different services to approximately 3,200 customers in all sectors in the logistics chain. The system is the digital connection to all Dutch ports, has national coverage, and is available for all port sectors: containers, general cargo, dry bulk, and liquid bulk. All entities in the logistics chain can exchange information through PCS easily and efficiently (Portbase 2018). Previously, companies had to organize matters such as pre-reporting a vessel, the status of a shipment, export documentation, loading/unloading papers or communication separately and by e-mail, fax, or telephone. Through Portbase, all these activities are merged into a single system. This results in increased efficiency, lower planning costs, better and transparent planning, faster handling, and fewer errors. All the links in the logistics chain can efficiently exchange information through these services, and each of these target groups is provided with a package of tailor-made services.

The main advantages of using the PCS are faster cargo flows (benefiting the utilization of infrastructure, modalities, and assets), time advantages, and efficiency gains for a large number of players throughout the entire supply chain. At the same time, the PCS has a clear positive impact on aspects such as sustainability, transparency, reliability, safety, and security (Port of Rotterdam Authority 2013). Security is at a very high standard, with features such as an information security manager and security audits, as well as an ISO-27000 certification for the system (data center security). Finally, the system has dual redundancy, so if one physical system fails, the other takes over in real time.

Portbase is a nonprofit organization. Users pay a fee for those services that provide demonstrable added value. The costs are relatively limited, compared with the advantages offered by the services. Research by PwC concluded that Portbase generates EUR 186.0 million per year in direct value for its users (Port of Rotterdam Authority 2013).

copies existing on different computer systems) that records information shared by a peer-to-peer network using cryptography and other techniques to create secure and immutable records of transaction. The blockchain application is expected to increase the speed of doing business while at the same time the costs related to the business are decreasing, as operational processes are simplified. Also, the need for human intervention declines, hence chances of human errors are reduced.

Blockchain technology could add important additional functionalities to transport and maritime information and communications technology and electronic data interchange systems, such as data verification and tracking and tracing. At the same time, it is important to develop and apply standards that facilitate the secure exchange of data between such technologies and all relevant stakeholders. Early-stage uses and pilot implementations of blockchain in supply chains and the transport and maritime industry include blockchain-enabled verified gross mass data exchanges, under the new International Convention for the Safety of Life at Sea requirements (SOLAS), which could lead to accelerated electronic data interchange standardization.

In practice, an example of the use of blockchain technology in the port sector is the recent collaboration by Maersk and IBM to improve transparency and decrease safety risk in container shipping. Additionally, other shipping lines, Hapag Lloyd, MSC, and CMA CGM, have also indicated the intention to invest in digitalization.

INADEQUATE STAKEHOLDER ENGAGEMENT

The relationship between the port and its stakeholders—including, but not only, the users of the port—is an essential component of good management and operation. However, it is not equally strong and formalized across the ESA ports. The relationship and cooperation between the port and its stakeholders is relatively good—and the most formalized—in Mombasa, Beira, and the two South African ports. In Mombasa, it takes place through the Mombasa Port Community Charter (although the Mombasa municipality is not part of the port charter). In Beira, there are port-consulting forums among CdM, CFM, the municipality, and port users that are used to balance the interests of all parties.

In the case of Durban, the Transnet eTheKwini Municipality Planning Initiative (TEMPI) was initially established as a planning document between Transnet and eTheKwini Municipality (eTKM), related to port-city infrastructure planning. As this document mainly concerned planning, not implementation, the TEMPI evolved to the current format, the "Transnet City Forum." Furthermore, TNPA and TPT engage with port users through the Port Oversight Committees.

In East London, port-related issues are discussed on a regular basis in the local Port Consultative Committee (PCC), which includes TPT, TNPA, local government, provincial government, national government, leasees, cargo owners, terminal operators, shipping lines, and the South African Maritime Safety Authority (SAMSA). All issues for which a solution cannot be found are passed on to the national PCC, which is chaired by the Minister of Transport.

The relationship with stakeholders, such as the city council, can also be regarded as good—although it is less formalized—in the ports of Djibouti, Port Louis, and Nacala. In Djibouti, DPFZA tries to involve shipping lines in the terminal projects to ensure buy-in on the development plans and to guarantee cargo flows. There is strong involvement of DPFZA through its subsidiaries PDSA and Great Horn Investment Holding (GHIH) in a shareholding position in all terminals in the port. Port Louis and the city are closely connected, and the developments at the port are closely coordinated between the MPA and the municipality of Port Louis. Furthermore, there is a strong relation between the MPA and its three main shipping lines (Maersk, MSC, and CMA-CGM) which jointly account for 92 percent of the container traffic in the port.

Also in the port of Nacala there is regular (although nonformalized) contact between the port and the municipality. In the port of Maputo, there is substantial informal communication and dialogue with the port users, driven by the need for MPDC to be customer-oriented, given its less-developed infrastructure compared with competitors (especially Durban and Richards Bay).

In the port of Moroni, there is relatively good dialogue between Bolloré, the PA, and the national government. In Toamasina, the operators are actively involved in SPAT's (*Société du Port à Gestion Autonome de Toamasina*, Autonomous Port Authority of Toamasina) planning practices (for example, Madagascar International Container Terminal Services Ltd.—MICTSL and

Société de Manutention des Marchandises Conventionelles [SMMC, General Cargo Handling Company] give their input to SPAT on port planning). There is also close collaboration between terminal operators, shipping lines, and importers/exporters.

The relationship with stakeholders remains more limited in the ports of Berbera and Dar es Salaam. In Dar es Salaam, although the port's growth is currently hampered by the lack of sufficient landside transport capacity, there is limited systematic dialogue or integrated planning between the PA and the urban authorities. Equally surprisingly, there is no systematic dialogue on the development of the port and hinterland connectivity with representatives of shipping lines, trucking companies, rail operators, forwarders, and cargo owners.

In Berbera, there is little to no communication between the port, the municipality, and other stakeholders on the development of the port. The large number of development agencies working on the port has brought some dialogue between the port and its stakeholders, but this has been on a case-by-case basis, and not institutionalized.

CONCLUSIONS

The ESA ports face many challenges, summarized in this chapter, some exogenous, such as the move to larger vessels in the pursuit of economics of scale and the cascading of vessels down routes and ports; and some endogenous, such as the need to improve spatial and operational efficiency, and introduce modern information technology systems, attracting specialist terminal operators, improving functional integration along the logistics chain, and improving landside access and the port-city interface.

Increasing maritime capacity to meet current and projected growth, without adequately considering both sets of issues, is likely to inhibit improved efficiency within a port, prevent the realization of the full benefit from the maritime capacity investments, and potentially undermine the strategic ambitions of a port. The next chapter reviews the prospects for the ESA ports, in terms of the predicted growth in demand, the potential contestability of their respective hinterland, the factors that influence port choice, and the resulting implications for each port.

NOTES

1. In addition, there still exist four shipping lines outside the alliances, namely, Hamburg Süd (acquired by Maersk), PIL, Wan Hai, and ZIM.
2. These figures are corrected for bunker vessels, which are significantly smaller than liquid bulk carriers.
3. Information retrieved from market consultation with TPT East London.
4. https://www.corridorperformancemonitoringsystem.com/.
5. Based on policy definitions by Torjman (2005), Cairney (2016), and OECD (2011).
6. *Stratégie de Croissance Accélérée de Développement Durable* ("SCA2D": National Five-Year Plan for Accelerated and Sustainable Growth). The current version covers the 2015–19 period.
7. Based on legal and regulatory framework definitions (United Nations 1995; World Bank 1998).
8. This issue was raised during interviews with PAs and terminal operators in Dar es Salaam, Zanzibar, Toamasina, Maputo, and Durban.

REFERENCES

African Development Bank. 2010. *Reforms and the Regulatory Framework of African Ports.* https://www.afdb.org/fileadmin/uploads/afdb/Documents/Publications/African%20 Development%20Report%202010_CH%203.pdf.

Álvarez-SanJaime, Ó., P. Cantos-Sánchez, R. Moner-Colonques, and J. J. Sempere-Monerris. 2013. "Vertical Integration and Exclusivities in Maritime Freight Transport." *Transportation Research Part E: Logistics and Transportation Review* 51: 50–61.

Baccelli, O., M. Percoco, and A. Tedeschi. 2008. "Port Authorities as Cluster Managers." *European Transport* 39: 44–58. https://www.openstarts.units.it/bitstream/10077/5984/1 /Baccelli_Percoco_Tedeschi_ET39.pdf.

Cairney, P. 2016. *What Is Policy?* https://paulcairney.wordpress.com/2016/03/04/what-is -policy-3/.

Crickmay & Associates. 2018. *Corridor Performance Monitoring System: Southern and Eastern Africa.* https://www.corridorperformancemonitoringsystem.com/about.

Department for Transport. 2012. *National Policy Statement for Ports.* Presented to Parliament pursuant to section 5(9) of the Planning Act 2008. London: The Stationery Office.

DPFZA (Djibouti Ports and Free Zones Authority). 2017. *About Us.* http://dpfza.gov.dj/?q=about-us.

Fitzmaurice, M., and O. Hartmann. 2013. "Border Crossing Monitoring along the Northern Corridor." Sub-Saharan Africa Transport Policy Program (SSATP) Working Paper no. 96, World Bank, Washington, DC.

Guiliano, G., and T. O'Brien. 2007. "Reducing Port-Related Truck Emissions: The Terminal Gate Appointment System at the Ports of Los Angeles and Long Beach." *Transportation Research Part D* 12 (7): 460–73.

Keceli, Y. (2014). "A Study on Port Community System Development Strategies in Turkey." *International Association of Maritime Universities* 7: 378–88.

Kenya Ports Authority. 2012. *KPA Master Planning for Ports.*

———. 2017. *Kenya Ports Authority Handbook 2017–18.* https://issuu.com/landmarine/docs /kpa_handbook2017-18.

Macauhub. 2017. "Railways: Mozambique and Malawi Approve Expansion of Nacala Development Corridor." https://macauhub.com.mo/2017/09/18/pt-mocambique-e-malaui -aprovam-expansao-do-corredor-de-desenvolvimento-de-nacala/.

Marine Insight. 2017. *Marine Insight.* http://www.marineinsight.com/shipping-news /containerships-24000-teu-possible-ship-size-approaching-limits/.

Ministry of Transport of Kenya. 2009. *Kenya Integrated National Transport Policy.* http://www .krb.go.ke/documents/mot.pdf.

Nathan Associates. 2011. *Definition and Investment Strategy for a Core Strategic Transport Network for Eastern and Southern Africa.* A study funded by the Public-Private Infrastructure Advisory Facility (PPIAF), World Bank Group.

OECD (Organisation for Economic Co-operation and Development). 2011. Policy Roundtable: Competition in Ports and Port Services. http://www.oecd.org/regreform/sectors/48837794.pdf.

———. 2014. OECD Investment Policy Reviews: Mauritius 2014. OECD Publishing. https://books .google.nl/books?id=qgHlAwAAQBAJ&pg=PA169&lpg=PA169&dq=road+network+mauriti us&source=bl&ots=nfUwkdH5PA&sig=QORxXghtMwiGvf0xQpZAQp47-rE&hl=nl&sa=X &ved=0ahUKEwji2Mey0szVAhWQL1AKHXwkDTsQ6AEIfzAO#v=onepage&q=road%20 network%20mauritius&f=false.

———. 2016. *Capacity to Grow Transport Infratrsucture Needs for Future Trade Growth.* OECD Publishing.

Port of Rotterdam Authority. 2013. *Where Would We Be Without.* https://www.portofrotterdam. com/en/news-and-press-releases/where-would-we-be-without.

Portbase. 2018. *Port Community System.* https://www.portbase.com/en/port-community -system/.

Portos do Norte. 2017. "Zambia Signs a Deal for Railway Construction Connecting to Port of Nacala." http://www.portosdonorte.co.mz/zambia-signs-a-deal-for-railway-construction -connecting-to-port-of-nacala/.

PwC. 2018. *Strengthening Africa's Gateway to Trade.* PwC.

Republic of Kenya. 2012. *Kenya Maritime Authority Act.* http://www.kma.go.ke/images/docs /KMA_ACT_2012.pdf.

Spasovic, L.N., B. Dimitrijevic, and J. Rowinski. 2009. *Extended Hours of Operation at the Port Facilities in New Jersey: A Feasibility Analysis.* New Jersey Institute of Technology.

Strategic Management Insight. 2013. *Horizontal Integration.* https://www.strategic managementinsight.com/topics/horizontal-integration.html.

Torjman, S. 2005. *What Is Policy?* http://www.sca2006.tic-educa.org/archivos/modulo_2 /sesion_1/what percent20is percent20policy.pdf.

Transnet Port Terminals. 2017. *Transnet Long Term Planning Framework.* http://www.transnet .net/BusinessWithUs/Pages/LTPF.aspx.

United Nations. 1995. *The Legal and Regulatory Framework of Public Administration.* http:// unpan1.un.org/intradoc/groups/public/documents/un/unpan000761.pdf.

USEPA (United States Environmental Protection Agency). 2006. *Glance at Clean Freight Strategies: Terminal Appointment Systems for Drayage.* SmartWay Transport Partnership.

Van de Voorde, E., and T. Vanelslander. 2009. *Market Power and Vertical and Horizontal Integration in the Maritime Shipping and Port Industry.* Available at: http://www.oecd -ilibrary.org/docserver/download/227458312782.pdf?expires=1505812436&id =id&accname=guest&checksum=8917C26FE1F3E5F5E4AABC79991263DC.

World Bank. 1998. *Creating a Legal Framework for Economic Development.* http://siteresources. worldbank.org/INTLAWJUSTINST/Resources/LegalFramework.pdf.

——. 2007. "Module 3 Alternative Port Management Structures and Ownership Models." In *Port Reform Toolkit.* Second edition. Public-Private Infrastructure Advisory Facility (PPIAF). https://ppiaf.org/sites/ppiaf.org/files/documents/toolkits/Portoolkit/Toolkit /module3/index.html.

World Cargo News. 2017. *Infrastructure Boom for East African Cargo Flows.* MTBS Database.

——. 2018. *First Freight on New Mombassa-Nairobi Rail Link.* http://www.worldcargonews .com/htm/w20180104.273142.htm.

World Maritime News. 2018. "MSC's Newbuildings Break 23,000 TEU Threshold." https:// worldmaritimenews.com/archives/249662/mscs-newbuildings-break-23000-teu -threshold/.

Xinhua. 2016. *Feature: Chinese-Built Railway Helps Propel Ethiopia's Industrialization Drive.* http://news.xinhuanet.com/english/2016-10/02/c_135729064.htm.

6 The Prospects for the ESA Ports

INTRODUCTION

This chapter reviews the prospects for the East and Southern Africa (ESA) ports in terms of the predicted growth in demand, their respective competitive environments, the factors that influence port choice, and the resulting implications for each port and its investment priorities.

PREDICTED DEMAND GROWTH

Africa's overall population is expected to quintuple between 2000 and 2100. This translates to a 2000–2100 compound annual growth rate (CAGR) of 1.7 percent, which is significantly higher compared with other continents' CAGRs, ranging from −0.1 percent for Europe to +0.5 percent for North America.

Between 2006 and 2016, ESA's gross domestic product (GDP) increased with a CAGR of 3.0 percent. Based on International Monetary Fund (IMF) projections for 2017–22 and linear growth assumptions thereafter, the economies of ESA countries are expected to maintain a robust growth rate of about 3 percent per year over the 2020–50 period.

Driven by these projections, the demand for ports and logistics services is expected to grow steeply. Total volumes in the ESA ports are predicted to increase with a CAGR of 3.76 percent, to 641.8 million tons in 2050 (figure 6.1). With a share of 40.2 percent of the total regional port volume throughput, containers are forecast to be the largest cargo type handled by the 15 ports in the study by 2050, carrying approximately 25.8 million twenty-foot equivalent units (TEU). The large share of containers in total port volumes is mainly attributed to the containerization effect, which is likely to be an important trend in the ESA port sector.

The second largest cargo type is dry bulk with 192.0 million tons in 2050, the equivalent of 29.9 percent of total port throughput. The Mozambican ports account for a third of these volumes, with large volumes of coal being exported

FIGURE 6.1

East and Southern African ports demand forecast up to 2050 (tons)

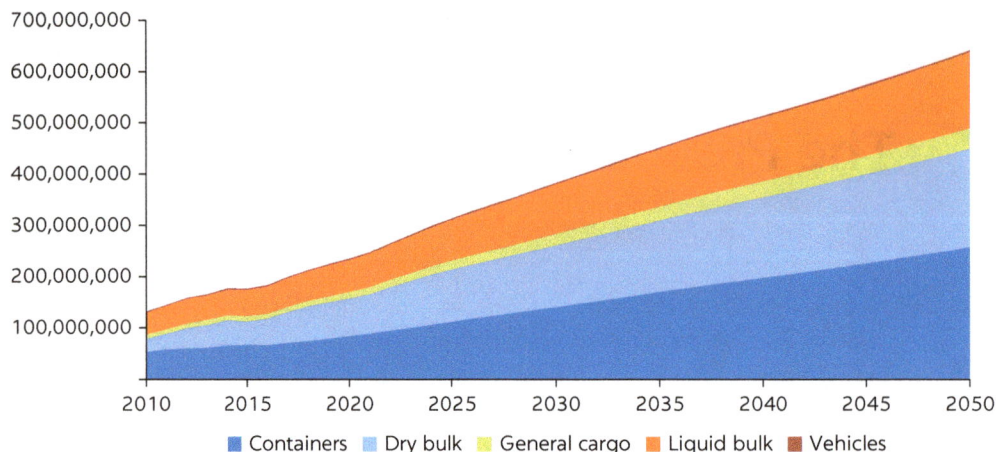

Source: World Bank analysis.

from the Moatize mines in the Tete province via the ports of Nacala, Beira, and Maputo. In addition, the ports of Mombasa and Djibouti are forecast to be large dry bulk ports, though mostly in the form of imports rather than exports. The forecast suggests Mombasa will handle 20.2 percent of total dry bulk volumes in 2050 and Djibouti 16.3 percent. With a total volume of nearly 150.0 million tons, liquid bulk is projected to be the third largest cargo type in the ESA port sector.

Even though potential export projects have been identified in Djibouti (liquefied natural gas [LNG]), North Kenya (crude oil), and Uganda (crude oil), these projects are yet to materialize, and are therefore not included in the forecasted volumes. Consequently, more than 90 percent of the volumes represent imports. General cargo is forecast to increase to 39.8 million tons in 2050, which represents 6.2 percent of the total port throughput. Last, total imports and exports of vehicles are expected to amount to just under 1.8 million units in 2050.

The relative tonnage share of containers and general cargo in overall flows is expected to remain similar in 2050 as in 2010; however, the share of dry bulk is expected to increase from about 20 percent in 2010 to about 30 percent in 2050, while the share of liquid bulk is expected to decrease from 33 percent to 23 percent.

The scale of demand growth is significant and presents a challenge for the region, given the currently available port capacities (or additional capacity that is certain to be added). For instance, the total container demand of nearly 26 million TEU by 2050 is more than double the ports' current total container handling capacity (11.4 million TEU). At the regional level, container demand will begin to exceed capacity by 2026–27, and by 2030 the gap between demand and capacity is predicted to reach about 18 percent.

In the other cargo sectors, the growth in demand relative to available capacity is expected to be particularly high. In the case of dry bulk, demand in 2050 will be nearly 100 million tons above current capacity. In the liquid bulk sector, demand will begin to exceed current capacity by 2025–26, and by 2050 the gap could reach 67 million tons (figure 6.2).

FIGURE 6.2

Expected regional growth in general cargo, liquid bulk, dry bulk, and vehicle demand, compared to total regional capacity (tons)

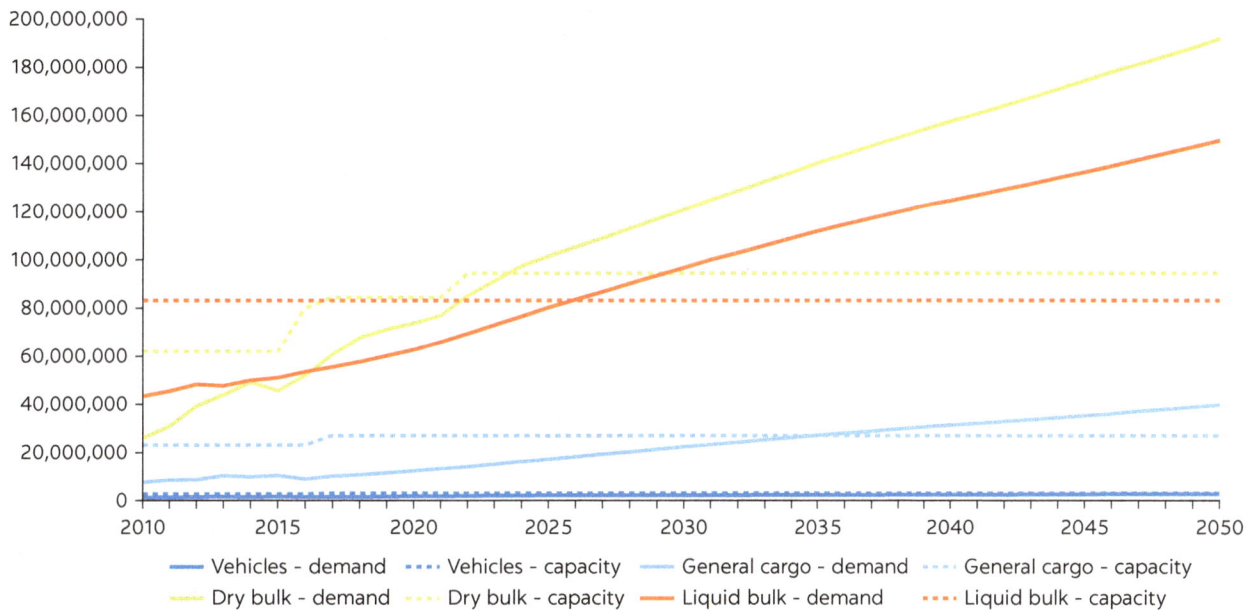

Source: World Bank analysis.

At an aggregate level, the Organisation for Economic Co-operation and Development (OECD) released a report which, using their global freight model, provided an estimate of the expected growth in global trade to 2050, and transport infrastructure needed to meet that growth (OECD 2016). The study predicts global growth will average 3.5 percent per year to 2050, slightly higher than the IMF forecast of 3 percent that underpins the commodity forecasts above. The report also suggests changes in the pattern and composition of trade: Asia and Africa are predicted to experience the largest changes, reflecting expected above-average growth rates, large market potential, and a shift toward services and industry. The report also goes on to predict that both current and planned port capacity in ESA will be close to exhaustion by 2030, and a significant increase in the capacity of hinterland connectivity will be required.

These changes, together with the trends noted in the previous chapter, will have a significant impact on the ESA ports, as all can expect demand growth. However, the nature and distribution of that growth is expected to vary. The following section looks at the competitive position of each port and the degree of competition, and tries to predict which ports will emerge as the comparative winners and which will be comparative losers as a result of the changes.

COMPETITIVE POSITION OF THE PORTS

The following subsection summarizes the competitive environment for each of the ESA ports, followed by a discussion of the factors that would improve their relative competitive position.

The advantage of location

By geographic location, Djibouti and Durban would appear to be the two ports best placed to develop into regional hubs and major transshipment ports. Located at the entrance to the Red Sea, the port of Djibouti enjoys an advantageous position along the main East–West shipping route, allowing services to transship containers to ESA without significant deviation from their routes. At the other end of the continent, the port of Durban enjoys a similarly advantageous position, allowing North and South American services to transship containers to Africa and the other way around, again without deviation.

Also, both ports benefit from a significant hinterland, allowing shipping lines to consolidate gateway cargo to and from the hinterland, with transshipment cargo. By contrast, the ports situated south of Djibouti and north of Durban, except possibly Port Louis, are further away from the main shipping routes, and in some cases are without a significant hinterland, making them less likely to attract relay transshipments. They are unlikely to develop into regional hubs.

This perspective is supported by the analysis of the formal indices of connectivity, presented in chapter 4. The Liner Shipping Connectivity Index, (LSCI) which captures how well countries are served by global shipping lines and their networks, stood at just 9 out of a 100 for the three Mozambican ports—Beira, Maputo, and Nacala—in 2017. This contrasts with a score of 30 or above for the ports of Djibouti, Port Louis, Durban, and East London (UNCTAD 2018). These latter ports are also the ones showing the most improvement over the last decade, with Djibouti improving from 20 in 2008 to 31 in 2017, and Port Louis from 17 to 32. The LSCI scores have, by contrast, remained nearly constant for Dar es Salaam, Maputo, Nacala, and Mombasa.

The competitive environment

The port of Djibouti functions both as a gateway port to Djibouti and Ethiopia and as a transshipment hub for East–West trade volumes. The port of Djibouti as a gateway port is currently almost entirely free of competition, with almost 95 percent of Ethiopian cargo passing through it. The remaining cargo passes through Port Sudan and Mombasa. However, competition for Ethiopian transit cargo is expected to increase, with planned development in Berbera and the involvement of DP World.

Further ahead, once constructed, the port of Lamu might also be expected to capture cargo from southern Ethiopia. The envisioned road and rail connection from the port of Lamu to southern Ethiopia would make it more efficient to import and export cargo via Lamu for this region of Ethiopia.

In terms of the transshipment volumes, Djibouti is in fierce competition with ports like Dubai, Salalah, and Jeddah, all of which have a similar advantageous location on the main East–West shipping route near the entrance of the Red Sea. This competition will continue and intensify, given the trends in the industry.

In its role as a gateway to Somaliland, the port of Berbera does not face any real competition, as it is the only port in that region that can handle vessels of a substantial size. Other ports in Somalia handle their specific hinterland markets (Puntland for Bosaso, and the rest of Somalia for Mogadishu and Kismayo), but the lack of infrastructure and geographical constraints preclude any competition. Berbera handles little transit traffic currently, but as mentioned above, that is likely to change with the planned developments in the port.

Inter-port competition in Kenya is nonexistent, as the port of Mombasa is currently the only deep-sea port in Kenya, and Kenya Ports Authority (KPA) is both the port authority (PA) and port operator. Mombasa's current competitor is the port of Dar es Salaam in Tanzania, which is competing for transit cargo to and from Uganda, the Democratic Republic of Congo, Burundi, and Rwanda. The completion of the port of Lamu is expected to intensify inter-port competition, with Lamu potentially attracting some of the cargo volumes that traditionally have passed through Mombasa, Djibouti, and Port Sudan.

With the Lamu Port–South Sudan–Ethiopia Transport (LAPSSET) Corridor linking the port of Lamu to Ethiopia and South Sudan, the port of Lamu is also expected to compete with the ports of Djibouti and Berbera for Ethiopian and South Sudan transit traffic. Market consultation with stakeholders from the LAPSSET corridor program has indicated that, given projected growth, they perceive the ports of Lamu and Mombasa to be complementary, with the former focusing more on Ethiopian, northern Kenyan, and South Sudanese traffic, and the latter primarily oriented toward Nairobi and hinterland markets.

In the past, Mombasa's transshipment function was limited from a lack of spare capacity, combined with relatively high prices. With the new Kipevu Container Terminal now operational, the KPA has set up a task force aimed at increasing transshipment volumes in the port of Mombasa (*IHS Fairplay* 2016). However, in addition to expanding port capacity, draft restrictions in the port need to be removed for transshipment volumes to potentially materialize.

Dar es Salaam is a gateway port that handles both domestic and transit cargo. The competitive environment for domestic cargo is limited, as the port of Dar es Salaam handles approximately 95 percent of Tanzania's international trade, with the secondary ports of Tanga and Mtwara handling the remainder. The share for Dar es Salaam port, albeit of a growing absolute volume, is likely to change if the proposed development of a new port goes forward at Bagamoyo.

The proposed development at Bagamoyo involves the dredging of the navigational channel, construction of a port and logistics park, and the development of a portside industrial free zone (Bagamoyo Special Economic Zone). The first phase of the project envisions the construction of four marine berths, two of which will be allocated to containers, one for multipurpose use, and the last one for support services. The first phase of the port will be developed in parallel with the supporting infrastructure, as well as the industrial zone connected to the port. However, the current status of the development was unclear at the time of this report.

Along with the development of Bagamoyo, another development is expected in the port landscape in Tanzania. A project agreement was signed in May 2017 between Tanzania and Uganda to develop an oil pipeline to enable Uganda to export oil in 2020 via the port of Tanga. The line, which is expected to become the longest heated pipeline in the world, at 1,445 km, will transport approximately 216,000 barrels per day from the remote Holma District in Uganda to Tanga. The project, reported at approximately US$3.5 billion, is expected to be completed by 2020 (*Hellenic Shipping News* 2017).

Regarding transit traffic, the competitive landscape is fierce: Dar es Salaam port serves the landlocked countries of Rwanda, Malawi, the Democratic Republic of Congo, Burundi, and Zambia, via the Central and North-South Corridors. Dar es Salaam is in direct competition with Mombasa, located only 450 km north of Dar es Salaam, and serving Northern Tanzania, Rwanda, and Burundi. Also, the Mozambican ports of Nacala and Beira aim to serve some of these landlocked countries.

Some traffic from the Democratic Republic of Congo, Malawi, and Zambia uses Durban port, even though the distance is almost twice as large. With the port of Dar es Salaam facing limitations in capacity, access constraints, and service quality on the publicly operated berths, the port's competitive position is under serious threat. The one comparative advantage, a specialist operator on the container berths 8–11, as reflected in the efficiency analysis in chapter 4, helps them compete now. A major reduction in operating efficiency on those berths would negatively affect the strategic role of the port.

The port of Zanzibar operates primarily as a gateway port to the island, and as such has no competition. The port handles approximately 90 percent of the cargo volumes entering Zanzibar (PMAESA 2017). Because of the current congestion problems near the port, a new multipurpose port near Maruhubi is being developed. Once completed, it is expected to handle the majority of container and bulk volumes destined for the island of Zanzibar. The Malindi Port will focus on passenger transport and small-cargo trade with the Tanzanian mainland and the surrounding islands such as Pemba.

The port of Moroni faces little competition, serving the island of Grand Comoros as its principal gateway port. Since the port of Moroni handles no transshipment cargo, it does not compete with the port of Mutsamudu or other transshipment ports in the region.

Toamasina, the largest port on Madagascar, also faces limited competition. The second largest port, Mahajanga, is not capable of handling vessels with a draft of more than 4.5 meters and focuses mainly on local traffic on Madagascar's West coast and the neighboring islands. Also, the port of Toamasina is connected via both rail and road links to the capital Antananarivo, further underlining its strategic position. As a result, Toamasina handles 90 percent of the container volumes and 85 percent of the total cargo volumes for Madagascar.

Port Louis serves as both a gateway to Mauritius and as a transshipment hub for both the neighboring islands and the East African mainland. As a gateway port it faces no competition and handles all international trade volumes of Mauritius that use maritime transport. Because of its position as a transshipment hub, it faces fierce and growing competition. Many ports either handle now, or seek to handle, transshipment cargo for the East African region, not only Djibouti and Durban, but also other Indian Ocean and Middle East transshipment ports, such as Djibouti, Salalah, and Colombo, and in the future Lamu and possibly Bagamoyo. Furthermore, the port of Reunion, located approximately 130 nautical miles southwest of the port of Port Louis, has expressed the ambition to develop the port as a regional transshipment hub, and transshipment volumes have increased 209 percent to 74,000 TEU in 2016, underlining the ambition.

The port of Nacala acts as the primary gateway port for the northern provinces of Mozambique, as well as for the landlocked countries Malawi and Zambia. The main competition for the gateway function comes from the ports of

Beira, Durban, and Dar es Salaam, which all fulfill the same function for the land-locked countries in Southern Africa, including Malawi and Zambia. One major advantage for Nacala is the construction of the railway and new coal terminal on the opposite side of the bay, ensuring that the port of Nacala will become a large center for coal exports that previously flowed through the port of Beira. Competition is minimal as the coal exporting company Vale invested in both the railway and the Nacala-a-Velha coal terminal.

The port of Beira has two functions. First, it acts as gateway port for cargo volumes to and from the greater Beira area, as well as the landlocked countries Zambia, Malawi, and Zimbabwe. Competition for these hinterland markets is fierce, with the ports of Nacala, Maputo, and Durban targeting a similar hinterland. Secondly, Beira serves as the traditional export port for Mozambican coal but is now experiencing significant competition from Nacala for this traffic, as mentioned earlier.

Maputo is the primary commercial cargo port for Mozambique, and a key transit port for South Africa, Zimbabwe, Botswana, and Swaziland. It also acts as commodity export port for South African coal and magnetite. For both functions, Maputo competes primarily with South African ports; it competes with Durban for commercial transit cargo, and with Richards Bay for coal and magnetite export.

The port of Durban is the largest and most important port on the East Coast of Africa, because of its relatively efficient port handling, strategic location, and hinterland connections. It is connected to landlocked countries in the region (Botswana, Zimbabwe, Zambia, and Malawi), and is the main gateway port for the industrial heartland of the Gauteng (greater Johannesburg) area. Despite port and infrastructure developments in various East and West African ports (Maputo, Beira, Walvis Bay, and Luanda), its dominant position is unlikely to be challenged, even if its market share may moderate.

The port of East London serves as a gateway to the Eastern Cape and focuses primarily on servicing the local automotive industry. Competition originates primarily from the port of Port Elizabeth, which is capable of handling larger vessels and consequently attracts certain volumes designated for the port of East London. With the port of Ngqura situated between Port Elizabeth and East London, and the expansion constraints in the port of East London itself, overall growth expectations are limited (Transnet National Ports Authority 2015).

DETERMINANTS OF PORT CHOICE

Given the predicted growth in port volumes and, in many cases, the increasing competition for that volume, understanding the determinants of port choice and port competition is important for estimating potential diversion of transit traffic between competing ports. The determinants provide an indication of the priorities ports should consider in their development plans, to protect and develop their strategic positions relative to other ports.

The literature on port choice and port competition is vast and ever expanding, to reflect the increasingly multifaceted nature of international logistics systems. Most of the literature that uses econometric modeling approaches considers ports in Western Europe, the Mediterranean, North America, or East Asia. This reflects both the origin of researchers and the differential availability of data. As a result, there is a clear knowledge gap in understanding of the structural factors of the maritime and logistics industries in other regions, such as Latin America, South Asia, and particularly Africa.

This section presents the results of a study (Thill 2018) of port choice in the context of the region of 10 countries that span Southern Africa. The study leveraged existing data on transportation infrastructure, trade, and logistical operations in combination with state-of-the-art econometric modeling. The study area of focus, because of data availability issues, is limited to the Southern Africa cone, composed of South Africa, Botswana, Namibia, Lesotho, Mozambique, Angola, Malawi, Zambia, Swaziland, and Zimbabwe, but the findings are considered transferable to other countries in the region.

Key drivers of port choice

The literature on port choice determinants has found that shippers, freight forwarders, and shipping lines make port choice decisions differently, and aim to reach different goals. Shipping lines make decisions to maximize scale economies and profits, and landside decision makers seek to minimize costs (Talley and Ng 2013).

Moreover, port choice may be determined by a range of factors, including those that are within the control of PAs (such as equipment availability at the port) and those largely beyond their control (e.g., maritime transit times and locations). The review by Moya and Valero (2017) finds that most studies on the topic of port choice—although focusing on regions other than Africa—find the factors within the PAs' control as being more important than the ones outside their control. Efforts made by PAs—including improvements in spatial and operational efficiency, infrastructure and superstructure, and investments in intermodality to improve access—are crucial factors in the competitiveness of any port.

The methodology of the study

Port-choice data used in this study consisted of shipment flows from location-verified physical origin points in 10 countries of Southern Africa—South Africa, Botswana, Namibia, Lesotho, Angola, Mozambique, Swaziland, Zimbabwe, Zambia, and Malawi—to their destinations in the United States. This data source encompasses those shipments (using bills of lading) originating in the identified countries and entering the United States between January 1 and July 31, 2017. It is derived from raw data comprising information submitted through both the U.S. Customs and Border Protection Automated Manifest System (AMS) and manifests submitted at the ports (Thill 2018).

After verification of the raw data, a data set consisting of 7,896 bills of lading was constituted, including 7,156 that were containerized (90.6 percent) and 740 that were not containerized (9.4 percent). This freight is shipped to the United States through 16 gateway ports located in the Southern African Cone, illustrated in map 6.1.

While the majority of these bills of lading are for direct service to the United States, a significant proportion of freight is transferred via some major ports in Europe, the Caribbean, or East or Southeast Asia, before completing its journey to the United States. Also, 15.8 percent of all bills of lading

MAP 6.1

Gateway ports in the southern cone

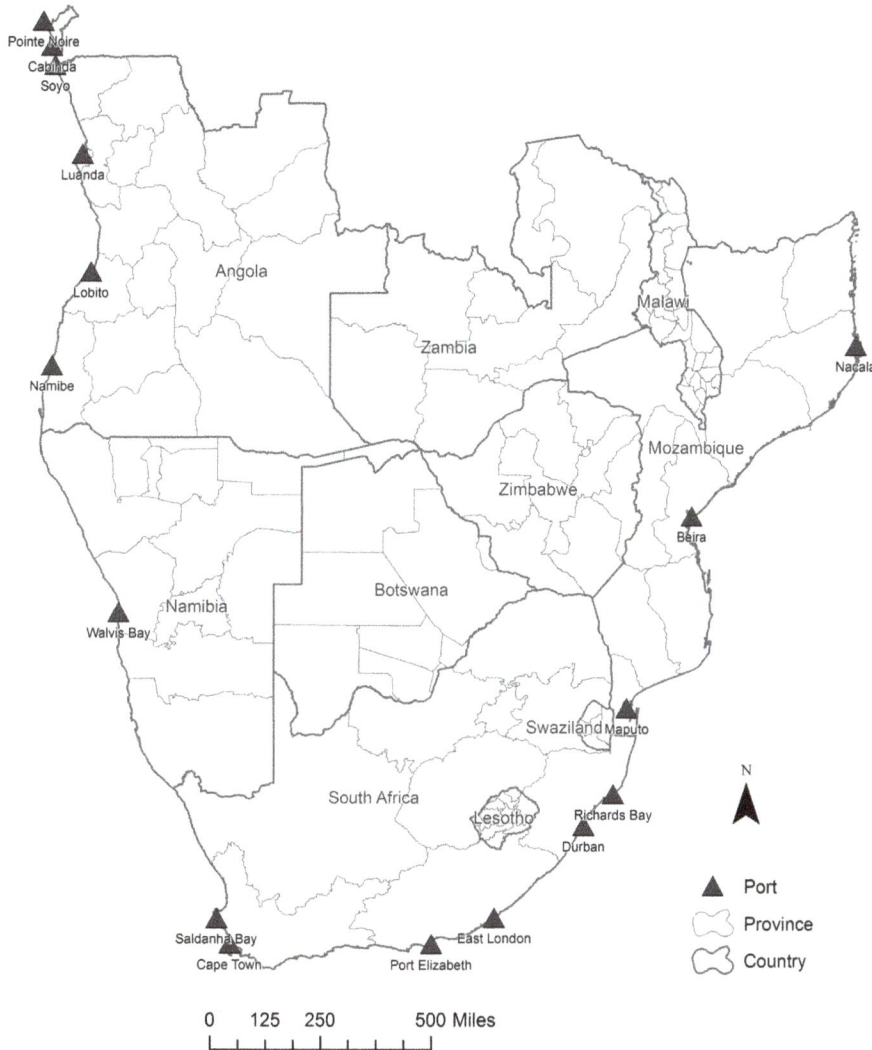

Source: World Bank.

(1,244 cases) underwent transshipment within a port in the Southern African Cone region, between a short-sea feeder service and the line-haul service to the U.S. port of entry.

The vast majority of Southern African exports to the United States originate from the Republic of South Africa. Map 6.2 depicts the geographic distribution of shipment origins by locality, where each locality is represented by a circle proportional to the shipment weight.

The analysis sought to explain port choices in Southern Africa through a number of possible factors. Key factors *a priori* were shipper attributes, shipment attributes, port attributes, and landside transaction costs from shipment origin to gateway port. The modelling exercise then sought to define the choice predictors.

MAP 6.2

Geographic distribution of shipment origins according to shipment weight

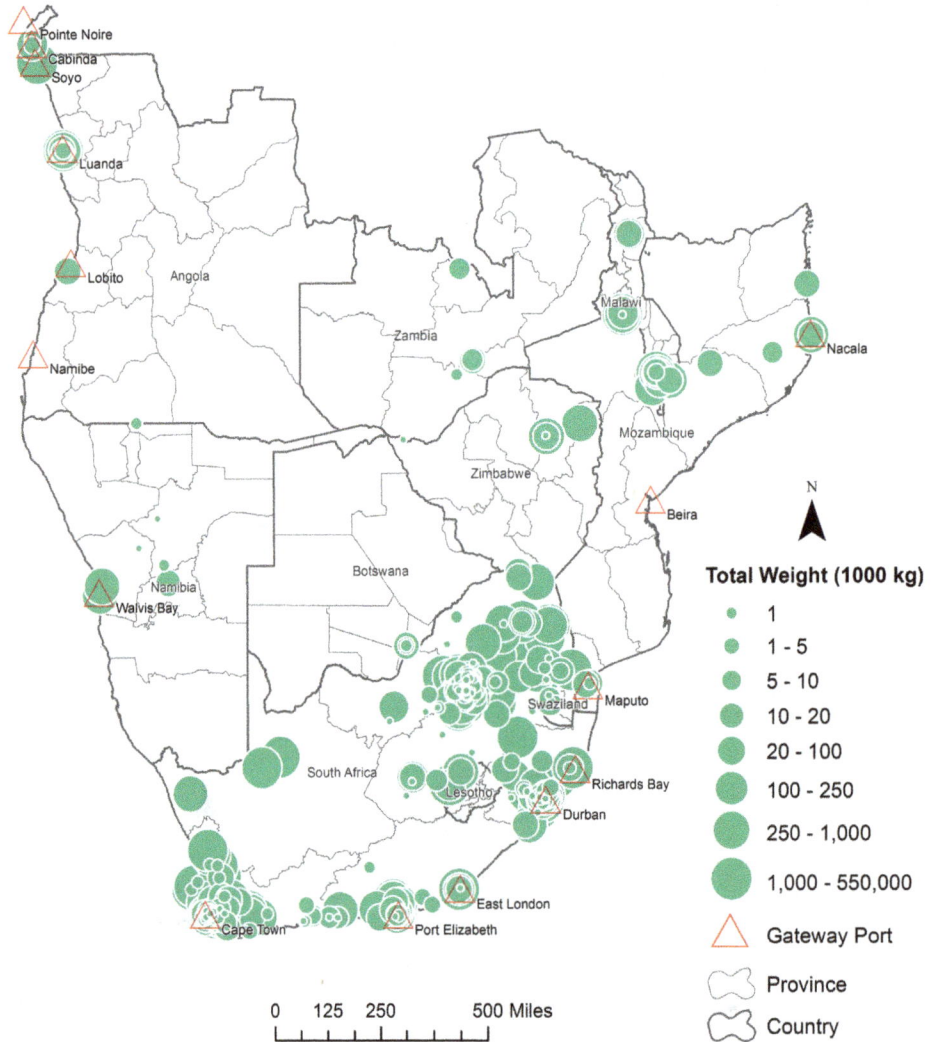

Source: World Bank.

The results of the study

The following represent the key findings from the analysis:

- Shippers show a clear preference for those ports that can be reached faster by road.
- Shippers show a strong preference for a port with good connectivity to the road transportation system.
- Shippers appear less concerned about landside traffic congestion.
- Shippers were concerned about delay at border crossings, which represented a significant deterrence factor in the choice of a port.
- Shippers were found to be even more concerned about the risk of extreme delay.

The next section draws together the information in the earlier sections, and, in forecasting market demand for the ESA ports, endeavors to predict the likely market share by commodity group for each port in the study.

FORECAST DEMAND FOR THE INDIVIDUAL PORTS

Domestic and transit containers

This study combined data from PA websites, transport corridor websites, and existing African transit studies to assign total gateway port throughput to the countries comprising the ports' hinterland. The approach used to forecast future throughput in the ESA ports followed the following steps:

1. The starting point of the demand forecast was to collect historical port statistics for each port. The data were gathered from PAs, corridor authority databases, or previous port studies conducted in the region. They were validated and complemented during site visits.
2. The second step was to determine the split between domestic, transit, and transshipment volumes handled in the ports. For example, this step involved determining Zambian cargo volumes handled in the port of Dar es Salaam.
3. Subsequently, the importance of this volume stream to the transit country itself was determined. This volume stream included both the imports and exports to and from the port. For example, this step entailed determining what share of total Zambian volumes is covered by the transit volumes originating from the port of Dar es Salaam.
4. The national volume demand was then calculated. Assuming the port of Dar es Salaam handled a total of 50,000 TEU for Zambia in 2016 and based on the assumptions gathered in step three that this represented 25 percent of the Zambian container demand, it can be calculated that the total Zambian container demand was 200,000 TEU in 2016.
5. Given this national demand projection for 2016, the country's container forecast could be calculated up to 2050, using its GDP projection and the GDP multiplier. This multiplier is the calculated difference between cargo growth and GDP growth.
6. Last, given the national demand projections up to 2050, market shares between ports were allocated. They were calculated on a yearly basis to account for expected shifts in the competitive environment between ports, and changes in the region's external trade environment. This approach was repeated for different cargo types.

The GDP multiplier (applied in step 5 above) is a factor representing the difference between the cargo growth and GDP growth in a country or region. Taking the example of containers, a GDP multiplier of 1.5 implies that for every one-percent increase in GDP, TEU growth is 1.5 percent. The GDP growth in developing countries is often lower compared with their TEU growth, as many goods are still being transported as general cargo. As developing countries evolve to more mature stages of economic development, cargoes are containerized more and more, to save costs. This trend, cargo containerization, is clearly visible in the ESA port sector, and is supported by many previously conducted studies.

Ideally, the regression analysis would be conducted for each country using a large set of data points. However, as the countries separately did not have many data points because of the lack of available transit information, the data points of the study area countries were combined to arrive at a regional GDP multiplier. The multiplier was calculated by dividing the CAGR of the specific cargo type (e.g., containers) by the CAGR of GDP over that same period. To calculate the CAGR of GDP, only that share of total GDP that was served by the ports in the analysis was considered. For example, 95 percent of Ethiopia's national volumes were served by ports within our scope. As a result, only 95 percent of the GDP volumes of Ethiopia were considered when calculating the regional multiplier.

For the island economies of Madagascar, the Comoros, and Mauritius, the multiplier was not calculated based on this regional multiplier and was hence not included in the GDP assessment for the regional multiplier, given that the volumes handled by the ports on these islands were destined solely to their respective island economies. As a result, the volumes denoted on the African mainland will be less correlated with the volumes denoted on the islands. Therefore, the multipliers for the island economies were calculated based on the historical multipliers observed in the main ports of the islands. A separate multiplier calculation was made for the port of Durban as well. This is because Durban represents more than half of all port throughput (excluding transshipments), while South Africa's GDP has a similar relationship to the study region's overall GDP. To avoid the port of Durban or South Africa's economy influencing the regional GDP multiplier too strongly, both were taken out of the calculation. A multiplier was separately calculated for the port of Durban by analyzing historical throughput and benchmarking it to GDP multipliers seen in other developed economies.

The port-demand forecasts stipulate four different traffic projections: a base case, a high case, a low case, and a market share shift case. The approach described above represents the "base case" approach for all five cargo types. The high and low case traffic projections were derived using increased (+1 percent) and decreased (−1 percent) GDP projections, respectively. The market shares for the high and low case are equal to the market shares applied to the base case. The market share shift case (MS Shift) is a traffic scenario in which market shares for transit cargo converge to a "natural equilibrium." In this case, transit cargo is (re)directed to the ports that are best situated to handle specific transit cargo. For example, historical figures show that the port of Durban handled more than 60 percent of Malawian cargo in 2016. However, it can be expected that in 20 to 30 years from now, the ports of Maputo, Beira, Nacala, and Dar es Salaam will take over a large portion of these transit volumes from the port of Durban, because of their favorable locations and the expected development of transport corridors in the region.

The rationale for applying and illustrating this case is to show the potential shift in cargo volumes handled by the ESA ports, given the fact that all ports are expected to develop and increase their competitive positions for captive cargo. Although specific projects in this regard may not yet have been identified, the MS Shift case provides an overview of cargo volumes should new projects in the ports materialize. For the dry and liquid bulks, the MS Shift case is not illustrated, as these goods are more dependent on dedicated infrastructure for handling the imports or exports (e.g., a rail line from Moatize mines to Nacala or oil pipelines to import or export crudes). As these projects are more difficult to ascertain, the MS shift case is not illustrated for these two cargo types.

Any incremental or currently untapped cargo demand from both landlocked and gateway countries is accounted for in the forecast via the GDP projections of the individual countries. Also, any incremental export demand, assuming this cargo can be transported in containers, is captured via the imbalance between import full and export full containers depicted in most African countries. This will not be reflected in the container volumes, as an exported 20 foot container counts as one TEU, regardless of whether or not the container is full.

Transshipment

The above methodology is applicable for forecasting gateway volumes (domestic and transit cargo). However, transshipment volumes are based on very different drivers. Here, it is assumed that transshipment relates to containers only, as transshipment is not seen in the ESA ports for other cargo types.

Whether a port can attract transshipment containers is dependent on several factors. A crucial feature of large transshipment hubs is their limited distance from arterial trade routes. The distance to the main maritime routes indicates the distance that a vessel is required to deviate from its route to call in the respective port. The lower the deviation, the lower the shipping costs, and thus the better a port is situated. An important factor stimulating the growth of transshipment volumes in a port is also the presence of a container terminal operator that is associated to a shipping line. As opposed to captive cargo, shipping lines can easily shift their container cargo from one port (or terminal) to the other. Also, a shipping line is more likely to remain committed to a terminal, if the shipping line or an affiliated terminal operator is (co-)owner of the terminal. However, as a result of alliances being formed among shipping lines, the group of potential clients is relatively small.

The distance of a transshipment hub to the main captive container markets is an important factor as well. The smaller the distance, the lower the feeder vessel costs and the more likely transshipment activities are to take place. This factor is related to the potential to consolidate volumes, or the possibility for a shipping line to combine transshipment volumes with large quantities of captive container volumes (e.g., at Djibouti and Durban). This is a major strength for a transshipment port, as it implies a minimum deviation from the shipping route.

Forecasting transshipment is complex and challenging for several reasons. First, transshipment traffic is known to be volatile and binary in nature. Volumes can increase or decrease dramatically in a short period of time, as has been demonstrated in African transshipment ports Ngqura and Walvis Bay. Second, although a container terminal might be able to create optimal conditions to handle transshipment, it remains an internal decision of shipping lines. These decisions are commercially sensitive to the shipping line and are therefore difficult to ascertain.

To forecast transshipment volumes in the ports, six successive steps were again applied:

1. Using a qualitative transshipment multicriteria analysis, the main ports that are likely to receive transshipment were identified. With the cascading effect of vessels continuing, shipping loops to Africa are expected to be concentrated around larger hubs, which subsequently are feeders of the containers

to smaller ports on the ESA coastline. This effect is strengthened by the fact that not all ports will be able to the receive larger vessels that are cascaded from the arterial trade routes—in terms of required depth, presence of ship-to-shore (STS) cranes, or other factors preventing the handling of large container vessels. Important transshipment factors were listed for each port, to identify the ports that are most likely to handle transshipment cargo. The ports of Berbera, Zanzibar, Moroni, Mahajanga, Toamasina, and East London were not included in this assessment, as these ports have little to no chance of attracting large volumes of transshipment given the absence of most transshipment criteria.

2. The historical transshipment volumes of the ports were analyzed to identify major events which have led to increases (e.g., dredging) or decreases (such as the opening of a competitive port) in transshipment volumes.

3. Any future port development plans were gathered. Known expansion projects that could impede or enhance the ability of each port to meet current or future transshipment demand were considered. These include, among others, terminal expansion programs and port dredging works.

4. Fourth, total transshipment demand for ESA was determined by using regional GDP forecasts to estimate the total transshipment volumes based on the main transshipment market served by a port. This distinction is required as the port of Djibouti serves a different transshipment market compared to the port of Durban, for example.

The level and allocation of transshipment cargo remains at the discretion of shipping lines, which might allocate transshipment containers to ports based on commercial rather than other logical reasons. Given the fact that shipping lines are reluctant to divulge this information, the forecasts are based on publicly available information. Transshipment is a way for shipping lines to meet cargo demand in the logistically most-efficient way. This means that, in the end, total transshipment volumes are related to GDP.

5. Fifth, the market shares of the identified transshipment ports were projected over the forecast period. This included an assessment of future port developments and their impacts on the competitive position of each port.

6. Finally, the projections were combined to arrive at the final transshipment forecasts, based on low, medium, and high case regional GDP scenarios.

The largest container vessels, currently having a maximum capacity of some 22,000 TEU, are predominantly deployed on the main East–West route, on which most of global cargo is transported. Consequently, the ESA ports are not projected to receive vessels upwards of 14,000 TEU in the short-to-medium term. To receive these vessels, ports should accommodate for a draft of at least 16.0 m and a length overall (LOA) of at least 365 m.[1] The only ports satisfying both conditions are the ports of Djibouti, Lamu, Durban, and Port Louis, with the port of Lamu having the best port characteristics. Although the ports of Mombasa, Bagamoyo, Dar es Salaam, and Nacala are just one or two meters shallower, they face LOA restrictions related to either their entrance channels or turning basins, making them less attractive as large-scale regional transshipment hubs.

For a port to develop as a regional transshipment hub, it is important to have ample terminal capacity, STS cranes, and a high quayside productivity to quickly load and unload boxes from the vessel to the quay, and vice versa. The ports of Durban and Djibouti have the highest capacity, the most STS cranes, and achieved the highest productivity in moves per crane per hour in 2016. The ports of Mombasa and Port Louis combine somewhat lower container capacities, with a productivity of 24 and 20 moves per crane per hour, respectively. The Mozambican ports have the least favorable infrastructure specifications, as all three ports have limited container-handling capacity; Nacala and Maputo have no STS cranes; and Nacala and Beira are characterized by relatively low productivity.

Sufficient terminal capacity is important, as transshipment activities are often the least value-adding activities in the port. This is because terminal handling rates for transshipment are often much lower than for gateway containers, as the competition in the transshipment market is higher. Without sufficient container capacity, ports might favor gateway boxes over transshipment boxes from one year to another. Recognizing the container terminal utilization rates, all ports have sufficient spare container-handling capacity to handle transshipment.

In terms of geographic location, Djibouti and Durban are the most favorable ports for both hub-and-spoke and relay transshipment. At the tip of the continent, the port of Durban provides a strategic position for transshipment from North and South American container services to Africa, and the other way around.

Finally, on connectivity, the port of Djibouti performs the best of all ports in the study area, having both a shipping-line-related container terminal operator (through China Merchants Port Holdings' [CMPH's] shares in Doraleh Multipurpose Port [DMP]) and the most container services calling its port. The ports of Durban, Mombasa, and Port Louis have many shipping lines calling them as well, yet have no relation to a shipping line, which could affect their competitive position in the transshipment market.

The qualitative multicriteria analysis, summarized in table 6.1, identified the ports of Djibouti, Lamu, Durban, and Port Louis as having the largest potential to develop as regional transshipment hubs. The ports of Djibouti, Durban, and Port Louis are perfectly located at minimum deviation of large trade routes, have ample container-handling capacity, and are well connected, making them the most suitable places to handle transshipments. The port of Lamu is also classified among these ports, despite being situated further away from the main trade routes, as the port has the lowest draft restrictions, once developed will have state-of-the-art facilities, and is situated closer to feeder ports along the eastern African coastline. Situated relatively close to each other, the port of Lamu is preferred over the ports of Mombasa, Bagamoyo, and Dar es Salaam because of its superior nautical accessibility and location. The Mozambican ports are not considered potential regional or subregional transshipment hubs, as they lack the required nautical accessibility and infrastructure.

Transshipment growth rates are calculated based on the growth rate of the transshipment market served by a port. If the port handles primarily hub-and-spoke or interlining transshipment destined for the African region, the African GDP projection is applied. Should the port also handle relay transshipment or interlining transshipment destined to other continents or regions, 50 percent of the projected world GDP growth and 50 percent of the projected African GDP growth is applied to calculate the transshipment growth rate for the port.

The ports are classified based on their location along main shipping routes and the current shipping services calling the port. The ports of Djibouti, Durban, and Port Louis receive shipping services that are destined for continents other than Africa, whereas this is not the case for Mombasa or

TABLE 6.1 **Transshipment assessment**

CRITERIA	UNIT	DJIBOUTI	LAMU	MOMBASA	BAGAMOYO	DAR ES SALAAM	NACALA	BEIRA	MAPUTO	DURBAN	PORT LOUIS
Nautical Accessibility											
Maximum draft[a]	m	−18.0	−22.0	−15.0	−15.0	−15.5	−15.0	−12.0	−14.0	−16.5	−16.5
Maximum LOA	m	300+	300+	300	n.a.	250	200	185	250	300+	300+
Maximum TEU vessel	TEU	14,000+	14,000+	6,000	6,000	6,000	6,000	3,000	5,000	14,000+	14,000+
Quay length	m	1,500	1,200	1,400	n.a.	1,200	375	650	300	4,150	800
Infrastructure											
TEU capacity	TEU	1,800,000	n.a.	1,650,000	n.a.	1,050,000	180,000	400,000	200,000	2,800,000	1,000,000
Container terminal utilization rate	percent	49.4 percent	n.a.	66.1 percent	n.a.	59.3 percent	39.5 percent	49.3 percent	64.9 percent	93.6 percent	51.1 percent
Quay equipment	# STS	12	n.a.	12	n.a.	9	–	4	–	30	5
Crane productivity	moves/crane/hour	34	n.a.	24	n.a.	17	10	12	22	25	20
Location											
Minimum distance to main trade route	–	✓	✗	✗	✗	✗	✗	✗	~	✓	✓
Minimum distance to feeder port	–	✗	✓	✓	✓	✓	~	~	✓	✓	~
Hinterland market	–	✓	✓	✓	~	✓	~	~	~	✓	✗
Connectivity											
Number of shipping services	#	21	n.a.	20	n.a.	12	7	5	4	18	16
Shipping line-related CTO	–	✓	✗	✗	✗	✗	✗	✗	✗	✗	✗
Transshipment potential	–	✓	✓	~	~	~	✗	✗	✗	✓	✓

Source: Data obtained from PAs, container terminal operators, and a variety of publicly available documents.

Note: ✗ = low/inadequate; ~ = moderate/inconclusive; ✓ = good/adequate; # = number; CTO = container terminal operator; LOA = length overall; n.a. = not applicable; TEU = twenty-foot equivalent unit.
a. including ongoing or planned dredging projects.

Dar es Salaam. Given the location of Lamu, it is not expected that transshipment to other continents will arise here. Based on these classifications, 100 percent of the African GDP growth projection is used for the latter three ports, whereas 50 percent of the world GDP projection and 50 percent of the African GDP projection is used to calculate transshipment growth rates for the former three ports.

These growth rates are applied to the actual transshipment rates observed in the historical figures to arrive at a total transshipment forecast for a particular region. Subsequently, market shares are allocated to competing hub ports to distribute the transshipment volumes. For the port of Djibouti, competition for transshipment cargo from African ports is limited. However, the port does compete with ports such as Jeddah, Salalah, and Dubai. Given the expanded container handling capacity, with the Doraleh Multipurpose Port extension inaugurated there in 2017, it is expected that Djibouti will keep a market share of 100 percent of its own volumes. Once fully developed and operational, the new greenfield ports of Lamu and Bagamoyo are projected to capture 80 percent of the transshipment market from the ports of Mombasa and Dar es Salaam respectively. This assumption is based on the previously conducted qualitative analysis. Port Louis is not expected to lose market share to the port of Reunion, despite improvements being made there. Lastly, the port of Durban is projected to see its transshipment market share reduced to 75 percent of the 2018 level because of improvements made in Mozambican ports that will limit the need for hub-and-spoke transshipment to these ports.

Dry bulk

As dry bulk exports are less correlated with national GDP projections, a different forecast method was applied to this segment: a bottom-up approach in which factors such as port- and infrastructure-handling capacity, mine capacity, and potential expansion plans were combined to estimate exported volumes. Data on the nature and origin of a specific export commodity were collected, which were combined with bottom-up information collected both via electronic sources and during site visits. The collected information is important to determine factors such as expansion plans, export volume targets, or infrastructure handling capacity.

Predicted growth in market share

The resulting projections by commodity group, by country, and by port, and the implications, are summarized here.

Overall, Durban, Djibouti, and Mombasa together are expected to represent 56 percent of the total volumes handled by the African ports in 2050 (figure 6.3). In the northern part of the project's geographical scope, Djibouti is expected to retain its position as leading gateway port. This is because of large port-and-hinterland infrastructure developments, which were recently completed in Djibouti. However, competition is expected to strengthen from both Berbera and Lamu for the Ethiopian market. Based on total throughput, the port of Djibouti is forecast to handle 17.0 percent of the ESA port throughput in 2050, followed by the port of Lamu with 4.3 percent, and the port of Berbera with 2.8 percent.

FIGURE 6.3

East and Southern African ports market share, 2050

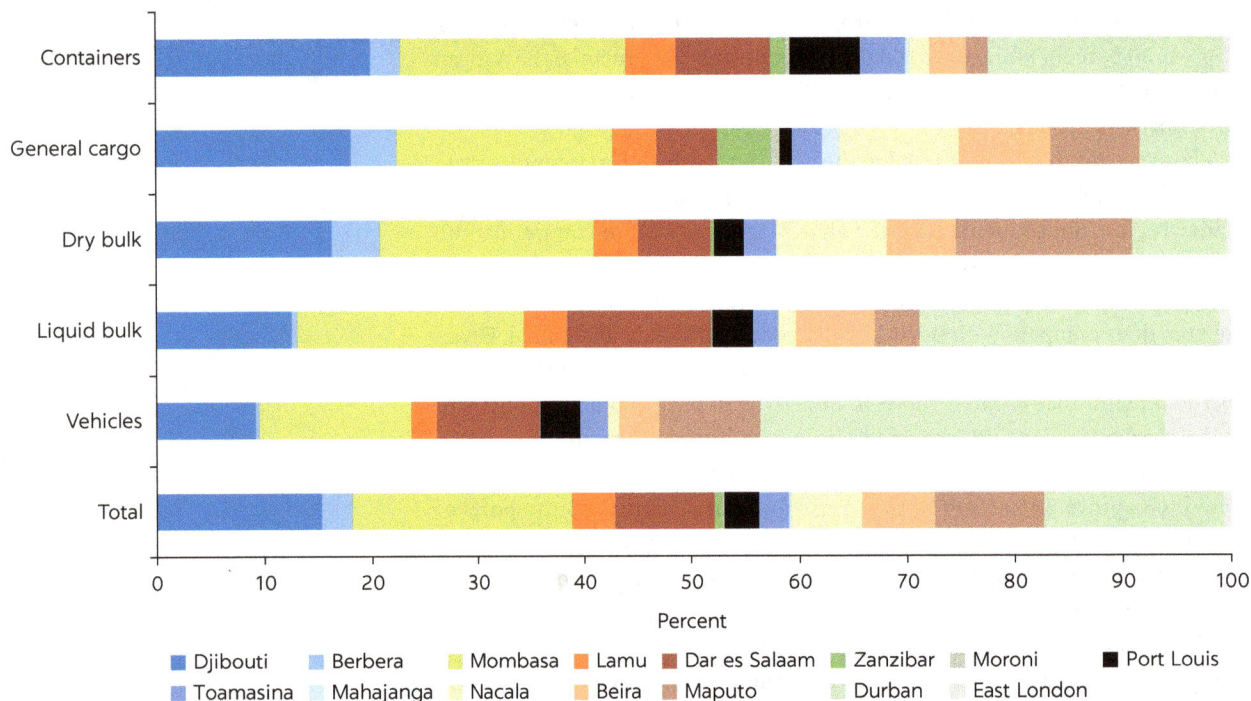

Both the port of Mombasa and the port of Dar es Salaam are projected to increase their market shares between 2016 and 2050 in terms of total ESA port throughput. The market share for the port of Mombasa increases from 15.1 percent in 2016 to 21.3 percent in 2050, whereas the market share for the port of Dar es Salaam increases a more modest 7.6 percent to 8.7 percent. Domestic competition is forecast to strengthen for both Mombasa and Dar es Salaam with the construction of the port of Lamu in Kenya, and the development plans for a large port in Bagamoyo, 65 km north of Dar es Salaam.

Lamu and Bagamoyo ports are projected to capture mainly market share for domestic markets, as the required connectivity with hinterland markets still runs behind in Kenya's and Tanzania's largest ports. One exception is the proposed rail-and-pipeline connections between the port of Lamu and Ethiopia and South Sudan. However, the development of standard gauge railways from the ports of Mombasa and Dar es Salam is further increasing their dominant positions in terms of hinterland connectivity. Consequently, the port of Mombasa is expected to maintain a dominant position in Uganda, South Sudan, and Kenya, while the port of Dar es Salaam retains it leading gateway role for Rwanda, Burundi, and Tanzania.

In Mozambique, the port of Nacala is projected to grow to be the largest general cargo port, the port of Beira the largest container- and liquid bulk–handling port, and the port of Maputo the largest dry bulk and vehicle port. With all volumes combined, the port of Maputo is forecast to become the largest Mozambican port, though dry bulks contribute significantly toward this.

For all three ports, large volumes of coal exports are forecast, with Nacala having commissioned its Nacala-a-Velha coal terminal and associated rail connection to the coal mines in Moatize, the port of Beira expected to rejoin the coal export market with the construction of the Essar Coal Terminal, and the port of Maputo continuing to export large quantities of coal and magnetite from mines in the southeast of South Africa.

The volumes handled in the port of Durban are projected to increase to just under 120 million tons in 2050. Durban is projected to be the largest liquid bulk and vehicle port in the study. With the limited GDP growth projected for South Africa and the increasing competitiveness of the Mozambican ports, the port is expected to see its total market share in the ESA port sector decrease from 36.6 percent in 2016 to 18.5 percent in 2050 based on the total throughput of all ports.

With the port of East London catering primarily to the local Mercedes-Benz factory, the port's growth projection is limited. Furthermore, expansion constraints in the port limit the potential of large expansion projects. As a result, the port is projected to grow at a CAGR of 1.8 percent, 2 percentage points below the average of 3.8 percent.

The ports of Moroni, Zanzibar, Toamasina, Mahajanga, and Port Louis all primarily serve the demand originating from their islands, with only the port of Port Louis handling volumes destined for other markets through transshipment. The ports are expected to grow at CAGR between 3.4 percent and 5.1 percent. Together, the ports are expected to represent 9.1 percent of the total port volumes handled by the ESA ports.

IMPLICATIONS FOR THE INDIVIDUAL PORTS

As noted earlier, container volumes in the ESA countries are predicted to reach about 26 million TEU by 2050, exceeding total available port capacity by nearly 14 million TEU. Depending on growth rates, overall container demand in the 15 ESA ports will begin to exceed current total capacity between 2025 and 2030.

In the case of the individual ports, available capacity in Djibouti is expected to be exceeded by 2028, while by 2050 the demand is expected to be more than twice the currently expected capacity level (approximately 5 million TEU compared with a capacity of about 2.2 million TEU. In Mombasa, the capacity to handle containers is below forecast demand by 2025, and the gap reaches 3 million TEU by 2050. The port of Dar es Salaam is predicted to hit capacity within the next three years.

The container capacity gap relative to expected demand is smaller in Port Louis, Nacala, and Maputo, where capacity in the base case scenario is expected to be adequate up until 2032–35. In the port of Durban, a capacity gap in container-handling operations is expected to emerge by 2028 and grow to about 2 million TEU by 2050.

In the case of general cargo, the capacity gaps are neither as large nor expected as soon. No gaps at all in the base case scenarios are expected for the ports of Djibouti, Berbera, Dar es Salaam, Maputo, Durban, or East London. On the other hand, Mombasa's capacity to handle general cargo is already considered insufficient, and the gap is expected to reach 5 to 6 million tons by 2050. General cargo capacity is also expected to be insufficient in Zanzibar, Moroni, and Mahajanga, and become insufficient in Toamasina and Port Louis by about 2030 and 2040, respectively. In Nacala, demand will start to exceed capacity by 2024, and the gap will reach about 3 million tons by 2050. In Beira, capacity gaps are expected by 2030 and will reach 2 million tons by 2050.

Dry bulk–handling capacity gaps are already seen and are expected to be the largest in the ports of Mombasa (30 million tons by 2050), Berbera (over 7 million tons), Dar es Salaam (8–10 million tons), Maputo (15 million tons), and Durban (about 5 million tons). While small in absolute terms, capacity gaps are also expected to be large relative to demand in the island ports of Zanzibar and Port Louis. In Djibouti, dry-bulk capacity gaps are expected to emerge by 2027–28 and reach 20 million tons by 2050. The port of Nacala is the only one where capacity is expected to be exactly in line with demand throughout the 2018–50 period, while at Beira the available capacity is expected to remain at about 5 million tons above demand.

In the case of liquid bulk, demand is expected to be above capacity in a number of the ports by 2020–25. The capacity gap by 2050 will be particularly large in absolute terms at the ports of Djibouti (about 18 million tons), Mombasa (20 million tons), Dar es Salaam (15 million tons), and Beira (8 million tons), and it will be large relative to available capacity at Port Louis and, especially, Toamasina.

On the other hand, liquid bulk–handling capacity is expected to remain adequate relative to demand in the ports of Zanzibar, Moroni, Durban, and East London, and it will remain nearly sufficient in Maputo. Finally, vehicle-handling capacity is considered sufficient to meet demand in all the study ports, with the exception of Port Louis and Durban.

CONCLUSIONS

The implications of the predicted growth are clear: there is a need for additional port capacity on the ESA coast, and the detailed planning and project preparation to expand port capacity in many of the ports needs to begin now, if it has not begun already.

It is a difficult balancing act, as the required capital investment is both substantial and lumpy, and there is always a risk that the capacity increment comes on stream during a downturn in demand. But in the case of a number of the ports, the delivery of necessary capacity increments already looks late. However, enhancing maritime capacity alone is insufficient, as chapter 5 made clear; improvement is needed in a range of areas in nearly all the ports.

The following chapter presents the conclusions and recommendations, and summarizes the necessary complementary measures, if not precursors, in nearly all the ports, to the proposals and initiatives to increase maritime capacity.

NOTE

1. Minimum draft restrictions depend on the vessel design, which is different for each shipping line. For example, 14,000 TEU ships exist with a depth of 13.0 m (MOL), whereas shipping lines such as CMA, CGM, and Evergreen have fleets consisting of 14,000 TEU ships with a depth of 16.0 m.

REFERENCES

Hellenic Shipping News. 2017. "New Pipeline to Enable Uganda to Export Oil by 2020." http://www.hellenicshippingnews.com/new-pipeline-to-enable-uganda-to-export-oil-by-2020/.

IHS Fairplay. 2016. "Mombasa Vows to Rebuild Transhipment Volumes." http://fairplay.ihs.com/ports/article/4276436/mombasa-vows-to-rebuild-transshipment-volumes.

Moya, J., and M. Valero. 2017. "Port Choice in Container Market: A Literature Review." *Transport Reviews* 37 (3): 300–21. doi: 10.1080/01441647.2016.1231233.

OECD (Organisation for Economic Co-operation and Development). 2016. *Capacity to Grow Transport Infratrsucture Needs for Future Trade Growth*. OECD Publishing.

PMAESA (Port Management Association of Eastern and Southern Africa). 2017. *Zanzibar Ports Corporation*. http://www.pmaesa.org/members/associate/zpc.htm.

Talley, W. K., and M. Ng. 2013. "Maritime Transport Chain Choice by Carriers, Ports and Shippers." *International Journal of Production Economics* 142 (2): 311–16.

Thill, J.-C. 2018. *Design and Estimation of Port Choice Models in Support of Transportation Infrastructure Investment in the Southern African Cone*. University of North Carolina at Charlotte.

Transnet National Ports Authority. 2015. *National Port Plans 2015*. South Africa. https://www.transnetnationalportsauthority.net/Infrastructure%20and%20Port%20Planning/Documents/National%20Port%20Plans%202015.pdf.

UNCTAD (United Nations Conference on Trade and Development). 2018. *Liner Shipping Connectivity Index*. United Nations Conference on Trade and Development.

7 Conclusions and Recommendations

This chapter presents the main findings and recommendations from the study, followed by the specific recommendations for each port.

THE MAIN FINDINGS

There is an urgent need to increase maritime capacity in all the East and Southern Africa ports, with certain caveats

The study has highlighted the growth trends across all the commodity groups in the East and Southern Africa (ESA) ports, and the resulting implications for capacity:

- Depending on growth rates, overall container demand in the 15 ESA ports will start to exceed current total capacity already by between 2025 and 2030;
- Dry bulk handling capacity gaps are already seen and are expected to be the largest in the ports of Mombasa (30 million tons by 2050), Maputo (15 million tons), Dar es Salaam (8–10 million tons), Berbera (over 7 million tons), and Durban (about 5 million tons);
- In the case of general cargo, the capacity gaps are neither as large nor expected as soon. No gaps at all in the base case scenarios are expected for the ports of Djibouti, Berbera, Dar es Salaam, Maputo, Durban, or East London;
- In the case of liquid bulk, demand is expected to be above capacity in a number of the ports by 2020–25. The capacity gap by 2050 will be particularly large in absolute terms at the ports of Mombasa (20 million tons), Djibouti (about 18 million tons), Dar es Salaam (15 million tons), and Beira (8 million tons), and it will be large relative to available capacity at Port Louis and, especially, Toamasina.

It is evident capacity enhancement is needed, and planning for the capacity enhancement needs to start now, if it has not already begun.

However, expansion and development plans of the individual ports need to reflect the trends in the shipping industry, the potential role of the port relative to both existing and new competing ports, and the landside access issues. Increasing maritime capacity without adequately considering these issues will undermine the efficiency of a port, prevent the realization of the full benefit from the maritime capacity enhancement, and subvert the strategic ambitions of a port.

There is a need to improve operating efficiency in all the ports

The analysis shows that the average technical efficiency of container terminal operations in the 10 ESA ports (Beira, Dar es Salaam, Djibouti, Durban, East London, Maputo, Mombasa, Nacala, Port Louis, and Toamasina) falls in a range of 44–53 percent for the 2000–10 data set. In other words, the ports in ESA are less than half as productive as the matched ports in the data set in terms of efficiency in container-handling operations. These matched ports are also not the global leaders, so performance gaps relative to the leading container handling ports would be even more significant.

The ranking is constant, more or less, across the different models; Durban, Mombasa, Dar es Salaam, and Port Sudan are the most efficient ports in terms of container handling, while Beira, East London, and Nacala are the least efficient. Globally, the port of Mombasa, based on this data set, is the most technically efficient port, and ranks as the 43rd most efficient container port in the global sample. Dar es Salaam and Durban follow at the 64th and 70th positions respectively for container operations.

The analysis also reveals that the main factors that drive the higher efficiency in container handling in these ports are the presence of a specialist private terminal operator, the existence of an effective rail connection to the port, the existence of transshipment traffic, a higher score on the Connectivity Index, and reduced vessel time at berth.

There is a need for greater integration in the supply chain

The global port industry has for some time been impacted by vertical and horizontal integration among producers (port operators and port authorities [PAs]), terminal operators, shipping lines, and land transport.

Within the maritime industry, key examples of horizontal integration are the container shipping alliances, where shipping lines pool together their respective fleets, moving containers for each other, to extend their service offerings and geographic coverage. In the port subsector, the most important horizontal integration trends are the development of global terminal operators (GTOs) that are operating port terminals globally, and the cooperation among PAs nationally and internationally (Van de Voorde and Vanelslander 2009).

The degree of horizontal integration is relatively high in the ports of Djibouti, Mahajanga, Maputo, and the two South African ports. Horizontal integration is also relatively strong in the port of Moroni. In the port of Maputo, DP World and Grindrod are present as port–terminal operators in multiple ports in the region, and CFM (Portos e Caminhos de Ferro de Moçambique) as a national PA is also involved in the other ports in Mozambique, in various public-private partnership (PPP) structures. In Durban and East London, Transnet National Ports Authority (TNPA) is the national PA of South Africa, and Transnet Port

Terminals (TPT) serves as the main operator of container, general cargo, and roll on–roll off (Ro-Ro) terminals in the country. Private operators Bidfreight and Grindrod, serving Durban, are large South African general cargo terminal operators that are also active in other ports on the continent.

The degree of horizontal integration is less advanced in Mombasa and Dar es Salaam. In the case of Mombasa, Kenya Ports Authority (KPA) is a nationwide PA that is also responsible for developments of other ports in the country (such as Lamu). In Dar es Salaam, Tanzania Ports Authority (TPA) is a nationwide PA that is also responsible for the development of ports in the country (e.g., Bagamoyo). But the specialization that would be expected from horizontal integration is not yet visible.

An example of vertical integration by public-sector entities in the port sector concerns the role of PAs or terminal operators (TOs) as cluster managers. In this role, PAs or TOs are involved in the development or the operation of rail and road hinterland links, logistics platforms, and port terminals to offer efficient and reliable transport services to shippers, and thereby maximize the flow of goods through the port (Baccelli, Percoco, and Tedeschi 2008).

In the ESA port sector, vertical integration is visible, but to a lesser extent than it is in the more economically developed countries. Furthermore, vertical integration in some countries in the project region is driven by the public sector authorities themselves, while in developed countries these trends are usually driven by the private sector.

The degree of vertical integration is strongest in the ports of Djibouti, Mombasa, Toamasina, Port Louis, Durban, and the three Mozambican ports. In Djibouti, logistics services are provided through a network of container depots and inland container depots (ICDs) in Djibouti and in Ethiopia, and the logistics services for hinterland transport are largely in control of a single entity: Ethiopian state-owned ESLSE (Ethiopian Shipping & Logistics Services Enterprise) can be regarded as a fourth-party logistics provider (4PL) that uses different service providers in Djibouti and asset-based Ethiopian trucking companies to provide their services to Ethiopian importers and exporters.

There is limited vertical integration in the port of Dar es Salaam, excepting the ICDs and container freight stations (CFSs) that are available, operated by TPA and by private logistics operators. The amount of systemic organization between terminal operations and landside transport is negligible. There is also no effective gate management system. Vertical integration is also absent outside Berbera, Moroni, and Mahajanga.

Improving landside access is crucial

One challenge that is faced by all the ESA ports, almost without exception, is the need to improve landside access. In the case of many, the issue of landside access is more important than improving maritime access and capacity. There are three main constraints: (1) limited or no intermodality, (2) poor-quality road connectivity and delays at the border crossing points, and (3) congestion at the port-city interface.

Limited or no intermodality

Current connectivity from ESA's ports to hinterland destinations still depends primarily on a road network of variable quality and coverage. Despite this, more than 70 percent of all cargo to or from the ports is carried by road transport. If one excludes South Africa, the figure increases to 90 percent. A significant part of the ESA railway network is in a poor state, and most rail lines are single track and not electrified, with the exception of South Africa.

Roads and borders

While the core regional road network on the main trading corridors is in good to fair condition, there are some sections in poor condition, and there are some missing links. But a major issue across the region is the efficacy and the efficiency of road maintenance. Despite the substantial investments made in road infrastructure in the past, limitations in management, inadequate enforcement of axle-load restrictions, inadequate maintenance practices, and inadequate resources have led to premature deterioration of the roads and increased transport costs in many countries.

Also, the border crossing points (BCPs), despite improvements in many locations, remain a significant point of delay and additional cost: an analysis of the road corridor on the Southern North–South Corridor revealed that border posts were responsible for 15 percent of the total monetary costs (comprising 1 percent, 1 percent, and 13 percent for Beitbridge, Chirundu, and Kasumbalesa respectively) and 37 percent of the total travel time (comprising 13 percent, 11 percent, and 13 percent for Beitbridge, Chirundu, and Kasumbalesa respectively) for the movement of a consignment between Durban and Lusaka.

The port-city interface

The final major challenge for many of the ESA ports in terms of access is the port-city interface. The evolution and development of ports creates a number of benefits for their host cities and countries, as ports and their related services and industries create substantial employment for local workers. As port traffic has grown, port-related labor demand has increased, usually unskilled and from the immediate vicinity of the port. While increased containerization and mechanization in a port has diminished the number of unskilled cargo handlers, ports generally remain significant local employers.

Despite the benefits, the negative impact of ports on cities—both direct and indirect—are substantial. These externalities range from environmental issues—air emissions, water pollution, or soil pollution—to congestion issues and safety risks. Port-induced city congestion is the most notable negative externality present in and around the ESA ports. Many cities grew around the existing port, with roads running through the city centers and suburbs, and few cities have attempted to address these concerns in a substantive manner.

There is a need to improve stakeholder engagement

The relationship between the port and its stakeholders—including, but not only, the users of the port, is an essential component of good management and operation. However, it is not equally strong and formalized across the ESA ports. The relationship between port and stakeholders is relatively good—and the most formalized—in Mombasa, Beira, and the two South African ports. In Mombasa, it takes place through the Mombasa Port Community Charter, although the Mombasa municipality is not part of the port charter. In Beira, there are port-consulting forums between CdM (Cornelder de Moçambique), CFM, the municipality, and port users that are used to balance the interests of all parties.

In Durban, the Transnet eTheKwini Municipality Planning Initiative (TEMPI) was initially established as a planning document between Transnet and eTheKwini Municipality (eTKM), related to port-city infrastructure planning. As this document mainly concerned planning, not implementation, the TEMPI evolved to its current format, the Transnet City Forum. Furthermore, TNPA and TPT engage with port users through the Port Oversight Committees.

The relationship with stakeholders is more limited in the ports of Berbera and Dar es Salaam. In Dar es Salaam, although the port's growth is currently hampered by a serious lack of sufficient landside transport capacity, there is limited systematic dialogue or integrated planning between the PA and the urban authorities. Equally surprisingly, there is no systematic dialogue on the development of the port-and-hinterland connectivity with representatives of shipping lines, trucking companies, rail operators, forwarders, and cargo owners.

In Berbera, there is little to no communication between the port, the municipality, and other stakeholders on the development of the port. The large number of development agencies working on the port has brought some dialogue between the port and its stakeholders, but this has not been institutionalized.

There is a need to introduce modern management systems

Despite the importance of comprehensive information management systems, in a number of the ports, the current method of operation in the terminals is characterized by operational and administrative procedures for which approval and information exchange is carried out on paper, in offices at multiple locations inside the port operations area. Also, import cargo is subject to customs inspection inside the operational area of the port, and agents and truck drivers walk between offices inside the operations area, resulting in operational delays and—with many trucks, cars, and individuals inside the operational area—causing safety and security risks as well as obstructing efficient cargo and equipment flow.

Although many ports in the ESA region provide services that could be part of a port community system (PCS) (single-window, tracking–tracing, automatic data interchanges, or truck appointment systems), there are only three that operate a full PCS similar to that of the Portbase system used in the Netherlands: Port Louis, Durban, and East London. The port of Djibouti is in the final phase of implementing its PCS by connecting private sector entities to the current public system. In the port of Maputo, Maputo Port Development Company (MPDC) and CFM jointly made investments in information technology (IT) and systems, such as the MCNET single-window system and terminal operating systems (Zodiac and CommTracTM).

Kenya's KPA and its partners (KENTRADE), as well as the government of Madagascar, have made substantial investments in IT and in single windows and terminal operating systems. In some cases, the private operators invested in terminal operating systems and gate management systems. In other ports, there is little movement toward a substantive PCS, with some terminals, operated by the port authority, still running inefficient paper-based systems that attempt to mirror a modern IT system; the publically operated berths in Dar es Salaam port are examples.

There is an overreliance on public investment in port development and expansion

Ports require considerable infrastructure in order to fulfill their function and compete successfully. The necessary infrastructure is large, lumpy in an economic sense, and expensive. Traditionally, the development of ports has relied on public investment, which remains the predominant approach in the ESA countries. However, elsewhere in the world, this reliance on the public purse changed from the 1980s onward, with private investment being utilized for equipment, the superstructure initially, and more recently in financing the construction of entire terminals, including quay walls, land reclamation, dredging, and the superstructure. The recent concession for Tema port in Ghana also included the construction of a new access road.

There is an advantage to utilizing the experience of specialist terminal operators

Ports and terminals benefit from the participation of private terminal operators, not only by leveraging private capital and reducing the level of necessary public investment, but also from the transfer of expertise, managerial incentives, and technologies. A transaction can be designed to protect the strategic interests of a country, but a specialist terminal operator can provide a port with a competitive edge relative to its regional peers. Many ports in West Africa have seen efficiency improvements after moving to a landlord model and bringing in a specialist terminal operator.

The institutional framework of all the ports needs improvement

The policy framework

The assessment reveals that the majority of the ESA countries perform poorly in terms of the policy framework, in the following respects: (1) policy documents are not regularly updated; (2) there is a lack of transparency in terms of the criteria for investment decisions and the financing of port investments; (3) the role of the private sector in financing and operating in ports is unclear; and (4) there is limited attention toward monitoring and evaluation.

The legal and regulatory framework

Madagascar, Mauritius, Tanzania, and South Africa perform best in terms of legal and regulatory practices for their port sectors. Djibouti, Kenya, and Zanzibar in Tanzania have suboptimal scores on the legal and institutional evaluation. Somalia, Mozambique, and the Comoros attain the lowest scores of the ESA countries. Djibouti, Somalia, and Mozambique all lack a port-sector regulator. Tanzania has a regulator, but as in many countries, capacity constraints and the asymmetry of information undermine the ability of the agency to fulfill the function of an independent regulator.

Most of the port acts—the laws providing the legal basis for port management, development, and operation—do not consider or enable modern PPP practices. Accordingly, the majority of the port acts in the region still prescribe that PAs are responsible for development, maintenance, and operations of ports, despite the opposite being the reality in many countries.

The port management models

The primary weakness in all the ESA countries, with the singular exception of South Africa, is the lack of an independent regulator with sufficient resources and capacity to ensure effective auditing, monitoring, and tariff regulation in the port sector. For example, in seven of the countries—Djibouti, Kenya, Zanzibar in Tanzania, the Comoros, Madagascar, Mauritius, and Mozambique—the PAs regulate themselves in terms of the scale and structure of tariffs.

Second, despite the explicit objective of a number of governments to move toward the landlord port management model, in many countries in the region, port operations are still carried out in whole or in part by the PAs themselves, using their own employees (Kenya and Tanzania in part plus Zanzibar), or by publicly owned companies working as operators (Mauritius and South Africa). While neither is ideal, the latter, at least, offers the advantage of transparency with regard to the profit and costs of port operations, and avoidance of implicit cross-subsidization.

Finally, the national policy-making and planning function, which would logically lie with the line ministry, in practice lies with the PA in five of the ESA countries—Djibouti, Kenya, Tanzania, Madagascar, and Mauritius.

Port tariffs

With respect to the structure and scale of tariffs, most of the ports in the region use a structure consistent with international norms, with certain exceptions.

- In a number of the ports, there are anomalies in the tariff structures, such as charging of berthing dues based on gross registered tonnage (GRT) per hour instead of the preferred meters per hour.
- In the port of Dar es Salaam, the wharfage charge included in the tariff book for noncontainerized cargoes is charged on an ad valorem basis, causing a double "tax" on the value of the cargo, from the charge of the PA and the customs authority.
- The ports of Berbera and the Comoros do not charge berthing dues per time unit but, instead, per vessel call.
- In the case of Djibouti, the fixed fees charged per volume class for pilotage, towage, and mooring services overcharge small vessels and undercharge large vessels.
- For several ports, parts of the tariff books are lacking completely.
- None of the ports apply an incentive-based tariff scheme to stimulate 24/7 operations on the port's landside.

THE SPECIFIC RECOMMENDATIONS FOR EACH PORT

This section summarizes the specific recommendations for each port, considered to be necessary complements, if not essential precursors, to maritime capacity enhancement. They are broadly categorized as short-term actions and medium-term actions. There is no suggestion that the former are greater priorities than the latter, merely a pragmatic assessment that they might be easier to introduce to begin to mitigate some of the challenges faced by the ESA ports.

Djibouti

Short-term actions

- Address the current weaknesses in the tariff book:
  - Despite making a broad distinction among the volume classes, the fixed fees charged per volume class for pilotage, towage, and mooring services overcharge small vessels and undercharge large vessels. Large vessels require more resources (more tug boats, more personnel for mooring) and should be charged accordingly.
  - The port tariff book does not charge the port's users for light dues.
- To reduce port-engendered congestion in the city, Djibouti Ports & Free Zones Authority (DPFZA) should introduce the following:
  - Terminal appointment system
  - Variable port fees as an incentive to use off-peak hours
  - Proper transport documentation required before gate arrival
- Introduce a more systematic, structured, and frequent meeting forum for port and city stakeholders to discuss port-city issues.
- Encourage greater modal shift: the new railway line from Ethiopia has the potential to transport substantial volumes, formerly carried by road haulage—and the port authority should focus on working with the terminal and rail operators to provide incentives for modal shift and ensure the last-mile connectivity is in place.

Medium-term actions

- Address the current weaknesses in the institutional framework:
  - Establish an independent port sector regulator in Djibouti.
  - Define and establish a clear national government policy on transport or the maritime sector in Djibouti.
  - Clarify the chain of command or collaboration between national and local policy makers.
  - Prepare clear guidelines on the type, size, or nature of private sector investments in the nation's ports and port sector and specify criteria.
- Further the implementation of the landlord management model in the port—the trend toward vertical integration in the container shipping industry underlines the importance of this move, both to improve efficiency and to ensure the status of the port in the hierarchy.
- Improve the landside access: As Djibouti's terminals are located outside the city, there is no immediate need to upgrade the port's immediate access road. However, the hinterland road network to Ethiopia needs to be upgraded.
- There are limited environmental measures taken to reduce the negative externalities for the adjacent city. Policy measures that could be implemented by the DPFZA include the following:
  - Introduce variable port fees as incentives for the use of less polluting vessels.
  - Regulate truck emissions through truck retirement programs.
  - Install facilities to cater to the "cold ironing"—shore-to-ship power—of vessels calling at the port of Djibouti.

Berbera

Short-term actions

- Address the current weaknesses in the tariff book:
  - o The berthing dues are currently not charged per time unit, but per vessel call. Vessels using a berth for a longer amount of time require more resources and should be charged accordingly.
  - o Mooring dues are currently independent of the size of the vessel. This also represents potential revenue that is not charged: larger vessels require more mooring operations and should be charged accordingly.
  - o There are no published storage tariffs for noncontainerized cargoes. However, it is likely that they are, in practice, applicable, so no opinion can be given on the missed potential revenues.
  - o There are no published gate-handling fees. The use of the port's entrance gates comes at a cost for the port authority, and therefore should come at a cost toward the port's users.
- Introduce a more systematic, structured, and frequent meeting forum for port and city stakeholders to discuss port-city issues.

Medium-term actions

- Address the weaknesses in the institutional framework:
  - o Establish an independent port sector regulator.
  - o Define and introduce an integrated policy for Somaliland's port sector.
  - o Ensure and clarify a clear chain of command or collaboration between national and local policy makers.
  - o Prepare clear guidelines and criteria on the type, size, or nature of private sector investments in the nation's ports and port sector.
- Try to deliver competitive logistics services: to provide competitive logistics services, an investment program in the transport sector is essential. The truck fleet is antiquated, and there is little or no use of modern IT systems in the transport sector. There are few, if any, independently operated warehouses, as all importers collect their cargoes themselves.
- Develop a national port master plan to reflect the link among the different developments. Planning of these ports has been undertaken in isolation by the PAs. This planning function should be improved, and the development of a port and logistics master plan that includes involvement of port stakeholders is regarded a necessity.
- Improve landside access: the hinterland network both within the country and the wider region, including Ethiopia, needs to be improved and upgraded.

Mombasa/Lamu

Short-term actions

- Facilitate modal shift from road to rail: the new railway line from Mombasa has the potential to transport substantial flows of cargo and enable a modal shift from road to rail. Rail is the preferred mode from an environmental and social perspective, and the port authority should focus on enabling this shift. Obligated modal shift agreements in the contracts of (public) terminal operators should therefore be considered.
- Improve the port's road connections: the current road network within Mombasa and across the causeway faces substantial issues associated with

truck traffic. This should be resolved in the short term in order for the port's hinterland connections to remain efficient or become efficient again.

Medium-term actions

- Address the anomalies in the institutional framework:
  - Clarify the policy goals; those set out in the National Transport Policy document are not bound to a timeframe and remain general statements (e.g., "Government of Kenya shall expedite plans to construct a new port at Lamu").
  - The National Transport Policy document does not provide an overview of financing principles for the sector, or a way in which the government plans to fund the policy goals.
  - The National Transport Policy document does not present criteria for investment decisions or proposed allocation of investments.
  - There are different legal and regulatory mandates for two major ports: according to the KPA Act, the KPA is fully responsible to maintain, operate, improve, and regulate all seaports in the country, but the development of the Lamu Port is allocated to the Lamu Port–South Sudan–Ethiopia Transport (LAPSSET) Corridor Development Authority under Gazette Supplement No. 51, Legal Notice No. 58, 2003.
  - Continue to implement the landlord-port management model: The possibilities to develop and implement port PPPs under the current legal and regulatory framework are unclear:
    - The KPA Act provides possibilities to outsource port activities.
    - The PPP legislation (PPP Act and Regulations) offers a valid legal ground for the design and the implementation of a PPP arrangement.
    - The Merchant Shipping Act states that shipping services providers cannot, directly or indirectly, be engaged in terminal operation services.
    - The KPA in its handbook states that it is not willing to move to a landlord port status.

Dar es Salaam

Short-term actions

- Address the anomalies in the institutional framework:
  - The berthing dues that are paid are based on GRT, while they should be directly related to the length dimension of the vessel.
  - The wharfage charge that is included in the tariff book for noncontainerized cargoes is charged on an ad valorem basis, causing a double "tax" on the value of the cargo because of the charges of both the port authority and the customs authority. This is not in line with activity-based costing principles and provides an overestimation of costs to port users.
  - Clarify and establish port safety and environmental protection responsibilities and measures.
  - Update the 2009 National Port Master Plan.
  - Remove the unjustified and expensive 100 percent scanning and 100 percent verification of all containers.
  - Remove the mandatory requirement for shipping offices to be open 24 hours if they have no vessel coming to the port.

- To reduce port-engendered congestion in the city, TPA should introduce the following:
  - o Terminal appointment system.
  - o Variable port fees as incentives for the use of off-peak hours.
  - o Ensure proper transport documentation before gate arrival.
  - o Introduce a robust and effective gate-management system.
- Introduce a more systematic, structured, and frequent meeting forum for port and city stakeholders to discuss port-city issues.
- Allow transit cargo to be nominated to one or more TPA-approved ICD(s), especially Congo cargo, which has 30 free days and cannot be sent outside the port. This action is important, because space issues are significantly negatively impacting the Tanzania International Container Terminal Services' (TICTS') ability to handle cargo efficiently.
- Introduce a one-stop shop for document checking in the City of Dar es Salaam instead of outside the TICTS main gates as is currently the case.
- Introduce better articulated and planned traffic management within the port area, especially related to imports and exports.
- Locate space to remove from the port area the unused TPA-owned equipment. This would allow TICTS to have an additional 110 m berth length and to berth a third ship.

Medium-term actions

- Address the anomalies in the institutional framework:
  - o The National Transport Policy document does not present criteria for investment decisions or proposed allocation of investments, nor does the National Port Master Plan.
  - o TPA has a major responsibility and power over the country's port sector, and currently provides numerous functions that a modern landlord is not expected to undertake (e.g., national port policy-making and planning function, internal legal practices, all port operators' functions, the nautical services function, and internal auditing practices).
  - o The TPA Act makes clear that TPA's function is not to provide port services (including terminal operations). It can only provide port services in case a contracted operator is not performing, and only for a period of up to 2 years, unless the Minister extends such period with a maximum of a further 2 years.
- TPA needs to continue to implement and extend the landlord-port management model and bring in more specialist terminal operators, including a second specialist container terminal operator, as part of the necessary expansion of the port.
- Strengthen the competitive position of the port with respect to transit cargo: the competitive position of Dar es Salaam for transit cargo is under pressure, hence TPA needs to
  - o Introduce the modern IT systems (PCS, port/terminal operating system [P/TOS]) that are currently completely lacking in the port.
  - o Engage in dialogue with the port stakeholders on the efficient integration of the ICDs to realize more capacity in the port.
- Improve hinterland connectivity:
  - o The current road network within and close to Dar es Salaam is heavily congested and needs substantive and substantial improvement.
  - o Facilitate a modal shift from road to rail, using incentives rather than mandates.

Zanzibar

Short-term actions

- Address the anomalies in the institutional framework:
  - The National Port Master Plan dates from 2006 and needs to be updated.
  - The berthing dues that are paid are based on GRT, which should be directly related to the length dimension of the vessel.
- Introduce a more systematic, structured, and frequent meeting forum for port and city stakeholders to discuss port-city issues.

Medium-term actions

- Address the anomalies in the institutional framework:
  - The National Transport Policy documents do not present criteria for investment decisions or proposed allocation of investments, nor does the Multipurpose Port Master Plan.
  - There are no clear guidelines on the type, size, or nature of private-sector investments in the nation's ports and port sector, nor have any criteria been specified.
  - The limited clarity on the designation of port managerial responsibilities and associated monitoring bodies, which in the Ports Act is described as "control," could be interpreted differently to "management."
  - The financing principles regarding port construction or development are not specifically drafted in the legal and regulatory frameworks of Zanzibar.

Moroni

Short-term actions

- Address the anomalies in the institutional framework:
  - The three autonomous port authorities currently tasked with executing the central port policy have no role in drafting any national or local policies.
- Improve spatial and operating efficiency:
  - Relocate the entrance gate of the port to the southern part of the terminal.
  - Develop the access roads to and from the port.
  - Pave the empty container yard and develop a container freight station.
  - Purchase additional tugs to enable faster operations for barges.
- Introduce a more systematic, structured, and frequent meeting forum for port and city stakeholders to discuss port-city issues.
- Ensure competitive port facilities and operations: the port-related aspects such as the available draft, quay length, equipment, and operations are currently at a very low level and cause substantial competitive drawbacks. To resolve this issue, the preparation for improvement in port infrastructure and equipment needs to begin now.

Medium-term actions

- Address the anomalies in the institutional framework:
  - The main shortcoming of the existing legal and regulatory framework is the absence of enforcement of the SCP (Société Comorienne des Ports) Act. The government has signaled its ambition to modernize the legal and regulatory framework by voting in favor of the act, but as of yet has not been able to implement the law.

- Ensure competitive logistics services: to provide these, an investment program in the transport sector for these ports is a must-have. The truck fleets are outdated and there are little or no IT systems used in the transport sector. There are often no independently operated warehouses, as all importers collect their cargo themselves.
- Engage in formal port master planning: planning has usually been done in isolation by the PA. This planning function should be improved, and the development of a port and logistics master plan that includes involvement of port stakeholders is regarded as a necessity.

Mahajanga

Short-term actions
- Address the anomalies in the institutional framework:
  - The main shortcoming of the Malagasy port sector policy framework is the lack of an official policy document at the national level. This is particularly surprising considering the vast population served by the country's ports.
- Improve port access roads: the quality of the port access roads is a major issue, on a local scale within the city and in the hinterland.
  - Create a dedicated truck waiting area to reduce congestion outside the main gate.
  - Assure proper transport documentation before gate arrival.
- Introduce a more systematic, structured, and frequent meeting forum for port and city stakeholders to discuss port-city issues.
- Ensure competitive port facilities and operations: the port-related aspects such as the available draft, quay length, equipment, and operations are currently at a very low level and cause substantial competitive drawbacks. To resolve this, the preparation for improvement in port infrastructure and equipment needs to begin now.

Medium-term actions
- Ensure competitive logistics services: to provide these, an investment program in the transport sector is a must-have. The truck fleets are outdated, and there are little or no IT systems used in the transport sector. There often are no independently operated warehouses, as all importers collect their cargo themselves.
- Engage in formal port master planning: planning of these ports has usually been done in isolation by the PAs. This planning function should be improved, and the development of a port and logistics master plan that includes involvement of port stakeholders is regarded a necessity.

Toamasina

Short-term actions
- Address the anomalies in the institutional framework:
  - The main shortcoming of the Malagasy port sector policy framework is the lack of an official policy document at the national level. This is particularly surprising considering the vast population served by the country's ports.

- To alleviate the congestion on the port access road, the following recommendations could be implemented:
  - Improve the rail infrastructure connecting the port of Toamasina to local markets and Antananarivo, and subsequently stimulate the modal shift from road to rail.
  - Construct a dedicated port access road.
  - Given the large peak of trucks during the day, the SPAT (Société du Port à Gestion Autonome de Toamasina) could implement terminal appointment systems or promote off-peak operating hours.
- Strengthen environmental measures taken to reduce the negative externalities for the adjacent city. Policy measures which could be implemented by the SPAT include the following:
  - Use variable port fees as incentives for use of less-polluting vessels.
  - Install facilities to cater for the cold ironing.
  - Measure and regulate noise levels.
- Introduce a more systematic, structured, and frequent meeting forum for port and city stakeholders to discuss port-city issues.

Medium-term actions

- Ensure a competitive approach toward transit cargoes: for the second-generation ports, transit cargoes are of enormous importance. Especially the hinterland connections can be strongly improved through the availability of proper rail connections.
- Ensure a modal shift.
- Continue port development based on formalized planning and a PPP focus.

Nacala

Short-term actions

- Address the anomalies in the institutional framework:
  - Some outdated policy and planning documents are in need of an update such as the National Transport Strategy (2009, with an updated presentation of 2013).
  - The current port tariff structure in Nacala lacks many of the preferred tariff structures that are typically charged to earn back certain infrastructure investments, especially in the vessel charge category, including port dues and berthing dues.
- Though the impact of the port on the environment is addressed by PdN (Portos do Norte) in their statements, additional measures could be considered to limit the port's impact on the local community:
  - Establish variable port fees as incentives to use less-polluting vessels.
  - Regulate truck emissions through truck retirement programs.
  - Introduce a more systematic, structured, and frequent meeting forum for port and city stakeholders to discuss port-city issues.
- Attract funding to develop ICDs to mitigate storage constraints at the port and terminals and reduce the truck traffic directed to the port.

Medium-term actions

- Address the anomalies in the institutional framework:
  - There is a lack of sustainable development plans toward the environment, which only exist at high level.
  - There is a lack of financing principles included in the policy goals. It is unclear how CFM or the government of Mozambique and its ministries

aim to finance the proposed port investment plans that are listed in the different policy documents.

- o There is a lack of guidance regarding the division of responsibilities of port development and port operations in the national policy documentation. CFM is a public company which oversees all Mozambican ports. However, for each of the different ports, a different port development and operational structure is used.
- o The National Transport Strategy document does not present criteria for investment decisions.
- o There is a lack of principles for the development of legislation regarding the port and transport sector.
- Invest in the rehabilitation and maintenance of the railway to Malawi and improve rail operations.
- Though the impact and maintenance of the port on the environment is addressed by PdN in their statements, additional measures could be considered to limit the port's impact on the local community:
  - o Install facilities to cater for the cold ironing of vessels calling the port of Nacala.
- Continue port development based on formalized planning and a PPP focus.

Beira

Short-term actions

- Address the anomalies in the institutional framework:
  - o Port dues are based on a fixed amount per vessel and are not linked to the vessel dimensions. Not only does this represent a potentially foregone financial gain, it also does not adhere to the principle of activity-based costing. Large vessels require more expensive port infrastructure and should be charged accordingly.
  - o Towage is charged per hour, irrespective of the number of tugs required for the operation.
  - o Mooring operations are charged as a single fixed fee and do not have any connection with the vessel dimensions.
  - o The cargo-handling costs consist of multiple elements, including the equipment charge, the stevedoring charge, and a terminal charge. These different charges overlap the cargo-handling costs and vessel-handling costs.
  - o The Beira tariff book does not include lighthouse dues, berthing dues, or a gate-handling fee.
  - o The National Transport Strategy (2009), with an updated presentation dating to 2013, is in need of an update.
- Strengthen environmental measures taken to reduce the negative externalities for the adjacent city. Policy measures which could be considered by CdM include the following:
  - o Introduce variable port fees as incentives to use less-polluting vessels.
  - o Install facilities to cater for the cold ironing.
  - o Measure and regulate noise levels.

Medium-term actions

- Improve the port's road connections.
- Monitor the improvements of the new truck-waiting areas and access roads to the port. Although this is envisioned to decrease the queue of

trucks outside the entrance of the port, it could be that the new operational procedures associated with this development are not in line with the projections.

- Connections to Malawi could be much improved if a 40 km rail track would be developed in Malawi. This would provide Beira a direct rail connection to Blantyre. Investments in the rail network would be needed, including proper rolling stock.
- CdM should focus on stimulating a modal shift from road to rail, especially if the rail corridor to Malawi materializes.
- Continue port development based on formalized planning and a PPP focus: the level of logistics services and terminal operations in many of these ports is currently at agreeable levels for the region. Still, these ports should ensure that they at minimum retain their positions and continue the development of ports and terminals as was done in the past decades.

Maputo

Short-term actions
- Address the anomalies in the institutional framework:
  - Some outdated policy and planning documents are in need of an update: National Transport Strategy (2009, with an updated presentation of 2013) and the Maputo Master Plan (2011).
  - The port dues (entry charges) are based on two categories: vessels larger than 500 GRT and vessels smaller than 500 GRT, whereby vessels larger than 500 GRT are charged a lower port entry fee. Not only does this represent a potentially foregone financial gain, it also does not adhere to the principle of activity-based costing. Large vessels require more expensive port infrastructure and should be charged accordingly.
  - The marine service tariff book of the MPDC includes a government charge (by INAHINA, Mozambique's National Institute of Hydrography and Navigation) of US$0.232 per GRT per entry, which is an uncommon charge in the preferred structure.
  - International Ship and Port Facility Security (ISPS) security charge of US$150 is added to the tariff book (inwards only).
  - A dredging fund charge of of US$810 is applied for vessels >5,000 GRT (inwards only).
  - A channel fee of US$0.40 per GRT is applied for vessels (inwards only).
- To limit congestion in the city, especially during peak hours, MPDC can impose the following regulations:
  - Establish terminal appointment systems.
  - Promote off-peak operating hours.
  - Assure proper transport documentation before gate arrival.

Medium-term actions
- Address the anomalies in the institutional framework:
  - There is a lack of sustainable development plans toward the environment, which only exist on a high level.
  - There is a lack of financing principles included in the policy goals. It is unclear how CFM or the government of Mozambique and its ministries aim to finance the proposed port investment plans that are listed in the different policy documents.

- There is a lack of guidance regarding the division of responsibilities of port development and port operations in the national policy documentation. CFM is a public company that oversees all Mozambican ports. However, for each port, a different port development and operational structure is used.
- The National Transport Strategy document does not present criteria for investment decisions.
- There is a lack of principles for the development of legislation regarding the port and transport sector.
- CFM's legal and regulatory mandate is defined in very broad, general terms. It does not specify clearly which roles and responsibilities shall remain with the public sector.
- There is no regulator in the port and railway sector that regulates the activities of CFM and its concessions.
- To facilitate a further shift from road to rail, inefficiencies with rail transport at the South African border posts need to be resolved.
- Relocation of specific bulk cargo storage areas should be priorities. This can reduce the number of vehicle movements within the port by limiting double-handling. As a result, carbon dioxide emission levels can be brought down and air quality around the port can be improved.
- In collaboration between CFM, MPDC, and the municipality, a common port-city master plan should be drafted to address specific topics such as port-city zoning and port-induced city congestion.
- Continue port development based on formalized planning and a PPP focus.

Port Louis

Short-term actions
- Address the anomalies in the institutional framework:
  - The policy documents do not present clear financing principles apart from statements that allocate the development tasks to Mauritius Ports Authority (MPA).
  - Some outdated policy and planning documents are in urgent need of an update, such as the National Development Plan, which dates to 2003, and then they need to be enforced.
  - There is a clear contradiction between policy statements and policy implementation on private-sector participation. It is recommended that the MPA present a single vision that is clear on its future as a landlord port, or as a port authority and shareholder at a terminal operator level.
  - Clarify the regulatory responsibilities in the sector: MPA is the landlord port authority, responsible for regular landlord tasks, and is also functioning as the port regulator.
- To limit congestion in the city of Port Louis, MPA can impose the following regulations:
  - Introduce terminal appointment systems.
  - Promote off-peak operating hours.
  - Assure proper transport documentation before gate arrival.

Medium-term actions
- Address the anomalies in the institutional framework:
  - The MPA has substantial freedom to invest as per section 18 of the Ports Act. This autonomy is generally regarded as positive, but in this case is

regarded as providing too much autonomy. For example, the MPA may do the following:

- Invest any sums not immediately required for the purposes of its business in any investment or loans.
- Acquire any land or building wherever situated, or any interest therein.
- Form or subscribe to the share capital of a company or enter into a management contract with any company or other person, for the purpose of managing its investments.

  o It is therefore recommended that the powers of the MPA be somewhat restricted, especially in terms of the above-mentioned clauses that could lead to investments of assets or entering into management contracts that are not necessarily required by a port authority.

  o The powers of the MPA over concessionaires are very strong in the current Act. In the current system where the port authority has a substantial shareholding in the single concessionaire of the port, this is not a major issue. If there were a desire to enter into more or other concession agreements with private operators, this would become a problem, as it is expected that private operators would not appreciate the differences in power between the MPA and a concessionaire, as per section 37 of the Act:

    - The Authority may at any time suspend or revoke a concession contract or license upon breach of any condition of the contract or license or upon any failure to comply with any provision of this Act or any regulations.
    - Where a contract or license is suspended or revoked, the Authority may—if it considers that such suspension or revocation would materially affect the movement of cargoes in the port—take temporary possession of any port facility or equipment and operate them; and engage any employee of the operator.

- Continue port development based on formalized planning and a PPP focus.
- Develop dedicated port-access roads, to reduce the wear of port-induced traffic on public roads and reduce air pollution emissions from congested port roads. Rail is not regarded as a solution for Port Louis, as the small size of the island—and the fact that the port is already located in the main economic center—makes rail an infeasible solution.
- Attract additional value-adding services, such as warehouse operations, to create even more employment locally.
- Further expand the port's Green Port Policy by
  o Imposing variable port fees as incentives for the use of less-polluting vessels
  o Installing facilities to cater for the cold ironing of vessels
  o Implementing environmental performance indices such as the Environmental Ship Index (ESI) or the Clean Shipping Index (CSI)

Durban

Short-term actions

- Address the anomalies in the institutional framework:
  o Port dues are partly charged based on a time dimension of a vessel call, while the dues should serve to recoup investments in infrastructure that vessels only use per vessel call (such as the entrance channel and turning basin).

  o Berthing dues are charged on a GRT basis, instead of a charge per LOA meter of the vessel or per berth.
  o There are no additional berthing dues for vessels over 53,000 tons, while these are usually the deep-draft vessels that require deep quays to be moored and that require substantial investments from a port authority.
- Introduce environmental policies promoting cleaner vessels:
  o Establish variable port fees as incentives for the use of less-polluting vessels.
  o Regulate truck emissions through truck retirement programs.
- Ongoing projects, which include the construction of ICDs, need to be prioritized. One of these projects includes the development of an ICD on the western boundary of the city. This will serve as a location for stuffing and de-stuffing of containers and will reduce the pressure on the local road network. There could be a dedicated railroad or a dedicated ICD access road connecting the port to this ICD.
- Along with developing additional ICDs, the port of Durban can control the queue of trucks on Bayhead Road by imposing terminal appointment systems or promoting off-peak operating hours.

Medium-term actions

- Address the anomalies in the institutional framework:
  o Excepting the local port master plans and the 2015–20 Strategic Plan, there is a lack of time-based policy goals. This should be resolved in order for policy makers to be accountable and responsible for their plans and to discourage making broad statements that are either achieved or not. For the local port policies within TNPA's National Port Plans, there is a clear timing: short term (2021), medium term (2044), and long term (>2044).
  o Criteria for investment decisions are not mentioned in the policy documents. It is unclear how investment decisions are validated by the government, and how a decision on whether to invest or not is made. A clear guideline with minimum requirements for government investments is regarded a necessity to ensure value for money for the government.
  o The legal framework has been developed with a focus on TNPA being positioned outside Transnet and becoming an independent National Ports Authority. Within this movement, additional private-sector involvement in port operations is being pursued. The legal documents that enable this move all date from the early 2000s, but so far the national ports authority is still part of Transnet, and all major terminals are still operated by TPT.
- With Durban's prime location and highly competitive nautical characteristics and terminal operations, the main actions—for the port to retain its current role as a major gateway port and transshipment hub for South Africa and the region—are based on the hinterland of the port. The following key actions are proposed for Durban to remain competitive:
  o Ensure a modal shift: Currently, 70–80 percent of boxes are stuffed or de-stuffed within the port's vicinity, causing huge flows of container trucks from the port to the stuffing and stripping areas, and huge flows of general cargo trucks between the city and the hinterland. Of the remaining 20–30 percent that moves in containers to Gauteng, only 12 percent is moved by rail, while there is railway capacity available for block trains to the hinterland. The rail capacity is substantial: 11 block trains in each direction are possible per day, each taking 100 TEUs. The total rail

capacity to Johannesburg is therefore around 800,000 TEUs per year. This capacity is currently underutilized. Obligated modal shift policies should therefore be considered.

o Improve the port's road connections: the current road network between the main highways and the port terminals is congested on a daily basis. The port of Durban and eTKM require assistance on arranging funding for the hinterland projects and road maintenance. Based on a meeting with eTKM, funding is a major issue: total investments needed add up to billions of South African rand.

o The port of Durban and eTKM require assistance to arrange funding from public and private sources for the hinterland projects and road maintenance.

o The current Cape-gauge railway needs to be upgraded to accommodate the transport of heavy loads. In addition, train schedules need to be optimized to make rail transportation more cost-efficient.

o As one of the most important hub ports in (South) Africa, the port of Durban could be a front-runner in promoting greener port policies such as cold ironing, liquefied natural gas (LNG) bunkering, or prohibiting the handling of commodities that are extremely polluting for the environment. The port of Durban is currently the only port in the study that offers environmentally differentiated port dues for specific liquid bulk tankers.

o In the long run, the development of Durban Dig-Out Port (DDOP) is inevitable. Although the project was postponed in recent years, the port will need additional capacity by about 2030. Developing the DDOP would require a full shift in the current port, and the development of new port areas. This plan should be accommodated with urban regeneration projects and waterfront developments, to transform the port areas that no longer have a function in the old port.

East London

Short-term actions

- Address the anomalies in the institutional framework:
  o Port dues are partly charged based on a time dimension of a vessel call, while the dues should serve to recoup investments in infrastructure that vessels only use per vessel call (such as the entrance channel and turning basin).
  o Berthing dues are charged on a GRT basis instead of a charge per length overall (LOA) meter of the vessel or per berth.
  o There are no additional berthing dues for vessels over 53,000 tons, while these are usually the deep-draft vessels that require deep quays to be moored and that require substantial investments from a port authority.
- Introduce environmental policies promoting cleaner vessels:
  o Establish variable port fees as incentives for the use of less-polluting vessels.
  o Regulate truck emissions through truck retirement programs.
  o Install facilities to cater for the cold ironing of vessels calling at the port of East London.

Medium-term actions

- Address the anomalies in the institutional framework:
  - Excepting the local port master plans and the 2015–20 Strategic Plan, there is a lack of time-based policy goals. This should be resolved for policy makers to be accountable and responsible for their plans and not make broad statements that are either achieved or not. For the local port policies within TNPA's National Port Plans, there is a clear timing: short term (2021), medium term (2044), and long term (>2044).
  - Criteria for investment decisions are not mentioned in the policy documents. It is unclear how investment decisions are validated by the government, and how a decision on whether to invest or not is made. A clear guideline with minimum requirements for government investments is regarded as a necessity to ensure value for money for the government.
  - The legal framework has been developed with a focus on TNPA being positioned outside Transnet and becoming an independent National Ports Authority. Within this movement, additional private-sector involvement in port operations is being pursued. The legal documents that enable this move all date from the early 2000s, but so far the national ports authority is still part of Transnet and all major terminals are still operated by TPT.
- Prioritize the development of the railway bridge to encourage the modal shift from road to rail.
- Continue port development based on formalized planning and a PPP focus.

REFERENCES

Baccelli, O., M. Percoco, and A. Tedeschi. 2008. "Port Authorities as Cluster Managers." *European Transport* 39: 44–58. https://www.openstarts.units.it/bitstream/10077/5984/1/Baccelli_Percoco_Tedeschi_ET39.pdf.

Van de Voorde, E., and T. Vanelslander. 2009. *Market Power and Vertical and Horizontal Integration in the Maritime Shipping and Port Industry.* OECD/ITF Joint Transport Research Centre Discussion Papers. OECD. http://www.oecd-ilibrary.org/docserver/download/227458312782.pdf?expires=1505812436&id=id&accname=guest&checksum=8917C26FE1F3E5F5E4AABC79991263DC.

Appendix A
The Review of the Institutional
Framework

TABLE A.1 Assessment of country policy framework in the port sector

CRITERIA	DJIBOUTI	SOMALIA	KENYA	TANZANIA	ZANZIBAR[a]	COMOROS	MADAGASCAR	MAURITIUS	MOZAMBIQUE	SOUTH AFRICA
Is initiated and documented by a government entity	✗	✓	✓	✓	✓	✓	✓	✓	✓	✓
Can be developed at different government levels: central government, regional governments, or decentralized	✓	✓	✓	✓	~	✗	✓	✓	✓	✓
Focuses on the longer term	✓	✓	✓	✓	~	✓	✗	✓	✓	✓
Is regularly updated	✗	✓	✗	~	✗	✗	✗	~	✗	✓
Presents goals with a clear timeframe to be achieved and defines a form of urgency	✓	~	✗	✓	~	✗	~	✓	~	~
Presents clear objectives and describes what is to be achieved	✓	✓	✓	✓	~	✓	~	✓	✓	✓
Presents sustainable development of a port toward its surroundings and the environment	✗	~	✓	✓	~	~	~	✓	~	✓
Contains corporate governance and structures of power in the port sector	~	~	~	✓	~	✓	~	~	✗	✓
Presents financing principles of the port sector, in particular related to the role of the government	~	✗	✗	~	✓	~	✗	✗	✗	✓
Presents division of responsibilities regarding port development and port operations	✗	✗	~	✓	✓	~	~	✓	~	✓
Presents possibilities and requirements for private sector involvement in the port sector	~	~	✓	~	~	~	~	~	✓	✓
Presents criteria for investment decisions	✗	✗	✗	✗	✗	✗	✗	~	✗	✗
Presents the principles for the development of legislation: policy is written, passed in legislation, and implemented by government bodies	✗	~	✓	✓	✓	✓	~	✓	✗	✓

Source: World Bank analysis.
Note: ✗ = does not meet the criteria; ✓ = meets the criteria; ~ = partially meets the criteria.
a. Zanzibar is a semi-autonomous region of Tanzania.

TABLE A.2 Overview of institutional roles and responsibilities in the port sector

CRITERIA	PREFERRED	DJIBOUTI	SOMALIA	KENYA	TANZANIA	ZANZIBAR[a]	COMOROS	MADAGASCAR	MAURITIUS	MOZAMBIQUE	SOUTH AFRICA
Landlord function: real estate management of port land and buildings	**Port Authority**	Ports and Free Zone Authority	Port Authority	Port Authority	Port Authority	Port Authority	Port Authority	(National) Port Authority	Port Authority	(Private) Port Authority	Port Authority
Local port policy-making and planning function: develop medium-to-long-term port plans	**Port Authority**	Ports and Free Zone Authority	Port Authority	Port Authority	Port Authority	Port Authority; Ministry of Transport	Ministry of Transport; Ministry of Finance	(National) Port Authority	External Communications Division; Port Authority	(Private) Port Authority	Department of Transport; Port Authority
Regulatory, supervisory, and surveillance function: ensuring legal/administrative compliancy of activities in the port perimeter	**Port Authority**	Ports and Free Zone Authority	Port Authority	Port Authority	Port Authority	Port Authority	Port Authority	(National) Port Authority	Port Authority	(Private) Port Authority	Port Authority

(continued)

TABLE A.2, *continued*

CRITERIA	PREFERRED	DJIBOUTI	SOMALIA	KENYA	TANZANIA	ZANZIBAR[a]	COMOROS	MADAGASCAR	MAURITIUS	MOZAMBIQUE	SOUTH AFRICA
Monitoring and promotion function: monitor own and other port performance	**Port Authority**	Ports and Free Zone Authority	Port Authority	Port Authority	SUMATRA	Zanzibar Maritime Authority	Port Authority	(National) Port Authority	Port Authority —	(Private) Port Authority	Ports Regulator Port Authority
Port training function: create a knowledge base in the port	**Port Authority**	Ports and Free Zone Authority	Port Authority	Port Authority	Port Authority	Not defined in ZPC Act. PPP Act notes this as a responsibility of a private partner	Port Authority	(National) Port Authority	Port Authority	(Private) Port Authority	Port Authority
National policy-making and planning function: develop policies and plans for the sector	**Ministry of Transport**	Ports and Free Zone Authority	Ministry of Transport	Port Authority Ministry of Transport	Port Authority Ministry of Transport	Port Authority Ministry of Transport	Ministry of Transport Ministry of Finance	(National) Port Authority	External Communications Division Port Authority	Ministry of Transport and Communications	Department of Transport Port Authority
Legal function: drafting, implementing, and monitoring laws	**Ministry of Transport**	Ports and Free Zone Authority	Ministry of Transport	Ministry of Transport Maritime Authority	Port Authority Ministry of Transport	Ministry of Transport	Ministry of Transport Ministry of Finance	Ministry of Transport Ministry of Finance and Budget National Regulator	External Communications Division	Ministry of Transport and Communications Maritime Authority	Department of Transport Department of Public Enterprises
International relations function: representation in multilateral/bilateral agreements	**Ministry of Transport**	Ports and Free Zone Authority	Ministry of Transport	Port Authority Ministry of Transport	Ministry of Finance	Zanzibar Maritime Authority	Ministry of Transport	Ministry of Transport Port Authority	External Communications Division Port Authority	Ministry of Transport and Communications	Department of Transport Port Authority

(continued)

TABLE A.2, *continued*

CRITERIA	PREFERRED	DJIBOUTI	SOMALIA	KENYA	TANZANIA	ZANZIBAR[a]	COMOROS	MADAGASCAR	MAURITIUS	MOZAMBIQUE	SOUTH AFRICA
Financing function: finance basic infrastructure and assess business plans	**Ministry of Transport**	Ports and Free Zone Authority	Ministry of Transport	Port Authority Ministry of Transport	Ministry of Transport Ministry of Finance	n.a.	Ministry of Transport Ministry of Finance	Ministry of Transport Ministry of Finance and Budget National Regulator	Ministry of Finance and Economic Development External Communications Division Port Authority	Ministry of Transport Private Sector	Department of Public Enterprises Port Authority
Port sector auditing function: independent monitoring	**Ministry of Transport**	Ports and Free Zone Authority	Ministry of Transport	Port Authority	Port Authority Ministry of Transport	Ministry of Transport	National Regulator	National Regulator	External Communications Division Shipping Division	n.a.	Ports Regulator
Port sector tariff regulation function: independent tariff monitoring	**Ministry of Transport/ Ports Regulator**	Port of Djibouti	Ministry of Transport/ Ports Regulator	Port Authority	SUMATRA	Port Authority	Port Authority	Port Authority	Port Authority	Port Authority	Ports Regulator
Cargo handling function: stevedoring and warehousing	**Private Operator**	Private Operator	Private Operator	Port Authority	Port Authority Private Operator	Port Authority	Private Operator	Private Operator National Port Authority	Public Operator	(Private) Port Authority Private Operator	Public Operator Private Operator
Terminal equipment function: acquire and maintain equipment	**Private Operator**	Private Operator	Private Operator	Port Authority	Port Authority Private Operator	Port Authority	Private Operator	Private Operator National Port Authority	Public Operator	(Private) Port Authority Private Operator	Public Operator Private Operator
Terminal development function: develop and maintain superstructure	**Private Operator**	Private Operator	Private Operator	Port Authority	Port Authority Private Operator	Port Authority	Private Operator	Private Operator National Port Authority	Public Operator	(Private) Port Authority Private Operator	Public Operator Private Operator

(continued)

TABLE A.2, *continued*

CRITERIA	PREFERRED	DJIBOUTI	SOMALIA	KENYA	TANZANIA	ZANZIBAR^a	COMOROS	MADAGASCAR	MAURITIUS	MOZAMBIQUE	SOUTH AFRICA
Terminal operations function: maintain a safe, secure, and environmentally friendly terminal	**Private Operator**	Private Operator	Private Operator	Port Authority	Port Authority / Private Operator	Port Authority	Private Operator	Private Operator / National Port Authority	Public Operator	(Private) Port Authority / Private Operator	Public Operator / Private Operator
Nautical services function: providing towage, pilotage, and mooring	**Private Operator**	Private Operator	Private Operator	Port Authority	Port Authority	Port Authority	Port Authority	Private Operator / National Port Authority	Port Authority	(Private) Port Authority	Port Authority

Source: World Bank analysis.

Note: n.a. = not applicable; PPP = public–private partnership; SUMATRA = Surface and Marine Transport Regulatory Authority; ZPC = Zanzibar Ports Corporation.

a. Zanzibar is a semi-autonomous region of Tanzania.

TABLE A.3 International maritime organization convention and agreement ratifications by countries in the study region

CONVENTION	DJIBOUTI	SOMALIA	KENYA	TANZANIA	ZANZIBAR[a]	COMOROS	MADAGASCAR	MAURITIUS	MOZAMBIQUE	SOUTH AFRICA
IMO Convention 48	✓	✓	✓	✓	✓	✓	✓	✓	✓	✓
SOLAS Convention 74	✓		✓	✓	✓	✓	✓	✓	✓	✓
SOLAS Protocol 78			✓			✓		✓		✓
SOLAS Protocol 88			✓					✓		
LOAD LINES Convention 66	✓	✓	✓	✓	✓	✓	✓	✓	✓	✓
LOAD LINES Protocol 88			✓					✓		
TONNAGE Convention 69	✓		✓	✓	✓	✓	✓	✓	✓	✓
COLREG Convention 72	✓		✓	✓	✓	✓	✓	✓	✓	✓
CSC Convention 72			✓							✓
Cape Town Agreement 2012										✓
STCW Convention 78	✓		✓	✓	✓	✓	✓	✓	✓	✓
SAR Convention 79	✓		✓	✓	✓	✓	✓	✓	✓	✓
IMSO Convention 76			✓	✓	✓	✓		✓	✓	✓
INMARSAT OA 76			✓	✓	✓			✓	✓	✓
FACILITATION Convention 65			✓	✓			✓	✓		
MARPOL 73/78 (Annex I/II)	✓		✓	✓	✓	✓	✓	✓	✓	✓
MARPOL 73/78 (Annex III)	✓		✓	✓	✓	✓	✓	✓	✓	✓
MARPOL 73/78 (Annex IV)	✓		✓	✓	✓	✓	✓	✓	✓	✓
MARPOL 73/78 (Annex V)	✓		✓	✓	✓	✓	✓	✓	✓	✓
MARPOL Protocol 97 (Annex VI)			✓				✓	✓		✓
London Convention 72			✓	✓						✓
London Convention Protocol 96			✓				✓	✓		✓

(continued)

TABLE A.3. *continued*

CONVENTION	DJIBOUTI	SOMALIA	KENYA	TANZANIA	ZANZIBAR[a]	COMOROS	MADAGASCAR	MAURITIUS	MOZAMBIQUE	SOUTH AFRICA
INTERVENTION Convention 69	✓			✓				✓		✓
INTERVENTION Protocol 73				✓				✓		✓
CLC Convention 69	✓		✓					✓	✓	✓
CLC Protocol 76								✓		
CLC Protocol 92	✓		✓	✓	✓	✓	✓	✓	✓	✓
FUND Protocol 76								✓		
FUND Protocol 92	✓		✓	✓	✓	✓	✓	✓	✓	✓
LLMC Convention 76							✓	✓		
LLMC Protocol 96			✓			✓	✓			
SUA Convention 88	✓		✓	✓	✓	✓	✓	✓	✓	✓
SUA Protocol 88	✓		✓	✓	✓	✓	✓	✓	✓	✓
SUA Convention 2005	✓									
SUA Protocol 2005	✓									
SALVAGE Convention 89	✓		✓				✓	✓		
OPRC Convention 90	✓		✓	✓	✓	✓	✓	✓	✓	✓
OPRC/HNS 2000	✓						✓	✓		
BUNKERS CONVENTION 01	✓		✓			✓	✓	✓		
ANTI FOULING 01			✓							✓
BALLASTWATER 2004			✓				✓			✓
NAIROBI WRC 2007			✓			✓				✓

Source: World Bank analysis.

Note: ✓ = meets the criteria; CLC = Civil Liability for Oil Pollution; CSC = International Convention for Safe Containers; COLREG = International Regulations for Preventing Collisions at Sea; IMO = International Maritime Organization; IMSO = International Mobile Satellite Organization; LLMC = Limitation of Liability for Maritime Claims; MARPOL = International Convention for the Prevention of Pollution from Ships; OPRC = Oil Pollution Preparedness, Response, and Co-operation; OPRC/HNS = Protocol on Preparedness, Response, and Co-ordination to Pollution Incidents by Hazardous and Noxious Substances; SAR = International Convention on Maritime Search and Rescue; SOLAS = International Convention for the Safety of Life at Sea; STCW = International Convention on Standards of Training, Certification and Watchkeeping for Seafarers; SUA = Suppression of Unlawful Acts Against the Safety of Maritime Navigation; WRC = Nairobi International Convention on the Removal of Wrecks.

a. Zanzibar is a semi-autonomous region of Tanzania.

TABLE A.4 Assessment of the legal and regulatory framework of the port sector

CRITERIA	DJIBOUTI	SOMALIA	KENYA	TANZANIA	ZANZIBAR[a]	COMOROS	MADAGASCAR	MAURITIUS	MOZAMBIQUE	SOUTH AFRICA
The legal and regulatory framework is consistent with and adheres to the different international treaties and agreements that a country signed or agreed to	✓	?	✓	✓	✓	✓	✓	?	?	?
The legal and regulatory framework uses policy as a basis and is driven by policy requirements: legislation is written to enforce policy goals	?	✗	?	✓	✗	✓	✓	✓	✓	✓
The legal and regulatory framework is consistent within the different bills, acts, rules, and regulations in a country	✓	?	?	✓	?	✓	✓	✓	✗	?
Designation of port regulatory responsibilities and associated monitoring bodies	?	✗	✓	✓	✓	✓	✓	✓	?	✓
Designation of port managerial responsibilities and associated monitoring bodies	?	✗	?	✓	?	?	✓	✓	?	✓
Designation of port development responsibilities, associated monitoring bodies, and options for the private sector in port development	✓	?	?	✓	✓	?	✓	✓	?	✓

(continued)

TABLE A.4, *continued*

CRITERIA	DJIBOUTI	SOMALIA	KENYA	TANZANIA	ZANZIBAR[a]	COMOROS	MADAGASCAR	MAURITIUS	MOZAMBIQUE	SOUTH AFRICA
Designation of port operational responsibilities, associated monitoring bodies, and options for private sector involvement in operations	✓	~	~	✓	✓	~	✓	✓	~	✓
Designation of port safety and environmental protection responsibilities and measures toward an independent entity	~	~	✓	~	✓	~	✓	~	✓	✓
Financing principles of the port sector	✓	✗	~	~	~	~	✓	~	~	~
Financing principles of the port sector's regulatory bodies	✗	✗	✓	✓	✓	n.a.	✗	✓	✗	✓
Requirements and possibilities for private sector involvement in the port sector	✓	~	✗	✓	✓	~	✓	✓	✓	✓

Source: World Bank analysis.
Note: ✗ = does not meet the criteria; ✓ = meets the criteria; ~ = partially meets the criteria; n.a. = not applicable.
a. Zanzibar is a semi-autonomous region of Tanzania.

TABLE A.5 Overview of the tariff structure applied in each port

	PREFERRED	DJIBOUTI	BERBERA	MOMBASA	DAR ES SALAAM	ZANZIBAR[a]	MORONI	TOAMASINA
Port dues	Vessel dimensions: GRT/GT	✓	✓	✓	✓	✓	~	n.a./✗
Light(house) dues	Vessel dimensions: GRT/GT	✗	✓	~	✓	✓	✗	n.a./✗
Wharfage	Cargo dimensions: ton/TEU/m³/unit	✓	✓	✓	~	✓	✓	✓
Berthing dues	Vessel dimensions per time unit: m/hr, berth/hr, or m/day	✓	~	✓	~	~	~	n.a./✗
Pilotage	Vessel dimensions per move/activity: GRT, LOA, or other vessel characteristics	~	✓	✓	✓	✓	~	n.a./✗
Towage	Vessel dimensions per move/activity: GRT/GT/LOA and number of tugs	~	✓	✓	✓	✓	✓	n.a./✗
Mooring	Vessel dimensions per move/activity: GRT/GT/LOA	~	~	✓	✓	✓	~	n.a./✗
Cargo-handling costs	Cargo dimensions: ton/TEU/m³/unit	✓	✓	✓	✓	✓	✓	✓
Storage tariff	Cargo dimensions per time unit: days per ton/TEU/m³/unit	✓	✗	✓	✓	✓	✓	~
Gate-handling fees	Cargo dimension per move: ton/TEU/m³/unit per move	✓	✗	n.a./✗	✓	n.a./✗	n.a./✗	n.a./✗

Source: World Bank analysis.

Note: ✗ = does not meet the criteria; ✓ = meets the criteria; ~ = partially meets the criteria; GRT = gross registered tonnage; GT = gross tonnage; LOA = length overall; n.a. = not applicable; TEU = twenty-foot equivalent unit.

a. Zanzibar is a semi-autonomous region of Tanzania.

www.ingramcontent.com/pod-product-compliance
Lightning Source LLC
Chambersburg PA
CBHW080551220326
41599CB00032B/6434